WAR IN THE PENINSULA

also by Jan Read

THE WINES OF SPAIN AND PORTUGAL

THE MOORS IN SPAIN AND PORTUGAL

WAR IN THE PENINSULA

by
JAN READ

FABER AND FABER
3 Queen Square
London

First published in 1977
by Faber and Faber Limited
3 Queen Square London WC1
Printed in Great Britain by
Latimer Trend & Company Ltd Plymouth
All rights reserved

© Jan Read, 1977

British Library Cataloguing in Publication Data
Read, Jan
  War in the Peninsula
  1. Peninsula War, 1807–1814
  I. Title
  940.2'7   DC231
  ISBN 0-571-10645-5

CONTENTS

Acknowledgements   9
Preface   13

PART ONE: THE ORIGINS

1. NAPOLEON DECIDES The Emperor's intentions, 1806–7   19
2. THE PRINCE OF PEACE Spanish politics to 1807   22
3. THE INVASION OF PORTUGAL France and Portugal; the occupation of Lisbon, 1807   32
4. THE PALACE REVOLUTION Ferdinand VII seizes power in Spain, 1807–8   38
5. BETRAYAL AT BAYONNE The abdication of the Spanish Bourbons, Spring 1808   46
6. BACKLASH IN SPAIN The rise of the Juntas, 1808   57

PART TWO: THE WAR

7. MEN AND ARMS Strategy, troops and equipment   65
8. 'WAR TO THE KNIFE' Bailén and the Spanish successes of 1808   73
9. 'A TIME TO STAND UP' The British entry into the war; Wellesley drives the French out of Portugal, 1808   84
10. NAPOLEON IN SPAIN The French counter-offensive of 1808; Sir John Moore's retreat to Corunna   92
11. 'PEPE BOTELLA' The trials of Joseph Bonaparte, 1808–13   107
12. RETURN OF AN IRON MAN Wellesley returns to Portugal; the battles for Oporto and French evacuation of Galicia   117
13. CATALONIA AND BEYOND The French offensive in the east, 1808–12   129

CONTENTS

14. SOUTH TO CADIZ   Talavera and the French occupation of Andalusia, 1809–10 — 141
15. THE LEOPARD AT BAY   Buçaco; Torres Vedras; Masséna's retreat from Portugal and its aftermath, 1810–11 — 155
16. THE GUERRILLAS 1808–13 — 169
17. THE LEOPARD FIGHTS BACK   Wellington's campaign of 1812; Arapiles; the French evacuation of Andalusia and counter-offensive — 182
18. VOICES FROM THE RANKS   The lot of the common soldier, 1808–13 — 195
19. FROM PORTUGAL TO THE PYRENEES   Vitoria and the Battle of the Pyrenees, 1813–14 — 207

PART THREE: THE AFTERMATH

20. A WAR FOR INDEPENDENCE   The repercussions of the war in Spain, Portugal and Latin America, 1807–24 — 225

Chronological Table 1788–1824 — 236

Napoleon's marshals in Spain and Portugal (and their titles) — 241

Bibliography — 243

Index — 249

MAP OF SPAIN AND PORTUGAL — 10

ILLUSTRATIONS

between pages 96 and 99

1. Queen María Luisa of Spain
2. King Ferdinand VII of Spain
3. The women of Saragossa man the guns
4. José Palafox
5. Soldiers on the march
6. The harbour of Corunna and the explosion of 13 January 1809
7. Pepe Botella
8. Napoleon
9. The Duke of Wellington
10. Spanish guerrillas casting bullets in the Sierra Tardienta
11. *Madre Infeliz*
12. The convocation of the Cortes of Cadiz in 1810

ACKNOWLEDGEMENTS

I am grateful to Mr. W. N. Hargreaves-Mawdsley and Macmillan & Co. for permission to quote from the translations of the Spanish despatch on the Battle of Trafalgar and Ferdinand VII's Declaration to the Americas, included among the interesting documents collected in *Spain Under the Bourbons 1700–1833*. Some of the translations from Napoleon's *Correspondance* are taken from Sir Charles Oman's *A History of the Peninsular War*, Oxford University Press, 1902–14. The verses of A. E. Housman's 'Grenadier' are reprinted from *Last Poems* by courtesy of Jonathan Cape Ltd. Short quotations from other authors are acknowledged in the text.

I am obliged to Don Xavier de Salas and the Museo del Prado for leave to reproduce the Goya paintings of Plates 1 and 2; to the British Museum for the print of his etching from the *Desastres de la Guerra*; to the Patrimonio Nacional for permission to reproduce the painting from the Casita del Principe (Plate 10); and to the Museo Romántico and the Museo Municipal, Madrid, for making available photographs of contemporary engravings from their collections.

PREFACE

In writing about the Peninsular War, Richard Ford, whose *Handbook for Travellers in Spain* of 1845 is itself a valuable source, says that the military authorities 'are necessarily of three classes: and belong to the invader, the *French*; the invaded, the *Spanish*; and the deliverer, the *English*. They correct and explain each other.' The French General Foy, for example, 'denies to the Duke the commonest military talent, attributes his successes to accident, and ascribes the valour of the British soldiers principally to "Beef and Rum" '. The Spanish, according to Ford, 'have two objects: one, to detail the ill usage which they have sustained from the invaders; the second, to blink as much as possible the assistance afforded by England, and to magnify their own exertions. . . . The traveller, when standing even on the battle-plains of Salamanca and Vitoria, will hear the post of superiority assigned to *Nosotros*.'

The difficulty in striking a fair balance persists even today: of all the many historians who have written about the war perhaps Sir Charles Oman came nearest to it—but his great *History of the Peninsular War* runs to seven volumes and 4,200 pages, and has for long been unavailable to the ordinary reader. Most modern histories in English are written strictly from the military standpoint and are largely confined to the campaigns of Sir John Moore and the Duke of Wellington, and the battles between the British and the French. In fact, it is a commonplace for their authors to disclaim any other intention, on the score that the Spanish war effort was too widespread and disorganized to permit of concise description. Yet this, as its Spanish name—*La Guerra de la Independencia*—implies, was a war for the independence of Spain and Portugal; and it was the common people of both countries who bore the brunt of it. Captain Liddell Hart has pointed out that the guerrillas inflicted immensely more casualties on the French than the British armies; and, dismal as was often the record of the Spanish generals and their regular troops after Bailén and the early successes of 1808, the refusal of the Spanish to surrender and the hydra-like emergence of new armies tied down scores of thousands of French troops across the length and breadth of the country. In short, Wellington, with an army that for most of the war amounted to no more than 40,000 British troops, would have had no chance of beating the French in open battle but for the relentless Spanish resistance—any more than the Spanish could have continued the fight without the inspiration of his victories.

There is perhaps a tendency to belittle what the Spanish regulars achieved in set combat: the sieges of Saragossa, Gerona and Ciudad Rodrigo immobilized thousands of men for long periods; La Romana in Galicia and Ballesteros in Andalusia achieved a great deal; when Graham hung back at Vitoria, it was Longa who cut the French line of retreat; and even General Blake, so regularly taunted with losing seventeen battles and winning one, came very close to inflicting a decisive defeat on Marshal Suchet at Sagunto. The Battle of Medellín was a nearer-run thing than is sometimes imagined; and perhaps the unkindest cut of all is that of Wellington's most distinguished biographer in describing Del Parque's resounding victory at Tamames in 1809 as a Spanish *defeat*!

All in all, a reassessment is called for; and however difficult the task, I have attempted a wide-ranging survey both of the operations of the guerrillas and of the more conventional Spanish forces. This has meant including less detail of Wellington's battles—available, in any case, in every standard military history—but I hope that, with the help of eyewitness descriptions, I have nevertheless given vivid and clear enough accounts of them. Overall strategy, both British and French, is analysed at some length. As always, the temptation to the historian is to criticize the commanders in the field. This is particularly evident in some modern Spanish books, where Wellington is taken to task for excessive caution and failure to exploit his successes. But it must be remembered that what is clear to the historian, writing with the benefit of hindsight, presented an entirely different problem to a general enveloped in the vastness of the sierras and beset with problems of supply. Thanks to the guerrillas, the French in particular were bedevilled by lack of up-to-date intelligence.

Of all wars, that in the Peninsula went far beyond a military exercise. It is because it was ultimately won in the hearts and minds of men that military histories dealing with the fire power of cannon rather than the inner fire of the human spirit seem so inadequate. For this reason I have written at some length on the plight of the ordinary Spanish and Portuguese; the *Levantamiento*; the spontaneous emergence of the Juntas; the painful gropings of the Regency and Cortes towards a revolutionary new Constitution; and the unavailing efforts of Joseph Bonaparte and his *afrancesado* followers to impose an alien regime, enlightened as it was in many respects, on a fiercely proud and patriotic people. The war began, not simply because Napoleon wished it, but as a consequence of the past mistakes of Spain's decadent Bourbon rulers. The politics of the preceding decade are, to my mind, a great deal more relevant than blow-by-blow accounts of individual battles. Again, the lasting significance of the Allied victory was not simply that the French were expelled from the Peninsula, but that the sacrifices of 1807–13 led to agonized reappraisal of the citizen's role *vis-à-vis* the State and the Monarchy. And, as I have tried to sketch in the last chapter, the Peninsular War began a revolutionary process, not only in Spain and Portugal, but in their South American empires.

It is not uncommon for English histories of the war to print a bibliography innocent of even a single Spanish or Portuguese source—and listing few enough French. The book list covers essential reading at least; the serious student may be referred to Volume XXVI of Espasa Calpe's great composite *Historia de España* for a detailed Spanish bibliography.

A book about the Peninsular War is not a novelty. What is, I believe, new, is a book for the general reader which focuses on the larger issues beyond the manoeuvring of armies and the winning of battles and on the stirrings of self-respect in an outpost of Europe that had sunk so low under its absolutist Bourbon rulers.

PART ONE
The Origins

Chapter 1

NAPOLEON DECIDES

*Je jurai dès lors qu'ils me la paieraient,
que je les mettrais hors d'état de me nuir.*
NAPOLEON to ARCHBISHOP DE PRADT

It was probably on the battlefield of Jena that Napoleon reached his decision to invade Spain. On 5 October 1806, a few days before the crushing defeat of the Prussians, Manuel Godoy, the favourite of Charles IV of Spain and virtual ruler of the country, had signed a manifesto calling the people to arms: 'Come then,' he declared, 'my loved fellow countrymen, come and swear allegiance beneath the banners of the most beneficent of Sovereigns, come and I will enfold you with my gratitude. . . .' The adversary was not named; but the proclamation demanded an immediate strengthening of the army. With the Spanish navy rotting in port, men and horses could hardly have availed against the English fleet.

Godoy had miscalculated the outcome of the battle and wrote post-haste to the Emperor assuring him of his absolute devotion to 'the most perfect model of a hero that History has to show'. Napoleon on his side affected to ignore the slight, contenting himself with a stern warning to the Spanish ambassador: 'I wish to tell you something which I want you to transmit in writing: in the sincere friendship of Charles IV for myself there is, as it were, a worm at work. An undefined fear and a certain distrust govern the heart of Spain in regard to my policies. If France went down in this struggle, Spain would go down too, and her fortunes would not be improved by it. If Spaniards are enjoying the sweets of peace in their homes, it is because France is their bulwark. Let this be clearly understood and let there be gratitude to me. . . .' For Godoy's benefit he added: 'Write also to your friend, the Prince of Peace. His position is such, if he can hold it, that History will acclaim him for having guarded his country from the revolution and wars which have everywhere desolated the nations—Let him be grateful for it, and let him take a piece of advice from me: if he wishes to live in safety, let him build no bridges with his enemies. His fall is certain if his policy shifts.'

After the victories of Austerlitz in 1805 and of Jena the only significant threat to Napoleon's complete mastery of continental Europe was from Russia; and this he neutralized at Eylau and Friedland in 1807. His real intentions towards Spain emerged in the subsequent negotiations with the Czar Alexander I. Apart from providing for an alliance against England, the Treaty of Tilsit embodied 'secret and supplementary' clauses which envisaged that the Balearic Islands should be taken from Spain and given to Ferdinand of Naples in return for his ceding Sicily to Joseph Bonaparte.

The invasion of the Peninsula was now indeed inevitable, if only because it was the final and logical step in completing the Continental System and denying the arch-enemy, Britain, the last of her trading facilities. In this respect the main offender was Portugal whose ports were still open to British shipping in accordance with the centuries-old Alliance between the two countries. Leaving aside the possibility of British military intervention in the Peninsula, of which there was yet no sign, it is more than doubtful whether a complete blockade of Europe would have damaged England more than France: English goods and commodities were much needed by France and her unwilling allies. In very similar circumstances Napoleon proved himself less astute than Adolf Hitler, who was content to rely on the tacit support of Spain and took advantage of Portugal's neutrality to import supplies of tungsten essential for the German war machine.

But in May 1806, Napoleon had written to his foreign minister, Talleyrand, declaring: 'I am not the heir of Louis XIV, I am the heir of Charlemagne.' Sir Charles Oman touches on the heart of the matter in pointing out that Napoleon no longer saw himself as 'the successor to the greatest of the Bourbons, but of the founder of the Holy Roman Empire. It is a very different thing to claim to be the first of the European monarchs, and to claim to be the king of kings.'

In pursuance of these ambitions he had already staked out various of his relations as rulers of puppet states, notably his brothers Joseph and Louis as kings of Naples and Holland. Naples was the former kingdom of the Bourbons, who had earlier suffered a crushing blow by the execution of Louis XVI during the early days of the Republic. Charles IV of Spain had retaliated by going to war with France; and the chequered course of the alliance which followed and the murder of another Bourbon, the Duke of Enghien, did nothing to reassure Napoleon as to the reliability of Spain while the dynasty survived. And Spain had proved a disappointing ally. Her fleet, on which Napoleon had pinned so much in his plans for invading England, had been destroyed at Trafalgar; her finances had for long been balanced only by the gold from the New World; and cut off from her American possessions by the British blockade, she had been able to provide pitifully little towards the coffers of war.

Looking towards his neighbour, Napoleon can have seen only an impoverished state with a badly equipped army and decadent court, headed by a half-imbecile king who had surrendered all real power to Manuel Godoy, the Prince of Peace, by all accounts his queen's lover. During his exile in St. Helena Napoleon was to declare that the decision to invade Spain was his cardinal mistake and indeed that the scheme was the brainchild of Talleyrand. This seems unlikely—the facts appear to disprove it—and in the heyday of empire Napoleon can have seen no reason to suppose that Spain and Portugal would not speedily suffer the same fate as Italy, Austria and Prussia before them. And if he saw the certainty of success, it is difficult to believe that any scruples of conscience or fair-dealing would hold back a man so ruthless and unscrupulous.

By the Treaty of Fontainebleau, signed on 27 October 1807, Spain agreed to the passage of 25,000 French troops for the purpose of attacking Portugal and so severing England's last contact with the Continent. It was agreed that a further 40,000 men should be held in Bayonne against any English counter-attack. By 20 November England had made no move, but a huge French army of 100,000 men was already launched across the Pyrenees and into Spain.

If Napoleon's motives and aspirations are clear enough, it remains to consider the course of events which had laid Spain open to an unopposed invasion, and in particular the role of Manuel Godoy. He has often been blamed for the whole débâcle. Could he, in fact, had he been stronger and less venal, have avoided it?

Chapter 2

THE PRINCE OF PEACE

The Spain which Manuel Godoy was to dominate for the sixteen years preceding the French invasion was a country in active process of transition. Charles III, the third of its Bourbon rulers, who died in 1788, was an enlightened despot. In the tradition established by the French advisers who came to Spain with his ancestor Philip V in the early years of the eighteenth century he ruled virtually without reference to the Cortes (or parliament) and by means of a Council of State, whose ministers were career diplomats. Many useful reforms were achieved: meandering country tracks began to give way to a system of modern roads radiating from Madrid; a much needed overhaul of the top-heavy Spanish administration of the overseas empire led to an improvement in trade with America; an attempt was made to stimulate agriculture by the sale of land in the open market; schools, universities and hospitals were built; and courageous efforts were made to curb the power of the Church and the Inquisition.

Far-reaching as these reforms were, they left the structure of power unchanged. At the top of the pyramid was the royal family, around whose court, rigid and stylized in etiquette and manners, revolved the grandees and higher nobility, following its ritual peregrinations from Madrid to the dusty would-be Versailles of Aranjuez, from Aranjuez to the summer palace of San Ildefonso near Segovia, from San Ildefonso to the gloomy half-monastery of the Escorial, and from there back to Madrid. It is on record that one-tenth of the public revenue went to support the court and its huge following of officials and retainers: 250 persons alone were required for the royal hunt; and the number swelled to 2,000 on special occasions when artillery was called up to decimate the game.

Out of a population of some six million in 1787 some half-million were *hidalgos*, the descendants of the Old Christians—those who, at the close of the Muslim era and the time of the expulsions, could claim that their blood was not tainted by Moor or Jew. As the Reconquest drew to an end it became a tenet of faith that it was beneath the dignity of a blue-blooded Christian to work with his hands, so entering into competition with the despised Moriscos, or to compete with the Jews in trading or professional activities. This tradition was still alive three centuries later and explains the almost complete absence of a middle class or upper *bourgeoisie*. The larger part of the country's commerce, especially in ports like Cadiz, was conducted by foreign merchants, often French. It was the hallowed custom among the lesser nobility for the estate to pass intact to the eldest son, or *mayorazgo*, leaving his younger brothers with a choice between becoming an officer in the army or navy, swelling the ranks of colonial administrators, joining the populous legal profession or entering the Church. The standing army, amounting to some 60,000 men, was in fact grossly over-officered, but, like the navy, poorly equipped.

Since the days of the great mediaeval pilgrimages to Santiago and the legendary apparition of St. James at the Battle of Simancas on his snow-white horse, the Roman Catholic Church had played a paramount part in the affairs of Spain. The whole course of the Reconquest was in the nature of a crusade. Although, in an age of 'enlightenment', its authority to intervene in matters of state was now being questioned, it still wielded enormous influence, and the mass of Spaniards—even the handful of intellectuals swayed by Voltaire and the Encyclopédistes—were devout Catholics. At this period the clergy numbered some 200,000 souls, of whom about half were monks and nuns. As it is to this day, the Church was actively involved in education, and its priests were the only educated people with whom the peasantry had regular contact. 'The real power in Spain', Wellington was to write, 'is in the clergy. They kept the people right against the French.'

Of the *comun*, or working classes, relatively very few were engaged in organized industry. There were then, as now, hardworking miners in Galicia and the Asturias, but the 300,000 workmen were in 1787 matched by an almost equal number of servants in the employ of the great families and lesser nobility. At least half the population were peasants, whether smallholders in the mountainous north, day labourers toiling in the summer heat of Andalusia or exposed to the biting winter cold of the

Castilian plateau, or the hardy fishermen of Biscay and the Mediterranean. It was among them that the will to victory, the stubborn refusal to accept foreign domination, took root and grew. No one has sung their innate dignity and worth better than Miguel Unamuno: 'A breed of men like vine shoots, grilled by the sun and tanned by the frosts, a temperate breed of men, product of an age-long selection made by the cold of the hardest winter and periodical famines; a breed of men made for inclemency of sky and bareness of life. The Spanish peasant is calm in all his movements, his conversation is deliberate and grave. You might think him an unthroned king. . . .'

Manuel Godoy was born in 1767 at Badajoz in the Extremadura, a deserted and mountainous region on the Portuguese border, its sallow ranges scattered with dark green clumps of cork oak. The acorns feed the wandering herds of pigs; and it is because the Extremadura is famed for its smoked hams and pork that in the days of his unpopularity he was dubbed 'the sausage-maker'. His father was an *hidalgo* with claims to nobility—flatterers were later to trace Godoy's descent to the Visigothic kings —but of modest means. At eighteen the young man, who was fair-haired, well-built and handsome enough, followed his elder brother to Madrid and, like him, obtained a place in the royal bodyguard. The court, at which within a few years he was to play the leading role, was eccentric to the point of decadence. Hunting was always a favourite pursuit of the Spanish Bourbons, but with Charles IV it was a mania. When preparing for the chase he was on one occasion informed that his child was dying. 'What can I do about it?' he replied and rode off. His other main interests were carpentry and shoe-making; affairs of state were left for his return from the hunting field, when after brief discussion with his leading minister, the Count of Floridablanca, he would sign the decrees already prepared.

United with this amiable, but near imbecile husband, his stronger-minded wife and first cousin, María Luisa of Parma, not surprisingly took an active and increasing role in the business of government: in fact, in imitation of their illustrious predecessors, Ferdinand and Isabella, '*Los Reyes Católicos*', the pair came to be known jointly as 'The Kings'. But María Luisa for her part displayed another of the penchants of the Bourbons—or at least those of the female line. Her sexual appetites were strong and evidently unfulfilled by her weakling husband: long before Manuel Godoy appeared on the scene, her affairs and her taste for young men were notorious. The handsome and personable young guardsman carried all before him; and during the next few years the Queen, sixteen years his senior, became whole-heartedly and lastingly infatuated with him. The surprising thing is that the King apparently accepted the situation and became as dependent upon Godoy as his wife: the unholy trio remained united even after Charles IV's abdication and their exile in France. The exact nature of the relationship remains something of a mystery to this day.

Among the most vivid contemporary accounts of the Spanish court is that of Lady Holland in her *Spanish Journal*. Her husband, Lord Holland, was of the Whig élite and a cousin of Charles James Fox. The couple were well known for their Spanish sympathies and understanding of the country's problems and paid two extended visits to Spain in 1802–05 and 1808–09, during which they had the entrée, not only to the court but to liberal circles, and were also on the closest terms with officers of the allied high command and British diplomatic representatives. Lady Holland was a reigning beauty and also a woman who knew her own mind—during an earlier visit to Italy, so as to avoid a daughter by her first marriage falling into the hands of her exhusband, she had smuggled the child out of the country while at the same time arranging for its mock funeral! Her day-to-day diary of events in Spain is as lively as it is well informed.

Of Godoy in 1803, she writes that he was 'a large, coarse, ruddy-complexioned man, with a heavy, sleepy, voluptuous eye', and of Maria Luisa that, 'The notoriety of the Q.'s amours is so great that it is not an unusual topic of conversation with the muleteers. Hitherto all ranks disapprove of the elevation of the P. of Peace, and ascribe his rise to the true reason. The dissolute manners of the women is disgusting; their excesses make them antidotes to the inclination they wish to inspire. Several of the highest rank, possessing youth, beauty, and consequence, have from their libertinage destroyed their health.' Returning to the subject, she adds: 'Such is the disposition of the P. of P. that *auprès de lui les femmes ont toujours raison*; suffice it that they complain, be it against husband, brother, father, son, they are sure of success. *Ainsi c'est le paradis des femmes*. Till I get to the fountain head, I shall suspend my belief in the various anecdotes about Court which people credit and retail.' But her curiosity was to remain unsatisfied: 'It is impossible with truth to ascertain, what are the ties between him and the Queen. He neglects, has insulted her, and possessed himself of the King's confidence, independent of her influence; and yet whenever he is hardly pressed by unpopularity or by French interference, she supports him effectually. . . .'

In the first flush of royal favour Godoy was appointed Adjutant-General of the Bodyguard in 1791, and further titles and honours followed thick and fast. His dominating position was confirmed in November 1792, when after the fall of Floridablanca and short-lived regime of the Count of Aranda, the young Duke of Acudía, as he had meanwhile become, was appointed principal Secretary of State. After the execution of Louis XVI in Paris, Spain was now on the verge of war with France. As the principal architect of the Treaty of Basel which brought the inconclusive hostilities to an end in July 1795, Godoy reached a pinnacle of popularity and the Spanish 'Kings' took the unprecedented step of joining him with the blood royal and creating him 'Prince of Peace'.

The Prussian ambassador to the court has left a vivid picture of his daily round at the time, quoted by Jacques Chastenet in his *Godoy, Master of Spain*, London, 1953: 'Godoy rises early and talks a little with his equerries and household staff. At eight o'clock he goes to the stables which the Queen visits regularly to see him get on his horse. . . . At one o'clock he goes to the palace, where he has his own office and bedroom, to be present in his capacity of Gentleman of the Household at the Queen's dinner. Afterwards, he descends to his own room, which is just below that of the Queen; there he dines alone, but is joined by the Queen who, when once the King has gone off hunting, arrives by a secret stair. It is in the course of these secret talks that the Queen and Godoy decide what proposals to lay before the King. Towards seven o'clock, Godoy goes off to get through the necessary work with the King and at eight descends again to his room, not without encountering in his anteroom thirty or forty women of every class and condition who assail him with their petitions. These audiences take up at least two hours and it is only between ten o'clock and midnight that he can get down to work with his clerks.'

After the Treaty of Basel Spain returned to her traditional

policy of friendship with France, and a year later the volatile Godoy was framing a typically bombastic ultimatum to his erstwhile ally, England: 'In the days since we concluded our Peace-Treaty with the French Republic, We have not only been vouchsafed solid evidence for suspecting an attack from England on Our possessions in the Americas, but We have been insulted in so direct a manner as to lead Us no longer to hesitate in believing Her determined to force Us to adopt a position contrary to that We should otherwise have adopted—and contrary to the interests of all humanity who have been decimated by this bloody war that grips the whole of Europe in its jaws. . . . Our Patience is spent, Our forbearance exhausted, and We must now turn Our gaze to the dignity of Our throne and to our duty of affording protection to Our subjects, and We must declare war on the King of England and the English Nation. . . .'

As the fortunes of the Republic waxed and Napoleon's grip tightened on Europe, Godoy was increasingly compelled to dance to a tune called by the First Consul. In 1801, at Napoleon's behest, he led an expedition against Portugal, called 'The War of the Oranges', because on crossing the frontier near the orange groves belonging to Godoy's family, a soldier broke off two branches from one of the trees and presented them to the Prince of Peace, who had them sent to the adoring Queen María Luisa in Madrid. Godoy fancied himself as a soldier and was painted by Goya in the resplendent uniform of commander-in-chief; but his victory was an empty one and led to the first cooling of relations with Napoleon.

Godoy had by now struck up a close friendship with Lucien Bonaparte, then French ambassador in Madrid. The two hatched a scheme for the premature ending of hostilities and a division of the lion's share of the spoils. Napoleon was infuriated, demanded that negotiations be reopened, and on hearing of Godoy's request for a portrait of himself, snapped back: 'Never will I send my portrait to a man who keeps his predecessor in a dungeon and employs the methods of the Inquisition. I make use of him, but I will feel for him nothing but contempt.'

But Napoleon was planning a much more damaging attack against England than the pantomime of a campaign in Portugal. During the brief interlude of peace with England that had followed the Treaty of Amiens in 1802, Godoy had been making attempts to secure Spain's neutrality during a resumption of the war, now plainly imminent, and had tentatively approached the British ambassador in Madrid, Hookham Frere. Whether or not Napoleon got wind of this, an ultimatum was delivered by the French ambassador, Beurnonville, on 14 August 1803, to the effect that a French army of 100,000 would enter Spain unless Frere was immediately handed his passports. On Godoy's demurring, Beurnonville was instructed by Talleyrand: 'You are forbidden to see or salute the Prince of Peace, who is an enemy of the French people.' He was further ordered to hand a personal letter from Napoleon to Charles IV. Godoy, to do him justice, had done his best to keep Spain out of the war, but was now obliged to climb down.

Napoleon had now decided on the outright invasion of England across the Channel, and the importance of Spain lay in her possession of a considerable, but ill-equipped fleet. This, Godoy was now ordered to put into fighting trim. In a rapid *volte face* and with a display of energy designed to placate and impress his French master, he set about the task with more haste than efficiency. The French Admiral Villeneuve collected half a dozen ships at Cadiz and after a brush with a British squadron off Cape Finisterre ran for shelter to El Ferrol near Corunna, where he made rendezvous with another ten Spanish ships. Napoleon's orders were for him to steer for the Channel, but Villeneuve, uneasily aware that he was being dogged by a British fleet under Nelson, put back towards Cadiz. It is perhaps of interest to quote from the official Spanish despatch on the ensuing Battle of Trafalgar by Rear-Admiral Antonio de Escaño, reproduced by W. N. Hargreaves-Mawdsley in *Spain Under the Bourbons 1700–1833*, London, 1973; it can have given its recipient in Madrid little inkling of the magnitude of the disaster:

> My most excellent Sir: The condition of Captain Federico Gravina, who was wounded in his left arm by grapeshot at the very close of the action yesterday, prevents him from sending your Excellency news of this bloody encounter [Admiral Gravina died of his wounds shortly afterwards].... That sad duty falls to me.... I have to inform you that all our endeavour and heroic unconcern for our lives did not prove sufficient to prevent our sustaining losses which would have been overwhelming had we not been convinced to a man that there was nothing more we could do and so come off with honour unscathed....

... At eight minutes to twelve in the morning, an English three-decker, with pennant flying at her topmast, cut our line at the centre with the support of those ships following at her stern. The leading vessel of each enemy column did likewise; one of them came round our rearguard and a third crossed between the 'Aquiles' and the 'San Ildefonso' and, from that moment on, the action was restricted to particular encounters, ship to ship, of a very bloody nature, and the greater part of them carried on by an exchange of pistol-fire. This between the whole of the enemy fleet and but half of our own, with the inevitable boarding of some ships. At the moment of writing, I am not in possession of the necessary and indispensable information about each of these separate actions that I would need to give your Excellency a full account, nor can I say anything about the movements of the vanguard, which I am assured came right round at the beginning of the action to sail to the aid of those under attack. What I can certainly assure Your Excellency is that every single vessel that I could see, be it French or Spanish, carried out its duty to the full in battle. ...

In printing this despatch in its issue of 5 November 1805, the *Gaceta de Madrid* adds that, 'The English have also suffered important losses in the battle, during the course of which Lord Nelson and other officers of distinction perished, according to a report from Gibraltar.'

With the British in complete command of the seas and his plans for an invasion of England in utter disarray, Napoleon was now to see little profit in maintaining relations with Godoy. And Godoy, thanks to his greed and nepotism and above all because of the bad blood between him and the popular heir to the throne, the Prince of Asturias, was becoming increasingly detested in Spain. Henceforth he was to devote his efforts to securing his own fortune with only a secondary regard for his country. With this in view he began a series of complicated intrigues to re-establish himself in the Emperor's favour. He was a not uncultured man—to his credit he initiated reforms in education and even, with considerable courage, attempted to put an end to bullfighting—and had formed a close friendship with a botanist, Eugenio Izquierdo, whom he sent to Paris as an intermediary. Izquierdo made contact with a French scientist, Lapécède, an intimate of the Emperor, and during the next few years letters and pleas from Godoy were to follow thick and fast. Thus, in 1806, he writes:

My security turns on the Emperor's protection. I may survive that great misfortune, the death of my Sovereigns, but, before that terrible moment comes, I am bound to assure myself of an existence which no violence can reach. I am ready to become the object of His Imperial Majesty's bounty and favour and also, provided that it is in conformity with his views, to be one element of the great political system which is to give back peace to Europe and secure to the world the freedom of the seas. Any suggestion of His Imperial Majesty will meet with acceptance from our Sovereigns.

Foremost among his own suggestions was a plan for the invasion of Portugal, from which he should benefit by being appointed regent of the country under French suzerainty. Notwithstanding his servile protestations, after the British occupation of Buenos Aires in September 1806 he was not averse to insuring against Napoleon's possible defeat at Jena by the famous, if obscure, proclamation of 5 October. It is hardly to be supposed that Napoleon placed the slightest reliance on Godoy's loyalty after that stab in the back. Nevertheless, with his mind made up to invade Spain and Portugal, it suited him to feed Godoy's ambitions and so to enter the Peninsula without resistance. On 28 July 1807 France delivered an ultimatum to Portugal and on 27 October a treaty between France and Spain was signed at Fontainebleau laying down conditions for co-operation between the two countries.

Both the Treaty of Fontainebleau and the Convention signed concurrently by Izquierdo on behalf of Spain and General Duroc on the part of France were secret: until the eleventh hour their contents were unknown even to the Spanish ambassador in Paris. The first three clauses of the Treaty provided:

Art. I   The province of Entre Minho and Duro, with the city of Oporto, shall be made over, in entire property and sovereignty, to His Majesty the King of Etruria, with the title of King of Northern Lusitania.

Art. II The province of Alentejo, and the Kingdom of the Algarves, shall be made over, in entire property and sovereignty, to the Prince of Peace, to be by him enjoyed under the title of Prince of the Algarves.

Art. III The provinces of Beira, Trás-os-Montes and the

Portuguese Extremadura shall remain undisposed of until there be a general peace, to be then disposed of according to circumstances, and conformably with what may be agreed upon between the two high contracting parties.

The first clause was framed to provide for the Queen of Etruria, a daughter of Charles IV and Maria Luisa, whose territories in Italy Napoleon wished to appropriate. As has been noted earlier, the Convention contracted for the passage of a French army of 25,000 through Spain and for it to be joined by a force of 11,000 Spanish infantry and cavalry, supported by artillery. A further French army of 40,000 was to stand guard at Bayonne in case of an English attack. However, Article VI specifically stated that, 'This additional corps shall not enter Spain until the two high contracting parties have come to agreement on that point.' In fact, Napoleon never implemented the Treaty and it seems highly unlikely that he ever had any intention of doing so: the Queen of Etruria lost her Italian kingdom and took refuge in Madrid; Godoy was left without his principality; and the French army at Bayonne moved into Spain without consultation or delay. As for Napoleon, with his Trojan Horse at full stretch, the agreements were so much waste paper.

Chapter 3

THE INVASION OF PORTUGAL

Since 1792, when it could no longer be disguised that Queen Maria I was insane, Portugal had been ruled in her name by her son, John, the Prince of Brazil. This Prince Regent, as he became known in 1799, was married to the Infanta Carlota, daughter of the 'Kings' of Spain. It was therefore with some heart-burning that they had agreed to the earlier French intervention in Portugal and to Godoy's 'War of the Oranges' in 1801. By 1807 neither the 'Kings' nor Godoy—if he had so wished—were in a position to oppose the new invasion. In any case, Carlota was not their favourite daughter.

Mme Junot, lively wife of the general commanding the French expedition and future Duchess of Abrantes, has left an unflattering portrait: 'Picture to yourself, reader, a woman four feet ten inches high at the very most, and crooked, or at least both her sides were not alike; her bust, arms, and legs, being in perfect unison with her deformed shape. Still, all this might have passed off in a royal person, had her face been even endurable; but, good Heavens! what a face it was! She had two blood-shot eyes, which never looked one way, though they could not absolutely be accused of squinting—everybody knows what I mean. . . . The dress of the Princess of Brazil was in *discordant* unison, if I may so express myself, with her person. . . . This dress, which was wretchedly ill made, very imperfectly covered an enormous bosom, and a chest all awry, while diamond brooches ornamented the sleeves, whose extreme shortness displayed a pair of arms which would have been much better concealed. . . . The exquisite beauty of these jewels, combined with the extreme ugliness of the person who wore them, produced an indescribably strange effect, and made the Princess look like a being scarcely belonging to our species. . . .'

The acid Mme Junot was equally downright about the Princess's morals—or lack of them—and hardly less disparaging about her husband: 'I had not then seen the Prince of Brazil, therefore I could not laugh as I afterwards did, when I beheld his corpulent figure, clumsy legs, and enormous head, muffled in a hussar uniform. His negro hair, which by the bye was in perfect keeping with his thick lips, African nose and swarthy colour, was well powdered, and pomatumed, and tied in a thick queue. The whole was surmounted by a shako, ornamented with a diamond aigrette, of great value. . . . I call up my recollection of him, at those gloomy moments when my spirits require to be rallied by a hearty laugh!'

The unfortunate young man was far from robust or well balanced. He was a hypochondriac who underwent moods of deep depression; and it was rumoured that he was mentally disturbed like his mother. Between the peremptory and menacing demands of the Emperor and her traditional alliance with England, Portugal stood in need of harder heads and stouter hearts than these; and in the event the Prince Regent proved himself indecisive and timorous.

From 1802 until 1805 the French ambassador in Lisbon was the fire-eating General Lannes, who soon obtained the dismissal of the foreign secretary and the chief of police, Pina Manique, on the grounds that they were unco-operative. Lannes secured an undertaking that British ships would avoid Portuguese ports; and as the price of her neutrality Portugal was required to pay a monthly contribution of a million livres. Incensed by his unpopularity and infuriated by the stoning of his residence, Lannes tightened the screw, and in December 1803 and under the threat of an invasion from Bayonne, the Prince Regent agreed to pay France a further subvention of sixteen million livres over sixteen months and to grant extended trading facilities. In April 1805 Lannes was replaced by General Junot, who brought with him a personal letter from Napoleon inviting the Regent 'to help in bringing England to saner and more moderate ideas'. This was met by a Portuguese declaration of neutrality; and when, as the war clouds gathered, an English fleet with nine battalions of troops on board anchored in the Tagus in September 1806, the Prince Regent made a hasty apology to Napoleon and sent the ships on their way.

It was becoming obvious that no concessions would satisfy the implacable Napoleon short of an outright declaration of war on England; and it is more than doubtful whether even this would

B

have saved Portugal from French occupation. The French ultimatum of 12 August 1807, after listing various fabricated grievances, continues: 'Therefore, the undersigned is ordered to declare that if on September 1st following H.R.H. the Prince Regent of Portugal has not manifested the intention of separating himself from English influence by immediately declaring war on England, dismissing the British ambassador and withdrawing his own from London, holding as hostages all Englishmen established in Portugal, confiscating English merchandise, closing his ports to English commerce, it will be understood that H.R.H. the Prince Regent of Portugal renounces the Continental cause. . . .'

The Regent was later to answer Napoleon's accusations and hectoring demands in a *Manifesto, or Justificatory Exposition of the conduct of the Court of Portugal* issued on 1 May 1808 during his exile in Brazil. With considerable acumen he points out that:

> France received from Portugal, from 1804 to 1807, all the colonial conditions and raw materials for her manufactures. The alliance of England and Portugal was useful to France; and in the depression suffered by the arts and industry, in consequence of a perpetual war by land, and a disastrous war by sea, in which he met only with defeats, it was certainly a great advantage to France, that the commerce of Portugal should suffer no interruption; undoubtedly it was useful to both countries. By ravaging Portugal, by subjecting her to excessive conditions, in an unheard-of manner, without war, or any resistance on her part, France has not obtained that advantage which a commerce useful to both countries would have procured her.

As to Napoleon's specific demands, he has this to say:

> The court of Portugal might then well have adopted the known maxim of the Romans, being convinced that disgraceful conditions frequently saved those who refuse them, and brought destruction upon those by whom they were proposed; but, on the one side, it could not believe that the Court of the Tuileries made in earnest proposals which committed both its honours and its dignity; and on the other side it hoped to ward off the storm, desirous of sparing the blood of its people; and placing implicit confidence in the friendship of his Britannic majesty, its old and faithful ally, it endeavoured to render the preten-

sions of the French government more moderate, by acceding to the shutting up of ports, and refusing two other articles, as contrary to the principles of public law, and to the treaties which subsisted between the two nations: and His Royal Highness the Prince Regent of Portugal had no hesitation to declare, that those articles wounded equally his religion and the principles of morality. . . .

The Portuguese Council of State in fact went most of the way to meet the French demands. It stopped short only at the actual arrest of British subjects, although, as the Prince Regent made clear, 'there was no longer any Englishman in Portugal who was not naturalized in that country, and all English property had been sold, and even its amount exported.' Napoleon prolonged the negotiations only to gain time for massing his armies; and on 1 October 1807 the French and Spanish ambassadors abruptly left Lisbon. The writing was on the wall, and the foreign secretary, António Araújo, was by now negotiating with the British minister, Lord Strangford, for naval assistance in evacuating the court and royal family to Brazil.

General Junot crossed the Bidassoa into Spain on 18 October and proceeded through Burgos, Valladolid and Salamanca towards the Portuguese frontier near Alcántara, so as to take the most direct route to Lisbon along the Tagus valley. The *Manifesto* describes his further progress: 'General Junot, without any previous declaration, without the consent of the Prince Regent of Portugal, entered the kingdom with the vanguard of his army, assuring the people of the country through which he marched that he was going to succour his Royal Highness against an invasion of the English, and that he entered Portugal as the general of a friendly and allied power. He received, on his journey, convincing proofs of the good faith of the Portuguese government; for he witnessed the perfect easiness which prevailed with regard to France, and that all the Portuguese troops were near the coast. His Royal Highness the Prince of Portugal, surprised in such an extraordinary manner, might have rallied around him the body of troops which were at a small distance from him, caused the English fleet to enter Lisbon, and thus cut to pieces the small and miserable corps with which General Junot was advancing, with a degree of temerity which would have been ridiculous, had not General Junot, whose conduct at Venice and Lisbon has but made him too well known, relied on the feelings of a virtuous prince, who would never expose his people to the most dreadful of calamities by a sure first success. . . .'

If the Prince Regent had been a bolder and more resolute man he might well have carried through the plan which, with the benefit of hindsight, he dreamed of in the safety of Rio de Janeiro. Junot was to discover that there was no road along the Tagus valley suitable for artillery or a baggage train. It rained in torrents; most of the horses died of cold, leaving the cavalry dismounted; cartridges were ruined by the wet; and his army melted away in search of food. But Junot, reassured by the absolute lack of resistance, pushed doggedly forward. An interview with Araújo, conducted beneath a tree in the driving rain, during which the cowed foreign minister offered yet more concessions, only strengthened his resolve. Had not the Emperor written to him: 'I will not have the march of the army delayed for a single day. 20,000 men can feed themselves anywhere, even in a desert'? It was with 1,500 men, tattered, shoeless and famished, that he finally entered Lisbon on 30 November 1807. The measure of Portuguese demoralization and of the legend of Napoleonic invincibility was that the capital should have fallen to this sorry band; it was not until Christmas that Junot had as many as 10,000 troops at his disposal.

Meanwhile a squadron of the Russian navy had arrived in the Tagus. The Czar had recently declared war on England; and on 17 November a British fleet under Sir Sidney Smith appeared in the mouth of the river and declared a blockade. Even at this eleventh hour the Prince Regent's fear of offending Napoleon was such that steps were taken to guard against an English landing; and Lord Strangford retired on board the British flagship, the *Hibernia*. Here, on 25 November, he received a copy of the Paris *Moniteur* in which Napoleon declared that 'the House of Bragança has ceased to rule in Europe'. At long last the Prince Regent was panicked into a decision; the whole royal household and other wealthy inhabitants of Lisbon, some 15,000 in all, took to ship with their treasure and belongings; and on the 29th, a day before Junot's arrival, the convoy of fifteen Portuguese warships and more than twenty merchantmen was escorted out to sea by the watching English.

Once in possession of Lisbon, Junot began by making some attempts to win the favour of its inhabitants. A programme of public improvements was announced, including the construction of roads and canals, so as to stimulate agriculture and industry. The Portuguese army was to 'form a single family with the soldiers of Marengo, Austerlitz, Jena and Friedland'; what in fact transpired was that the militia was suppressed and all regular soldiers with less than one or more than six years' service were disbanded. The remainder of the army was reorganized and put at Napoleon's disposal; its last remains, under the Marquis of Alorna, perished in the snows of Russia during the retreat from Moscow in 1812.

On his flight from Portugal Prince John had left a Council of Regency, but this was soon dissolved and it was announced that the country would be governed on behalf of the Emperor by Junot as general-in-chief of the French forces. Portuguese collaborators were not wanting among the bureaucrats and civil servants; and to his discredit the Archbishop of Lisbon lent his support to the new regime. Only the common people of Lisbon displayed any spirit of resistance. The hauling down of the Portuguese flag from the Castle of St. George and other buildings and its replacement by the tricolour led to violent riots, and Junot's attempts at conciliation were brought to a summary end by orders from Napoleon. These bade him expropriate the property of all the 15,000 persons who had taken refuge in Brazil with the Prince Regent and levy a general fine of a hundred million francs—an impossible task, since the refugees had taken with them about half the money in circulation. The French army and, more discreditably, its officers on their own behalf, then took to sacking churches of their gold and silver relics. It was a pattern which was to be repeated throughout the Peninsular War and, together with the savagery of the French troops in the country districts, soon brought the country to a state where all that was lacking to fan the smouldering flames of revolt was effective leadership.

Chapter 4

THE PALACE REVOLUTION

One member of the Spanish royal family who did not share his parents' admiration for Manuel Godoy was the heir to the throne, Ferdinand, the Prince of the Asturias. He was not María Luisa's favourite, as Lady Holland recounts, reporting on a visit to court: 'The Queen calls her favourite child, the Infante Don Francisco, a pretty, lively boy, bearing a most indecent likeness to the P. of Peace. She enumerated the children she had, and those she had lost, 22!! 6 only remaining. "My eldest son whom you are going to see you will find ugly, he is the counterpart of myself."' Ferdinand's mother-in-law, the Queen of Naples, describes him as 'hideous to look at, with tubby shape, round knees and legs, a small, delicate voice—and utterly dull'. For all this, the Prince of the Asturias was a stronger character than his father and, though in later days he proved to be a bigoted and reactionary ruler, he was soon to become the idol of the Spanish people and the 'Desired One' of the Peninsular War.

His mother frequently remonstrated with him over his dislike for Godoy, but his feeling only deepened and became one of utter loathing when Godoy took steps to separate him from his tutor, Escoiquiz, a canon of Toledo, and to replace his entourage by creatures of his own. Perhaps not without justification, Ferdinand suspected that Godoy wished to disinherit him and take his place. The breach only widened when in 1802, at the age of eighteen, the Prince was married to Maria Antonia of Naples. Soon the Queen was talking of 'this rascally Court of Naples, and this slut who fans the flames, my daughter-in-law'. Lady Holland, writing in January 1804 about a new grant of lands and titles to Godoy by the King, elaborates on the feud.

'The wording of the decree is whimsical; it is almost a threat of his indignation should his successors infringe these rights. They call it here a *billet d'enterrement du Roi*, as it confirms the belief of his illness and approaching danger. It is a great proof of the folly, vanity, and egotism of the P. of the P. Folly to imagine that such a measure could in any way bind hereafter the Prince of the Asturias, should he be inclined to pluck this fat bird; and of vanity, to obtain an additional Grandeeship merely because others who have several are addressed as *double* Grandees in memorials; egotism, at this crisis when fresh taxes and scarcity already oppress every class to get favours merely to enrich himself. His policy is unaccountable. In his conduct towards the P. of A., instead of conciliating or even demonstrating the usual tokens of respect due to his rank, he offends, and has insulted him by slights. The consequence is what might have been foreseen, that he has made an implacable enemy, who will not delay showing his resentment by overturning this formidable rival....'

Shortly before the tubercular Princess of the Asturias died in 1806, Queen Maria Luisa was so involved in the quarrel as to describe her as 'that off-scouring of her mother, that poisonous viper, that animal bursting with spleen and venom in place of blood, that half-dead toad, that diabolical serpent'. Escoiquiz, on the other hand, roundly declared that 'the sausage merchant' had poisoned the Princess; and when Godoy, proffering a belated olive branch, suggested that the Prince should now marry the sister of his own wife, María Teresa of Bourbon, Ferdinand burst out: 'Let me rather remain a widower all my life, or become a monk, than be brother-in-law of Manuel Godoy!' Godoy retaliated by making a clean sweep of the Prince's household. The repercussions led to a swiftly mounting crisis, which was to give Napoleon the pretext for overturning the Bourbon dynasty and occupying Spain.

A group of Ferdinand's discredited supporters, including the Duke of Infantado, the Marquis of Ayerbe and the Count of Orgaz, made an approach to the new French ambassador, the Marquis François de Beauharnais, and secretly introduced him to Escoiquiz. It was suggested to the ambassador that ties between the countries might be strengthened and Godoy's position undermined if the Prince were to marry a relation of the Emperor's—in the person of Marie Stéphanie Tascher de la Pagerie, a young cousin of the Empress Josephine. Charles IV had not, of course, been informed of the intrigue; and Napoleon's first reaction was a brusque refusal to be involved. However, on second thoughts, he told Beauharnais to get the Prince of the Asturias to make the request in writing. Escoiquiz, with the help of the ambassador, drafted a letter in the most unctuous terms, which was duly signed by Ferdinand and despatched.

It was now mid-October of 1807—the signature of the Treaty of Fontainebleau and Junot's march into Spain were to follow at the end of the month—and the court had taken up residence at the Escorial. Ferdinand, at his own request and so as to be as far removed as possible from his parents, was lodged in the part of that cold and gloomy building occupied by the monks. At twenty-three he was still very much the dependent child in the presence of his parents and must have been uneasy enough about taking such an unprecedented and unauthorized initiative when he went to pay his nightly visit to the King and Queen on 27 October.

They had been informed in an anonymous letter—probably written by Godoy—of the intrigue and were in a state of pent-up emotion and anger. Ferdinand's chamber was ransacked, and after the 'Kings' had examined his private papers he was locked into a closely guarded cell. There was apparently nothing definitely treasonable among the documents, but the King was agitated enough to send a frantic letter to Napoleon. 'Alas!' he wrote, 'My heart bleeds in recounting such a hideous crime! My first-born son, the heir presumptive to my crown, has cruelly intrigued to dethrone me; he has even gone to the extreme of plotting against the life of his mother. Such a horrible outrage deserves to be punished with all the rigour of the law. His title to the succession must be revoked: one of his brothers will be more worthy to take his place in my heart and on my throne. At this moment I am engaged in seeking out his accomplices so as to plumb the depths of this blackest and most evil plan and I do not wish to lose a single moment in informing His Imperial Majesty and in begging his enlightenment and counsel. . . .'

On receipt of this and a further letter from the King complaining of Beauharnais's backstairs manoeuvres, Napoleon summoned the Spanish ambassador and in a towering rage bade him: 'Send a courier to your Court without delay and instruct him to declare that never has the Prince of the Asturias written to me and that my Ambassador has embarked on no sort of intrigue. Tell him that, as from now, I take the Prince under my protection and that if violence, however slight, is used against him, or if any insult is offered to my Ambassador, or if the army now mustered does not immediately set off for Portugal as arranged between us, I will declare war on Spain.'

Godoy, who had almost certainly stage-managed the episode to discredit the Prince, now decided that matters had gone far enough. Immersed as he was in his own intrigue for securing a principality in Portugal, it was not in his interest to offend the Emperor. It was therefore arranged that Ferdinand should write an abject letter of apology to his father—no doubt drafted by Godoy so as to put him in the worst possible light:

Sir:
    Dear Papa: I have done wrong, I have sinned against Your Majesty both as king and father; but I repent and offer Your Majesty the most humble obedience. Nothing should have been done without Your Majesty's knowledge; but I was caught unawares. I have denounced the culprits, and beg Your Majesty's pardon for having lied the other night, at the same time seeking permission as your grateful son to kiss your royal feet.

                                                             Fernando
San Lorenzo, 5 November 1807

Later, after his temporary rise to power in March of the following year, Ferdinand caused a long statement to be printed in the *Gaceta de Madrid*, retracting what he had said and attacking Godoy. The King meanwhile professed himself satisfied and made public a proclamation pardoning the Prince. It begins: 'The voice of nature stays the hand of vengeance, and when an oversight calls out for pity, a tender father cannot withhold it....' Nevertheless, all the former charges were repeated in detail, and neither María Luisa nor Godoy were content to let the matter rest. Escoiquiz, the Duke of Infantado and the other conspirators were put on trial for high treason; but the proceedings were hamstrung from the beginning because of Napoleon's determination that his ambassador should not in any way be implicated. In spite of the pressure put upon them, the judges decided that there was insufficient evidence to convict any of the accused, and they were set at liberty. Charles IV at first professed to be delighted with the verdict, but later, at the insistence of Godoy and the Queen, banished the accused men to the provinces. Godoy, whose object had been to discredit the Prince for good and all, had badly miscalculated. The only lasting result of the affair was to encourage popular agitation in favour of the Prince and to goad his aristocratic supporters into new activity.

Godoy was by now faced with much more serious worries than this storm in a court teacup. On 22 November, with Junot now in Portugal and approaching Lisbon, Napoleon moved a second army of 25,000 into northern Spain under the command of General Dupont. This was done in flagrant violation of the Treaty of Fontainebleau, without prior consultation or any sign of English attack. On the implementation of the other clauses of the treaty and the partition of Portugal the Emperor remained silent; instead, his mouthpiece, the Paris *Moniteur* indulged in systematic abuse of the Prince of Peace as a false and untrustworthy ally. In January 1808 a further force of 30,000 crossed the Pyrenees into Biscay and Navarre, while Dupont's troops fanned out into Old Castile and took up positions at Burgos and Valladolid. Finally, in February, General Duhesme crossed the Pyrenees at the southern end with yet another 14,000 men and began an advance towards Barcelona. The French had at first been welcomed as friends and allies; they now threw off all pretence of being anything but foreign invaders. The first incident occurred at Pamplona, where a party of French soldiers who had pretended to be snowballing outside the fortress suddenly rushed the gate and turned out the Spanish garrison. The citadel of Barcelona was occupied by a similar treacherous ruse: General Lecchi marched a column of troops past the fortress, apparently on the way out of the city, then gave sudden orders to wheel and occupy it. Other strongpoints in the north were then seized, either by trickery or direct assault. Having secured his base, Napoleon now put his brother-in-law, the dashing and ambitious Murat, who from being a Gascon innkeeper had been ennobled as Grand-Duke of Berg, in overall command of the armies in Spain with instructions to march on Madrid.

In the forlorn hope of propitiating the Emperor, Godoy and the court had refrained from issuing any orders for resisting the French advance. The Spanish army was in any case in no shape to oppose the massive influx, if only because 15,000 of its best troops under the orders of the Marquis of La Romana had been sent to the Baltic in March of the previous year in response to a peremptory demand from Napoleon. This had left its remaining squadrons depleted and disorganized. Godoy can hardly have been reassured by an order of the day issued by Murat from

Burgos on 13 March, enjoining his troops to 'treat the estimable Spanish nation as friends, for the Emperor sought only the good and happiness of Spain'. It was obviously prompted by the looting and other savagery now rife in the occupied territory; and when Marshal Bessières crossed the Pyrenees with a further *corps d'armée*, bringing the total of French troops in the country to 100,000, Godoy finally took action.

The court was now in *sitio* at the palace of Aranjuez, south of Madrid. Urgent consultations with the Queen resulted in a decision to follow the Portuguese example and to evacuate the royal family to America. Charles IV, after all, was King of the Indies, and both he and Godoy had everything to gain by transferring to Buenos Aires or Mexico where they would be beyond Napoleon's clutches. Troops had already been drafted from the capital, and Godoy gave orders for the Madrid garrison to leave on 18 March and to escort the royal family to Seville preparatory to sailing.

Emotions were now running high. It was almost universally believed that Godoy had been acting in collusion with Napoleon and that he was personally responsible for the unpreparedness of the Spanish army. This was not the case. He had made sporadic efforts to turn to England, but in each case had been forced back into a dangerous game of politics with the Republic: Napoleon held all the cards and it was inevitable that he should win. It was not within the nature or capabilities of a Godoy or Charles IV to take the bold decisions or embark on a radically different policy of rapprochement with England which would have made possible effective resistance. Sir Charles Oman puts the position squarely in saying that 'upstarts who guide the policy of a great realm for their private profit must naturally expect to be misrepresented, and there can be no doubt that the Spaniards judged Godoy to be a willing helper in the ruin of his master and his country'.

Lady Holland has left a vivid description of the little town of Aranjuez, with its palace, grounds and pleasantries: 'Houses are low, streets excessively wide and covered with a white loose sand over the pavements; houses built of white stone which reflects powerfully the heat and the light. The walks and roots of the trees are regularly watered, which gives a coolness to the air, almost pernicious from the damp feel which it emits. It is a healthy and pleasant residence till ye end of May, but it then

becomes hot, and from the marshy ground in its neighbourhood, the people suffer from agues etc. The air is in some places infected with putrid matter; as it is not allowed to bury any body or animal at the *sitio*, therefore they are thrown on to a heap and allowed to rot. The King besides, is not averse to the custom, as the carcases serve for food to crows, etc., which is so much fish to his net, as he is indifferent to the quality of his *chasse*. . . .'
With its somewhat *manqué* atmosphere, Aranjuez formed a not unsuitable background for one of the last acts in the decadent regime of Charles IV.

On the evening of 17 March 1808 the place was thronged with soldiery, with palace retainers, with the great nobles and their servants and with an excited crowd which had streamed out of Madrid on rumours of the royal family's imminent flight. Mingling with this mob and fanning the growing uproar were various supporters of the Prince of the Asturias, among them the Count of Montijo, disguised as a priest. The riot began with the arrival at Godoy's house of a carriage and the appearance of a heavily veiled woman—in all probability his mistress, the notorious Pepita Tudo—who was swiftly driven away. It spread like wildfire that Godoy was smuggling out the King and Queen. The doors of the house were broken down and the mob surged in, smashing the magnificent furniture and tearing down paintings, in a wild search for the detested Prince of Peace. Balked of their quarry, the crowd streamed over to the palace and with cries of 'Long live Ferdinand' clamoured for their favourite.

Meanwhile, the uppermost thought of the King and Queen was for the safety of Godoy and they implored their son to intervene. For the Prince, it was the long-awaited moment of revenge: having obtained the assent of his quaking father, he stepped out on to the balcony and to thunderous cheers announced that the Prince of Peace had been disgraced and dismissed. The following morning the decision was confirmed by the signature of a decree in which the King declared: 'Desiring to command in person the Army and Navy, I relieve of his commands Don Manuel Godoy, Prince of the Peace, whom I allow to retire to whatever place he chooses.'

But where was Godoy? For a full thirty-six hours he had lain hidden and undiscovered under a pile of carpets in one of the attics of his house. At length he was driven out by hunger and attempted to slip away, but was immediately recognized and arrested by the soldiers guarding the house. It required their best efforts to prevent his being lynched on the spot, and only after he had received a severe battering and a knife wound in the face, was he able to limp away, supporting himself on the bridle of a horse, escorted to a place of safety by the soldiers. A pitiful appeal to the Prince of the Asturias resulted only in Ferdinand's shouting to the crowd: 'Gentlemen, I answer for this man. He shall be tried and his punishment shall fit the gravity of his offences.'

Ferdinand's supporters now advised him that he must grasp his opportunity. They were abetted by the Minister of Justice, Caballero, who, trimming his sails to the wind, announced to the King and Queen that their own lives were in danger and that Godoy could only be saved if Charles were to abdicate in favour of his son. A Council of State was hastily summoned and the King thereupon signed a proclamation drafted by Caballero:

> My habitual infirmities not permitting me to support any longer the important weight of the government of my kingdom; and having need, in order to re-establish my health, to enjoy private life in a more temperate climate, I have decided, after the most minute deliberation, to abdicate my crown in favour of my heir, my most beloved son, the Prince of the Asturias.
>
> Consequently, it is my royal will, that he be forthwith acknowledged and obeyed as king, and natural lord of all my kingdoms and sovereignties; and that this royal decree of my free and spontaneous abdication may be exactly and directly fulfilled, you will communicate it to the Council, and to all others whom it may appertain.
>
> (Signed) I, the King

Given at Aranjuez, 19 March 1808

Chapter 5

BETRAYAL AT BAYONNE

> How carols now the lusty muleteer?
> Of Love, Romance, Devotion is his lay,
> As whilome he was wont the leagues to cheer,
> His quick bells wildly jingling on the way?
> No! As he speeds, he chants 'Viva el Rey!'
> And checks his song to execrate Godoy,
> The royal wittol Charles, and curse the day
> When first Spain's queen beheld the black-
>   eyed boy,
> And gore-faced treason sprung from her
>   adulterous joy.
>
> BYRON, *Childe Harold's Pilgrimage*

While Aranjuez celebrated the palace revolution, Murat was pursuing his purposeful way to Madrid in the belief that he was to replace Godoy and rule in his place as Lieutenant of the Emperor. The *coup d'état* occasioned urgent reappraisal of the situation on both sides. It was all very well for Ferdinand to appoint a new Council of State, headed by his loyal and tried supporters, Infantado, San Carlos, Escoiquiz and Ceballos; the crucial question was the attitude of the French, and in particular Napoleon. Two policies were possible: either to fall back, offer what resistance was possible and if necessary to fly the country, as previously envisaged by Goody; or to placate the Emperor, whatever the price. Escoiquiz pointed out that the troops immediately available to the court numbered only 3,000 or 4,000, whereas the French had 60,000 in the field. In the circumstances Ferdinand wrote a humble letter to Napoleon, pledging his co-operation and once again asking for the hand of a French princess. He meanwhile entered Madrid on 24 March 1808 amidst public acclamation—thus placing himself within the power of Murat, who had arrived the day before with more than 20,000 troops.

Murat, uncertain of Napoleon's reaction, but rightly guessing that it would be unfavourable, was distant and, like his colleague Beauharnais, careful not to acknowledge Ferdinand as

King. There was almost immediately to be a new development, of which Murat was quick to see the possibilities. María Luisa's daughter, the ex-Queen of Etruria, sent him a messenger begging protection for her father and mother and claiming that they had been forcibly deposed. This was later followed up by no less than seventeen letters from María Luisa herself, of which the first begins:

> The King, my husband, asks me to write, not being able to do so himself because he is ill and his right hand is swollen, and asks if the Grand-Duke of Berg can intercede with the Emperor to safeguard the life of the Prince of Peace and to send some servants or priests to him. If only the Grand-Duke could go and see him or, at least, console him, since the Prince pins all his hopes on one whom he regards as his true friend.
> .... Our one desire is that the Grand-Duke obtains permission from the Emperor for the King, my husband, myself and the Prince of Peace to live together, all three, in some place beneficial for our health, without authority and free from intrigues, which assuredly we do not wish. The Emperor is generous; he is a hero; he has always supported his faithful allies and those in trouble.... Of my son we can never hope for anything but miseries and persecutions. Both to the public and the Emperor, he has begun and assiduously continues to misrepresent that innocent and passionate friend of the French, the Grand-Duke and the Emperor—the poor Prince of Peace. It is all untrue....

Her subsequent pleas were in similar abject vein, and Murat's response was to write to Napoleon recommending a course of action which was soon to be implemented to the letter: 'The spectacle of a king despoiled of his crown calls in question the position of his son, who can only be regarded as a rebel, if it is true, as the Queen's letter seems to prove and as is generally believed, that he forced his father to abdicate the crown. If he presents himself at my headquarters I will send him to Your Majesty, and then Spain would really be without a king, since the father has abdicated and you would be within your rights not to recognize the son, who is like any other usurper. I believe additionally that I ought not to recognize the Prince of the Asturias as king until Your Majesty has considered the matter.'

Without waiting for a reply Murat went a stage further by despatching his aide-de-camp to Aranjuez with the drafts of two documents ante-dated 21 March for Charles's signature. The first was a personal letter to Napoleon in which the deposed King protests about the events of 17 March and declares that 'full of confidence in the generosity and genius of the great man, who has at all times declared himself my friend, I have taken my resolution to resign myself into his hands'. The second was a short proclamation withdrawing the abdication:

> I protest and declare, that my decree of the 19th of March, in which I renounce my crown in favour of my son, is a deed to which I was compelled in order to prevent greater calamity and spare the blood of my subjects. It is therefore to be considered as of no authority.
>
> (Signed) I, the King

Without publishing the papers, which he withheld for possible later use, Murat sent copies to Napoleon on 24 March. At the back of Murat's mind was the conviction that once the Spanish throne was declared vacant there was only one suitable candidate for it—himself. Napoleon had, in fact, been thinking along similar lines himself, but with one important difference—witness a memorandum of the same date, drawn up by the French foreign minister, Champagny, but corrected in the Emperor's own hand. It sets out the necessity for the throne to be occupied by one of Napoleon's own brothers and continues: 'The Emperor for his part, and as arbiter, considers it impossible to re-establish Charles IV in the face of public opinion or to recognize Ferdinand VII, risen in rebellion against his father and supported by the English, and even less to subject Spain to anarchy at the hands of the English. . . . I have expressed to Your Majesty the circumstances which necessitate an important decision. Politics make it advisable, justice authorizes it, the disturbances in Spain underline the necessity. Your Majesty ought, then, to look to the safety of his empire and save Spain from the schemes of the English.'

Napoleon forthwith took steps to put this plan into operation. On 27 March he wrote to his younger brother, Louis Bonaparte, whom he had installed as King of Holland, offering him the throne of Spain: 'You say that the climate of Holland does not suit you. Besides the country is too thoroughly ruined to rise again. Give me a categorical answer: if I nominate you King of Spain will you accept; can I count on you?' Louis prudently declined; and it was his older brother Joseph who was later to accept, his throne of Naples going to the disappointed Duke of Berg as a consolation prize.

But of these developments Murat was as yet unaware, and it seems unlikely that when Napoleon's special envoy General Savary, the Duke of Rovigo, arrived in Madrid on 7 April he enlightened him as to the full extent of the Emperor's intentions. Meanwhile, Murat, in full expectation of being nominated himself, sent back over-optimistic reports on the state of the country and his own grip of the situation and pushed ahead energetically with plans for securing the removal of all the members of the royal family to France.

Ferdinand had already been told that Napoleon was projecting a visit to Spain and would be travelling to Bayonne. He was in a fever to clarify his own situation, which remained entirely insecure until he had received the Emperor's blessing. Unlike Murat and Beauharnais, Savary addressed Ferdinand as 'Your Majesty' and, though he was later to deny it, led him to believe that Napoleon would recognize him as King once they had met. One of Ferdinand's advisers, Ceballos, was later to write that 'it was, in fact, very difficult to suppose that a general sent by the Emperor should come determined to cheat'. On 10 April the King set out for Burgos in company with Savary and all his closest advisers, including Infantado, Ceballos, Escoiquiz, Labrador and Ayerbe. On reaching Burgos Savary professed himself disappointed that Napoleon had not yet arrived there and encouraged the party to proceed to Vitoria. At this point the Marquis of Urquijo, more perspicacious than his colleagues, suggested turning back; but escape was no longer possible from the heart of French-occupied Spain, and encouraged by a reassuring letter from Napoleon, Ferdinand crossed the Pyrenees into Bayonne on 20 April.

The King and his advisers had been so hoodwinked as to Napoleon's real intentions that they had left in Madrid only the most ineffectual *Junta de Gobierno* in charge of the country's affairs, headed by Ferdinand's uncle, Don Antonio, whose capacities may be judged by Talleyrand's account of his subsequent captivity at Valençay: 'The Infante spent much of his time cutting up picture books with scissors, so as to excise any illustrations that offended his morals or religion.'

Murat had little difficulty in securing the Junta's agreement to the release of Godoy, who, rescued from the fury of the Madrid mob by his intervention, had been languishing in prison at the castle of Villaviciosa. 'The vermin [María Luisa]', wrote Don Antonio to his nephew in a letter quoted by Jacques Chastenet, 'writes gleefully to the Grand-Duke of Berg and has obtained from him the sausage-selling Prince; but it is your ineffable father who begged more warmly still that the sausage-seller might be freed and not have his head cut off. The tender pair [the ex-King and Queen] are still at the Escorial, guarded by those traitors of carabiniers and the French soldiers. . . . Those who demanded Godoy's liberty are my brother and the vermin, who was ready to burst into tears and go on her knees, and the Frenchman who had undertaken to save the prisoner. . . . The bodyguards would have freed him only to the gibbet. However, our friend is now in the hands of Colonel Manhès and you will soon be seeing him at Bayonne. . . .'

Godoy had in fact been released in pursuance of Murat's plan for assembling the royal family—of whom Godoy ranked as one —at Bayonne. He was despatched by coach from Madrid on 22 April; and the old King and Queen, at Napoleon's behest, followed him a few days later. Of the royal family there now remained in the capital only the effete Don Antonio, the Archbishop of Toledo (a second cousin of the King), Ferdinand's younger brother Don Francisco and his sister, the ex-Queen of Etruria and her children. It was felt that Don Antonio and the Archbishop were of little consequence, but it was essential to Napoleon's machinations to remove any member of the ruling Bourbon dynasty around whom resistance might later crystallize. News of his double-dealing at Bayonne was now reaching the capital, already restive after the release of Godoy. The Queen of Etruria and her children departed without disturbance on the early morning of 2 May; she was in any case unpopular for having sided with Godoy and María Luisa. What kindled the flames was the arrival of another coach outside the royal palace to carry away the Infante Don Francisco. A master locksmith, one Molina Soriano, raised the first shout of *'traición!'* A group of about fifty people then burst into the palace and the presence of the Infante, whom they urged to a window. His appearance only increased the tumult in the street below; an aide-de-camp sent by Murat was set upon and rescued with difficulty; a battalion of grenadiers was called up; and it required three fusillades to disperse the crowd, who left some dozen dead and wounded behind them.

If Murat thought that the affair was now over, he was to be disillusioned speedily. This was only the overture to the famous revolt of *El dos de mayo*, depicted in all its savagery by Goya in those great companion pieces, *La Lucha con los Mamelucos* and the *Fusilamiento de Moncloa*. Armed with any weapon that came to hand—knives, muskets and stones—the inhabitants emerged into the streets with pent-up fury, falling on any detached French soldiery. But Murat had some thousand disciplined troops in the city and within the hour called up thousands more from the camps outside. Only in the great square of the Puerta del Sol and the Artillery Park of Monteleón were the disorganized Spaniards able to offer effective resistance to the French squadrons moving inexorably in from the perimeter and clearing the streets with their withering fire. It was at the Artillery Park that the French suffered their heaviest losses.

In obedience to orders from the Junta the regulars of the Madrid garrison had not joined the revolt, but the officers in command of the arsenal, Daoiz and Velarde, disarmed the small French contingent and opened the gates to a mob in search of weapons. Pouring volleys of grape shot into the advancing French troops, they repulsed two attacks, capturing the commander of the second column, Colonel Montholon. Murat finally threw in a force of almost 2,000, which overwhelmed the defenders, killing Daoiz and Velarde and their 40 soldiers, who together with some 500 civilians had held out for four hours.

The Imperial troops now proceeded to the ruthless house-to-house extermination of the insurgents, described by Pérez de Guzmán as 'a hunting party directed against balconies and windows'. In an order of the day Murat ordered the summary execution by firing squad of 'all who have been taken during the riot with arms in their hands', of persons found in possession of arms without a licence and of the sellers and distributors of seditious literature, at the same time making parents and the heads of households responsible for their dependents. Estimates of the casualties vary widely according to the source. Murat declared that he had lost only 80 men; Sir William Napier in his *History of the War in the Peninsula* puts the French dead at 750. As regards the Spanish casualties the *Moniteur* reported that 2,000 'criminals' had been cut down, while the Junta, anxious to restore calm in Madrid, announced that only 150 of its citizens had fallen.

The news of the revolt was to have dramatic repercussions at Bayonne, where negotiations had meanwhile reached stalemate. On the arrival of Ferdinand and his party on 20 April, Napoleon entertained them to dinner at the castle of Marrac, but refused to be drawn into discussion. Later the same night Savary presented himself at the King's quarters. It was only a day or two before, according to Ceballos's account, that he had declared: 'I am ready to have my head taken off if, within a quarter of an hour of your majesty's arrival at Bayonne, the Emperor has not saluted you as King of Spain and the Indies. . . . The whole negotiations will not take three days, and your majesty will be back in Spain in a moment.' He now announced to the incredulous Spaniards that the Emperor had decided that the Bourbon dynasty was to be removed from the throne of Spain. Heated, and on the Spanish side, indignant, argument now ensued at various levels.

It emerged that Napoleon was proposing that Ferdinand should exchange the kingdom of Spain for that of Etruria—from which his own sister had just been evicted by the Emperor! Ceballos made a firm statement of the Spanish position to his French counterpart, Champagny: 'The King could not renounce his crown in favour of another dynasty without failing in his duty to his vassals and at the expense of his own reputation; neither could he do it without prejudice to the members of his family and the fundamental laws of his kingdom; still less could he countenance the reign of another dynasty, which could only be called to the throne by the Spanish nation in virtue of its native rights to choose another family, should the reigning one be extinguished.' Ceballos refused to budge from this position; Napoleon soon lost patience with him; and Labrador and Escoiquiz were successively sent to reason with him—with equal lack of success. Escoiquiz, in his *Memorias*, has left a complete record in dialogue form of his discussions, which at this stage, as the concluding exchanges show, were conducted with elaborate urbanity, Napoleon familiarly tweaking the canon's ear—although neither man would depart one iota from his position:

The Emperor: (smiling and tugging forcibly at my ear) But, worshipful Canon, will you not accept my ideas?

Escoiquiz: (also smiling) I wish with all my heart—even at the expense of my ears—that His Majesty would agree with mine. But our interests are opposed, and I regret this all the more, since my admiration and affection for His Majesty has grown since he did me the honour of granting an interview. It would give me the greatest satisfaction to comply respectfully with all his august wishes; but I am bound by a sacred obligation, as His Majesty will understand.

The Emperor: Yes, I understand. Your worship conducts himself like a man of honour and a faithful vassal.

Although there was some division of opinion among Ferdinand's entourage about the expediency of accepting Napoleon's offer of Etruria, the majority, like Escoiquiz, was solidly behind him and against his abdication. Exasperated by Ferdinand's unexpected obduracy and in possession of Charles's letter repudiating his abdication at Aranjuez, Napoleon now resorted to new tactics and sent for the ex-King and Queen. They arrived on 30 April and, in marked contrast to the treatment of their son, were received with every mark of attention and respect. Their first thought, as always, was for Godoy. Noticing that he was not seated at the table of honour at the banquet given on their arrival, they at once obtained Napoleon's permission for him to join them. Charles's subsequent actions were dictated throughout by hatred for his son and without regard to the interests of Spain. On 2 May he signed a letter, no doubt dictated by Napoleon, in which, having reaffirmed that his abdication was invalid, he went on to declare that, 'The King Carlos . . . has for the present resolved to cede to His Majesty the Emperor Napoleon all his rights to the throne of Spain and the Indies.'

Ferdinand had meanwhile continued asserting his own right to the crown and had even smuggled out a letter to the Junta in Madrid, calling upon it to declare war on France. But by now Napoleon was in no mood for further parleying. On 5 May he called a meeting of all the parties, at which Charles IV rose and in the most abusive terms accused his son of stirring up the riot which had led to so much bloodshed in Madrid. It was then made brutally clear to Ferdinand that he must either abdicate or 'be dealt with as a traitor and a rebel'. At this point, according to the *Memorias* of Escoiquiz, his assembled advisers 'abandoned the young king and his brother [Don Carlos] to their own counsels'. In a letter dated the following day Ferdinand renounced the crown, at the same time making plain his feelings: '... Your Majesty thought proper to insult me in the presence of my venerable mother, and of the Emperor, by appellations the most humiliating; and not content with this, you require my renunciation without any conditions or restrictions, under pain that I, and those who composed my council, should be treated as conspirators. In such circumstances, I make the renunciation which Your Majesty commands. . . .'

With his brother Joseph waiting in the wings, Napoleon was now impatient to complete the transfer of sovereignty. It required another five days before Ferdinand was induced to sign away his remaining rights as Prince of the Asturias; in the meantime a stream of letters, directives and proclamations issued from Bayonne. On 4 May Charles wrote to the *Junta de Gobierno* in Madrid with instructions that it should instal Murat as president; as a result, the Infante Don Antonio shrugged off all further responsibility and left for Bayonne. By the same token the ex-King also wrote to the Consejo de Castilla, the supreme legislative body, announcing his abdication, and issued a proclamation to the Spanish people urging cooperation with the French. A convention signed by General Duroc and the Prince of Peace on 5 May set out the terms of the abdication in detail. Charles IV agreed that 'the prince whom His Majesty the Emperor Napoleon shall judge proper be placed on the throne of Spain', making only two material conditions: that 'the integrity of the kingdom shall be maintained' and that 'the Catholic, Apostolic and Roman religion shall be the only one in Spain; no reformed religion shall be tolerated there, and still less infidelity, according to the usage now established.'

On 8 May 1808 King Charles issued his last proclamation to the Spanish people, referring to 'my ally and dear friend the Emperor of the French' and urging complete subservience to his wishes. Shortly afterwards he set out, in company with the Queen and the Prince of Peace, for the exile in France, and later in Italy, from which none of them were to return. Ferdinand, together with his brother Don Carlos and uncle Don Antonio, were separately confined at the castle of Valençay under the custodianship of Talleyrand—a step which Napoleon later described as 'a practical joke', since his former foreign minister was now completely out of sympathy with the Emperor's policy in Spain. Ferdinand was to remain at Valençay for almost six years, until, with the decline of Napoleon's fortunes in 1813, he was released to reoccupy the throne.

To give some semblance of legality to his brother's accession, Napoleon now required the *Junta de Gobierno* to submit to him a petition for a new king. Its new president, Murat, duly saw to it that it both acceded to his 'request' and suggested Joseph Bonaparte. Murat further advised Napoleon on the desirability of convoking the Cortes (or Spanish parliament) in Bayonne to solemnize Joseph's enthronement and to ratify a new constitution, 'so as to demonstrate the joy of all Spain, to manifest the ills which the previous regime had caused her, and the reforms and remedies most appropriate for ending them throughout the nation at large and in each individual province'.

Murat forthwith canvassed 150 members of the clergy, the nobility and the community at large, as representing the three estates. The last were to be drawn from the universities, the army and navy, commerce and the deputies from the different metropolitan provinces and the Americas. In fact, only 94 representatives agreed to make the journey to Bayonne, a notable absentee being the Bishop of Orense, who in declining the summons paid lip service to Napoleon, but continued: 'At present Spain cannot but behold him under a very different aspect. She sees, or thinks she sees in him the oppressor of her princes and of herself. She looks upon herself as enchained and enslaved, when happiness is offered to her. More than is worked by artifice, is done by violence, and by an army which has been admitted as a friend, either by indiscretion or timidity, or perhaps by a vile treason which serves to give an authority that cannot easily be esteemed legitimate....'

On 15 June the sixty-five deputies who had by then arrived in Bayonne began detailed consideration of a draft constitution already prepared by the Emperor. The sessions lasted for twenty-three days, with the Spaniards making suggestions for modifying clauses which in their opinion ran counter to Spanish tradition and institutions. Some of their proposals found their way into a final draft submitted to the Emperor, who simply pencilled *approuvé* or *refusé* against them. On 8 July Joseph Bonaparte solemnly pledged himself to observe the new constitution, and the deputies swore loyalty to him. He then named his first cabinet, which was headed by the Marquis of Urquijo and included Pedro de Ceballos, Miguel José de Azanza, Gonzalo O'Farril, José de Mazarredo, the Count of Cabarrús and Sebastián Piñuela. The patriot Gaspar Melchor de Jovellanos, later to play a dominant role in forming a free Cortes at Cadiz, honourably declined Joseph's invitation. The others, whose motives, though mixed, were by no means entirely venal, formed the nucleus of the so-called *afrancesados* (or 'French-influenced'). Misguided they may have been; but, as will appear, they hardly deserve Sir Charles Omans's sweeping denunciation as a miserable 'traitor faction'.

On 9 July 1808 Joseph Bonaparte crossed the frontier to take possession of his new kingdom. He can have had little idea of what he was to find. Napoleon consistently underrated the problem of occupying the country and thanks to the erroneous reports of Murat was under the impression that 'the affairs of Spain are going off wonderfully well'. Only a week or two before he had informed Escoiquiz that 'countries full of monks like yours are easy to subdue. There may be some riots, but the Spaniards will quieten down when they see that I offer them the integrity of the boundaries of the monarchy, a liberal constitution, and the preservation of their religion and their national customs.' What Joseph was actually to enter into was a Spain in which spontaneous revolt had flared up from the Asturias and Galicia in the north to Seville and Cadiz in the far south.

Chapter 6

BACKLASH IN SPAIN

The apparatus of government which proved so helpless in the face of *force majeure* from Bayonne was authoritarian and had evolved as a means of implementing the decisions of an absolute monarch. With the head—in the form of the King—cut off, it is not surprising that the limbs should cease to function. Decisions made in the first place by the King and his council of ministers were communicated to the Council of Castile, whose function was to enact them. It has been defined by a French historian, Desdevises du Dézert, as at once 'a legislative committee, a political council, and a supreme tribunal of justice, civil and criminal'. One of its responsibilities was, from time to time, at the King's wish, to convoke the Cortes. To describe the Cortes, which worked on a regional basis, as a 'parliament' is perhaps misleading; it was rather an assembly of representatives from the three estates—clergy, nobility and commons—with very limited advisory powers.

Events in Bayonne had demonstrated the moral bankruptcy of the old regime and the incapacity of the central organs of government. The *Junta de Gobierno*, ostensibly ruling in the name of the King, and the Council of Castile were almost completely cowed by the Duke of Berg. The Spanish people could now only turn to the local organs of government in their deep-seated determination to resist the invader.

The different provinces of the country were each administered by a Captain General, or military governor, who was also the president of the *Audiencia*, a committee responsible for civil government. In the first instance the Captains General and the bureaucrats of the *Audiencias* displayed as little fighting spirit as their opposite numbers in Madrid and contented themselves with posting the edicts of the Council of Castile and the *Junta de Gobierno*. As Miguel Artola Gallego has written in Volume XXVI of the *Historia de España*, 'they were not traitors, nor were they sold to the French, but they failed to rise to an historic responsibility, as much for reasons of legality as for an understandable fear of the likely consequences of being dragged down in a general débâcle'. They were officials schooled to rubber-stamp any document presented in the prescribed form, whether signed by Charles IV, the Prince of Peace or Murat; and as members of the Establishment were more afraid of a state of public anarchy than of the French army. The orders from Madrid were to preserve the peace at any cost, and these they slavishly followed.

The mass of ordinary Spaniards were patriotic to a degree and believed in the near sanctity of their monarch. So it was that a ruler as ineffective as Ferdinand, when forcibly wrested from them, could become the 'Desired One' of the Peninsular War. At the time of his enforced departure for Bayonne the people of Vitoria had attempted to cut the traces of his coach; and plans for a popular uprising were only abandoned when he made plain his express wish to meet the Emperor. The timid reaction of the authorities to the betrayal of Bayonne led to a mounting outcry.

Open revolt first broke out in the isolated northern province of the Asturias; it is perhaps significant that it was from the fastness of its mountains that the legendary King Pelayo mounted the first counter-attack on the Moors. On 9 May 1808 the *Audiencia* in Oviedo received decrees issued by Murat, the Council of Castile and the *Junta de Gobierno*, together with orders for their immediate publication. This resulted in immediate uproar, and the *Audiencia* was forced to adjourn amidst cries of '*a las armas!*' ('to arms!'). An emergency meeting of the *Junta General del Principado*, a form of assembly dating from mediaeval times, was called for that same evening; and the old Duke of Santa Cruz sounded a dramatic call for 'the conservation of the Monarchy and the defence of the country'.

The two bodies had a number of members in common, and the Junta, proceeding with due regard for the authority of the *Audiencia*, allowed the offending decrees to be publicly posted and temporarily suspended its session after a vote weighted by the members of the *Audiencia*. Matters took a new turn when orders arrived from Madrid for the execution of fifty-eight members of the Junta and the intervention of the army. An arms factory was stormed; and the rebels forced the military governor, La Llave—who throughout took the side of the *Audiencia* and the Madrid authorities—to convene what was to become a Supreme Junta 'with all the attributes of authority'. Article 8 of its constitution called for the immediate declaration of war on Napoleon, and all its members were required to pledge themselves 'to sustain the liberty and independence of the Nation against the infamous aggression of the Emperor of the French until the restoration to the throne of Ferdinand VII, the only king recognized and sworn to by the Nation'. All the members, including the recalcitrant deputies of the *Audiencia*, took the oath, with the exception of La Llave, who preferred to resign.

The formation of the Supreme Junta on 21 May was accompanied by a general uprising in Oviedo and the surrounding countryside, a gesture of great courage considering the proximity of strong French armies in the provinces to the east. One of the first actions of the Junta was to despatch a letter to the Magnanimous Monarch of Great Britain, in which the Principality 'through its deputies furnished with full powers presents itself to solicit from Your Majesty the succours necessary in its present situation'. The deputies, one of whom was the Spanish historian the Count of Toreno, reached London on 7 June after a passage on a Jersey privateer. Five days later the foreign secretary, George Canning, assured them that military supplies would be shipped immediately to the port of Gijón, adding that, 'Every ulterior effort will be cheerfully made by His Majesty in support of so just a cause. I am commanded by his Majesty to declare to you his Majesty's willingness to extend his support to all other parts of the Spanish monarchy, as shall shew themselves to be actuated by the same spirit which animates the inhabitants of Asturias. . . .' It was in fact the plea from the Asturians which first set in motion British military intervention in the Peninsula.

The Junta meanwhile sent representatives to the province of Galicia neighbouring the Asturias on the west. The opposition of the authorities was more stubborn, but after an army revolt and the flight of the Captain General, Filangieri, who was later assassinated, another Supreme Junta was declared on 30 May. Here, as elsewhere, what began as a popular uprising was fairly soon supported by the authorities on the spot.

The Asturians were as yet unaware of what was happening elsewhere, but spontaneous uprisings were soon to result in the formation of Supreme Juntas in Oviedo, Badajoz, Seville, Valencia, Catalonia and Saragossa. They were achieved only at the expense of considerable bloodshed and the murder of former supporters of Godoy and officials, who, because of their procrastination, the insurgents suspected of favouring Murat. Many high-ranking army commanders displayed little enthusiasm for lending support to what they evidently regarded as a revolutionary mob. The only commander to join in the *Levantamiento* spontaneously and without hesitation was General Castaños, the future victor of Bailén. At Valladolid in Old Castile the aged General Cuesta, who was later to infuriate Wellington with his lack of decision before the Battle of Talavera, came near to paying for his hesitation with his life. General Solano at Cadiz persisted in defying an excited crowd, stirred to revolt by the arrival of emissaries from the Seville Junta, and obstinately maintained that they had only to look to the ships of the blockading English fleet to see their real enemies. He was chased from his house and later stabbed to death—perhaps by a friend, to save him from a worse fate at the hands of the mob. Various other Captains General were killed, including Francisco de Borja at Murcia and Torre del Fresno in the Extremadura. In Catalonia, with its capital, Barcelona, occupied by Duhesme, some of the Spanish officials actively supported the French; and local Juntas were set up at Lérida, Manresa, Tortosa and Villafranca del Panadés only after the assassination of their governors.

The most powerful of the Juntas were those of Seville and Galicia—for the same reason: that both had fairly powerful armies at their disposal and also naval bases, El Ferrol and Corunna in the north, and Cadiz in the south, through which they could be supplied and reinforced from England. The Seville Junta, proclaimed on 26 May 1808, was soon to take the lead by assuming the title of *Junta Suprema de Gobierno de España e Indias* and despatching deputies to organize resistance in neighbouring provinces. This unilateral declaration of supremacy was later to cause friction elsewhere, culminating in the dissolution of the Central Junta in January 1810.

Meanwhile, on 29 May it issued a proclamation requiring that, 'In cities and towns consisting of 2,000 or more householders, a junta shall be established, which shall superintend all arrangements, and shall be obeyed by all the inhabitants', and specifying what these arrangements were to be. On 6 June, on behalf of Spain and Spanish America, it formally declared war on Napoleon and France, further declaring that 'there shall be open and free communication with England, that we have contracted and will keep an armistice with her, and that we hope to conclude a durable and lasting peace. Moreover we protest, we will not lay down our arms till the Emperor Napoleon the First has restored to Spain our king, Ferdinand the Seventh, and the rest of the royal family; has respected the sacred rights of the nation, which he has violated, and her liberty, integrity and independence.'

Although the *Levantamiento* took place without a tithe of the bloodshed of the French Revolution, it was a true popular revolution; and from this it derived its strength and its weakness. Among its leaders it numbered patriots like Joseph Palafox, the hero of the sieges of Saragossa, experienced in politics but out of favour with the old regime; but in general the men at its head were unused to governing and found it easier to issue resounding proclamations than to organize effective resistance to the invasion. After the first mass uprising and the demonstrations in the streets the ordinary people, from whom the movement derived its support, tended to leave the day-to-day conduct of the Juntas to people who had been carried willy-nilly by the wave of popular indignation rather than to those who had instigated it. The military had in the first place been undecided; and it is significant that most of the real successes in the field were to be achieved by the irregulars, among them the fiercely independent *miqueletes* and *somatenes* of Catalonia, rather than by regular troops officered by *hidalgos* representative of the traditional ruling classes. The Juntas, in pledging their loyalty to the exiled Ferdinand VII, may not have been fully aware of the revolutionary step that they had taken; one thing is certain: that, although Ferdinand VII was finally restored to his throne, Spain was never again to be satisfied with the forms of government of the old Bourbon monarchy.

The Peninsular War proper began with the successive declarations of hostilities by the different Juntas; and it is of interest to summarize the strategic position at the outset.

Apart from the isolated forces of Junot in Portugal and Duhesme in Barcelona, the French were solidly established in the north of Spain at San Sebastián and Pamplona and in secure possession of the main road to Madrid through Vitoria and Burgos. They had thus cut the north of the country in half. Napoleon's main preoccupation was with the threat to his right flank from the well-equipped army of Galicia. There was little to fear on the left, since Joseph Palafox, the newly appointed Captain General of Aragon, had only 2,000 regulars and a single battery of artillery at his disposal—and was soon himself to fight a desperate battle for Saragossa. The Spanish forces in Valencia and Murcia were also relatively weak; and the first major trial of strength was to be with the armies of Andalusia, which on 15 June 1808 had already captured the remnants of the French fleet defeated at Trafalgar in the harbour of Cadiz.

PART TWO
The War

Chapter 7

MEN AND ARMS

All who run or ride through the Peninsula, will read thirst in the arid plains, and hunger in the soil-denuded hills, where those who ask for bread will receive stones. . . . Hunger and thirst have ever been, and are, the best defenders of the Peninsula against the invader. On sierra and steppe these gaunt sentinels keep watch and ward. . . .

RICHARD FORD, *Gatherings from Spain*, 1846

It is the habit of military histories, of which this is not primarily one, to line up the combatants, to enumerate their numbers, equipment and tactics—and then, with mathematical precision to analyse the outcome, as if war were a game of chess. The Persians may indeed have devised chess in the guise of a war game; but Spaniards are not chessmen, nor is Spain a chessboard. The temptation, especially for the English historian, basing his account on the numerous memoirs and eye-witness reports of officers engaged in the campaign, is to describe the Peninsular War in terms of a series of set battles between the armies of Wellington and the French, with the Spaniards and Portuguese playing an ineffectual peripheral role. Liddell Hart, in *The Strategy of Indirect Approach*, is much nearer the mark when he remarks that 'by treating the Peninsular War as a chronicle of Wellington's battles and sieges it becomes meaningless', or again that, 'Wellington's battles were perhaps the least effective part of his operations. . . . The overwhelming majority of the losses which drained the French strength, and their morale still more, was due to the operations of the guerrillas, and of Wellington himself, in harrying the French and in making the countryside a desert where the French stayed only to starve.' It was, in fact, his long-drawn-out strategic retreats, so much criticized at the time both by Spanish patriots and an English public hungry for victories in the field, which were to be a determining factor in the defeat of the Imperial armies.

The Iberian Peninsula is one of the most mountainous regions in Europe. At its centre is a bleak plateau, bitterly cold in winter and without shelter from the beating summer sun, criss-crossed by great mountain massifs with foothills running down to the sea. A low-lying coastal fringe is of considerable width around Cartagena and Valencia, extends up the Guadalquivir valley into Andalusia as far as Cordoba and into southern Portugal; elsewhere it is narrow. The Pyrenees effectively barred the French access to Spain except at either end near the coast; from Madrid at the centre it is almost impossible to travel towards the coast in any direction without crossing a mountain barrier; and Portugal is screened by a range of mountains running from north to south along the frontier, through which only the valleys of the Guadiana and Tagus in the south and centre, and of the Duro and Minho in the north, afforded access, difficult at that, to an army and its baggage train. It was only because of this natural obstacle that Wellington, greatly outnumbered by the French for most of the campaign, was able to strike into Spain, to retire and regroup, and strike again when opportunity offered.

On geographical grounds alone Napoleon disastrously underestimated the difficulties of conquering the Peninsula. It was one of his cardinal precepts—and one that had served him well in Italy and Germany—that an army should live off the countryside. This proved to be totally impossible in Spain, where in the larger part of the country the peasants found it difficult enough to feed themselves, let alone an invading horde. The measure of the problem facing an invader is the bitter adage: 'In Spain large armies starve and small armies are defeated.' As Richard Ford well put it, 'The knife and fork question has troubled every warrior in Spain, from Henri IV down to Wellington; "subsistence is the great difficulty always found" is the text of a third of the Duke's wonderful despatches.'

Of all the commanders in the field, Wellington had the firmest grasp of this essential requirement, although he could not always provide against contingencies. 'If you mean to dine,' he writes to General Hill from Moreleja, *'you had better bring your things,* as I shall have nothing with me.' Even after his personal intervention during the campaign of 1808, Napoleon remained under the delusion that, 'Spain is a much better country than he had ever supposed, and that he had no idea of what a magnificent present he had made to his brother Joseph till he had seen it.'

The Spaniards themselves were the least organized; and the recurrent defeat of their regular armies during the early stages of the war very largely stemmed from throwing away hastily recruited and ill-equipped troops with only the scantiest provision for supplying them. The most terrible example of the losses suffered by an ill-provided army is that of Marshal Masséna's during his Portuguese offensive of 1810/11. Out of an original 65,000 officers and men, 2,000 were killed in action and 8,000 were captured by Wellington (half of them already hospitalized). A further 15,000 men died of starvation and illness, among them many stragglers who had broken away from the main force in a desperate search for food and were butchered by the revengeful Portuguese peasantry.

If Napoleon failed to grasp the problems of his marshals in provendering their men and animals, he was still less aware of the appalling system of communications. The one good military road was that from the north through Burgos, which he travelled himself during his march on Madrid in the winter of 1808. Elsewhere the natural obstacles of high passes and rivers, impassable during the winter floods except by narrow and infrequent bridges, were made worse by the lack of anything except winding cart tracks following the lie of the land and often unsuitable for the passage of an army and its baggage train. Even the English, with the goodwill and advice of the native Spanish and Portuguese, made serious miscalculations—hence Sir John Moore's disastrous decision before the retreat to Corunna to march to Salamanca by one route and to send his artillery by another, which, in the event, proved far worse.

In practical terms one result was the near impossibility of co-ordinating the movements of the different French armies and arranging for their massing at a given place and time; another was the terrible toll taken of stragglers, the interception of despatches by roving bands of guerrillas and the impossibility of movement except in force. Perhaps the most glaring example of Napoleon's unfamiliarity with the difficulties of the terrain was his order to Marshal Soult after the evacuation of the British army from Corunna. Assuming that the Marshal would arrive at Lugo, in the far north-west of Spain, on 9 January 1809, the Emperor gave orders that he was to occupy Oporto on 1 February and Lisbon about the 10th. Soult's army was in fact so exhausted by hunger and lack of supplies that he did not leave Corunna until 20 February and was not able to take Oporto until 29 March; he had still made no further progress towards Lisbon when he was driven out of Oporto by Wellington on 12 May.

In the halcyon days of July 1808, with Joseph Bonaparte on the high road to Madrid and Murat reporting that 'the country was tranquil, the state of public opinion in the capital far happier than could have been hoped', the Emperor was far from foreseeing these grim developments. The north-east was firmly in his hands and his plan was to despatch flying columns to the remaining centres of resistance. With the provincial capitals in French hands, and in the light of his successes elsewhere in Europe, by all the rules the country must then lay down arms. The reality was far different. As the French armies fanned out, still further extending their long lines of communication, one of their officers wrote: 'the march of our army reminds me of a ship at sea, creating a wake, which disappears without trace of its passage'.

If hunger, cold, disease and the sheer size and impenetrability of the occupied territory were to be enemies that Napoleon could no more overcome than during the retreat from Moscow, more conventional military considerations played an important part, especially when the Spaniards attempted to fight Napoleon on his own terms with regular troops. It was only after their armies had suffered a series of defeats that might well have crushed any other nation that they took to guerrilla operations on a large scale. And without the intervention of Wellington, constantly drawing away large bodies of troops from garrison operations, the guerrillas would not have been left with sufficient freedom of action to harry those that remained. Fighting the same war in very different ways, Wellington and the guerrillas in fact complemented one another by ensuring that the French could rarely achieve overwhelming superiority in any given area of operations.

When the Juntas declared war in the early summer of 1808 the nominal strength of the Spanish army was some 100,000 regulars, but of these 15,000 of the best troops under the Marquis of La Romana had been creamed off by Napoleon to fight in the Baltic. The Marquis was soon to extricate 9,000 of them from Denmark in a daring amphibious operation undertaken with the help of the British navy. Thirty thousand auxiliaries, comprising urban militia and wounded veterans, were assigned to garrison duties. There were also some 13,000 foreign mercenaries, mainly Swiss and Germans, who also formed the core of the so-called 'Walloon Guards' originally recruited during the Hapsburg domination of the Low Countries. The Irish regiments of Hibernia, Irlanda and Ultonia (Ulster) were also a survival from an earlier period after the siege of Limerick, when the vindictive Penal Code of a Protestant parliament had forced thousands of young Catholics abroad to seek service against England in the armies of France and Spain. At the time of the Peninsular War these regiments were much under strength and short of Irish recruits; most of their men, the sons and grandsons of the original emigrants, were Spanish-speaking and Irish only in name and descent. The army was disproportionately weak both in cavalry and artillery: the 17,000 troopers disposed of only 9,000 horses, and the 6,500 artillerymen were equipped with only 216 guns and 400 beasts of draft to draw them.

Contemporary English observers spoke disparagingly of the officers, thus the Earl of Munster: 'We should not have been dissatisfied with our allies, *malgré* their appearance and their rags, if we had felt any reason to confide in them. The men might be "capable of all that men dare", but the appearance of their officers at once bespoke their not being fit to lead them in the attempt. They not only did not look like soldiers, but even not like gentlemen. . . .' Sergeant Surtees of the Rifle Brigade comments that, 'Most of the Spanish officers appeared to be utterly unfit and unable to command their men. They had all the pride, arrogance, and self-sufficiency of the best officers in the world, with the least of all pretensions to have a high opinion of themselves.' This state of affairs was the legacy of Godoy and of the habit of granting commissions on the score of birth and influence rather than of ability. But it must be added that there *were* officers who displayed great bravery, if not matching tactical skill; a surprising proportion were hereditary soldiers of fortune of Irish blood, notably Blake (pronounced 'Blacké'), the O'Donnells, O'Donovan, O'Daly, O'Neil, Lacy, Sarsfield and O'Donahue (hispanicized as 'O'Donaju').

The 116,000 troops with which Napoleon began the campaign were a very mixed lot, reflecting his opinion of the weak opposition that he expected in Spain and Portugal. Only about a third, mostly with Junot in Portugal and Duhesme in Barcelona, were veterans. The remainder were raw conscripts who had been under arms for less than a year. The 16,000 men of the 'legions of reserve' had seen at least a year's service as integral units, but the 'provisional regiments' and '*régiments de marche*', which between them made up about a third of the French strength, had been hastily thrown together with detachments of recruits drawn from the depots of southern France. A further 14,000 foreign troops from occupied Europe were scattered in single battalions among the five armies commanded by Junot, Dupont, Bessières, Moncey and Duhesme. Only under General Lecchi in Catalonia did the Italians and Neapolitans form a national division of their own.

Napoleon's contempt for his opponents and his employment of green troops undoubtedly contributed to the early reverses of Dupont and Moncey at Bailén and Valencia. The position was to change radically when after these defeats he himself crossed the Pyrenees in November 1808 and, at the expense of weakening himself in Central Europe, transferred 200,000 of his finest troops to Spain.

Napoleon normally employed a much larger ratio of cavalry and artillery to infantry than either the Spanish or the British. The French cavalry were to prove far more effective against the Spanish, whose generals would recklessly commit their men to battle in open country, than against the English. Because of the difficulty of hauling heavy artillery over mountain passes and along the appalling Spanish roads, the 'undergunning' of his opponents was not to play a large part in the outcome of the campaign—though when the English appeared on the scene, they were repeatedly handicapped by the lack of a siege train capable of breaching strong defences.

During the Revolution the French army had evolved the concept of the 'division', a very large, self-sufficient body of troops supported by the necessary cavalry and artillery. Napoleon's doctrine of living off the land was designed still further to increase striking power and mobility by reducing the number of non-combatants; and the rate of march of the infantry had been increased to 120 paces a minute as against the 70 habitual with other Continental armies. The purpose of these measures was to achieve rapid concentration of troops on the battlefield: superior mobility could make up for numerical inferiority or increase the disparity, as in Spain, where the French initially outnumbered the Spanish regulars by three to two.

The favourite tactic of Napoleon and his marshals, which had gained them so many victories in Italy, Austria, Prussia and Russia, was to attack in column. The main force was preceded by a screen of *tirailleurs* or skirmishers, whose object was to disorganize the enemy and distract his attention. The main force then advanced in column of companies, the whole weight of the battalion, regiment or brigade being thrown behind a front of forty men in a single long column. Often the mere impetus of this great battering ram was enough to carry it through the enemy lines. Against any but the steadiest troops drawn up in line, the effect was to throw them into confusion, so that they either took to their heels or could be taken from the rear and shot down in detail; and this was what almost invariably happened in confrontations between the French and Spanish armies.

Wellington's troops were far better officered and trained than the Spanish, and this enabled him to find an effective answer. His favourite method was to station himself above the enemy and to draw up a long double line of infantry just *behind* the crest of the position. To protect his lines he sent forward dispersed companies of riflemen to engage and repulse the *tirailleurs*, so that by the time the main French column advanced through the skirmishers it was unprotected, while his own lines remained intact. This was often achieved only with cruel loss of the riflemen; but if the *tirailleurs* could be held back, the main column was then open to a withering fire. Only the front two ranks of the column, 80 men in all (or 160, if as sometimes happened, a column of double companies was employed), could use their muskets; in return all his own men, usually 800 of them two deep, could pour bullets into the head of the column, bringing down the front ranks, halting the men behind, and exposing the struggling mass to withering flanking fire. So successful were Wellington's tactics that he never saw the need to change them in set encounter. At least one French general, Foy, admitted their superiority in his private journal, but not, presumably, to the Emperor's face—at any rate Napoleon stuck to his methods to the last, so that on the field of Waterloo Wellington was to remark: 'The French came on once more in the old style, and we beat them off in the old style.'

Overall figures for the nominal strengths of the French, Spanish and Anglo-Portuguese armies over the course of the war are of interest—if only because, in general terms, they demonstrate the enormous disparity between the numbers of French and British until the latter stages.

	French	Spanish	Anglo-Portuguese
June 1808	165,000	140,000	—
October/November 1808	300,000	217,000	33,000 (Moore)
February 1809	289,000		
May 1809			27,000 (Wellesley)
November 1809		119,000	
January 1810	325,000		
June/September 1810		100,000?	
September 1810			61,500 (including 25,000 Portuguese)
November 1810			67,000 (including 25,000 Portuguese and 8,000 Spanish)
July 1811	354,000		
June/September 1811		90,000?	
September/October 1811			63,000
October 1812	260,000		
May 1813			81,000 (including 29,000 Portuguese)
June/July 1813		99,000	106,000

This table is based on those printed on page 265 of Volume XXVI of the *Historia de España*. The number of Spanish 'effectives' fluctuated wildly according to the fortunes of war. It is obviously impossible to be precise; and these figures do not include the guerrillas.

Chapter 8

'WAR TO THE KNIFE'

Once the provincial capitals are in our hands, the country will be pacified; but if the revolt continues, a few mobile columns, destroying the centres of resistance and making an example of them, will restore order.

MARSHAL BESSIÈRES, in a letter
to NAPOLEON dated 16 April 1808

Napoleon's plan for subjugating Spain was imposing in its simplicity: Bessières was to ensure communications with France by disposing of the threat to the Madrid highway from Galicia on his right flank and Aragon on his left, at the same time despatching a brigade to capture Santander on the north coast; Moncey was to advance from Madrid and seize Valencia and the naval base of Cartagena with help from Duhesme, who was to march down the coast road from Barcelona and to join him; while it fell to Dupont to move forward from Toledo and to occupy Andalusia and the south, eliminating resistance in Seville, Córdoba and Cadiz.

Bessières accomplished two of his objectives without undue difficulty. General Cuesta, perhaps of all the Spanish commanders consistently the most incompetent, gave battle with his embryo 'Army of Castile', numbering some four or five thousand volunteers, to a professional force of twice the size. He was at once routed, with the loss of Valladolid to the French. In the meantime General Blake, a younger and more competent soldier, had been reorganizing the not inconsiderable Army of Galicia and joined forces with Cuesta and the wreck of his battalions. Unabashed by his defeat a month earlier, Cuesta, who was much senior to Blake, insisted on a pitched battle with Bessières on open ground. It took place on 14 July near the town of Medina de Río Seco and resulted in a further and more serious Spanish rout. The road to Madrid was now entirely safe, and Joseph Bonaparte and his entourage were able to make their entry into the capital on 20 July 1808. It was a somewhat hollow triumph: the streets were lined with French troops and loud with military music, but the inhabitants kept to their houses and even the servile Council of Castile refused to swear the oath of allegiance. Ten days later Joseph, his court and the French garrison were in full retreat up the road by which he had just come.

Bessières achieved the second of his objectives on 23 July, when General Merle, brushing aside resistance in the mountain defiles around Reinosa, emerged on the shores of Biscay and occupied Santander. Bessières's last task, the dispersal of the Spanish forces in Aragon, on his left flank, was seemingly the easiest, since Joseph Palafox in Saragossa disposed of only 1,500 men, comprising some 900 volunteers, 300 cavalry with only 90 horses between them, and 250 artillerymen and engineers. In the event the siege of Saragossa was to be one of the epics of the war, all the more important because it foreshadowed the only way in which the Spaniards were to offer effective resistance—with the active participation of civilians fighting in their own houses or in their native woods and mountains.

Joseph Palafox came of an aristocratic Aragonese family and was of the party that had accompanied Ferdinand VII to Bayonne. Disgusted by the betrayal, he succeeded in escaping to Spain, and at twenty-eight was appointed Captain General of Aragon when its capital rose in revolt. Although, like Godoy, he was a member of the Royal Bodyguard and only a chocolate soldier at the time, he at once set to work to organize the kingdom's defences, to such effect that by the end of the siege he had raised 30,000 volunteers and started factories for the manufacture of gunpowder and small arms.

At the time, Saragossa was a city of narrow streets and solidly built houses of some 60,000 inhabitants. It was surrounded by a high brick wall, which may have afforded some protection at the time of the Moors, but was only the flimsiest of defences against the French artillery. To the north it was protected by the wide Ebro river, across which a single bridge, commanded by artillery, connected it to the suburb of San Lazaro. To the south and west it lay wide open to attack, the only outlying defences being the old Moorish castle of the Aljafería, the monastery of Santa Engracia and the hill of Monte Torrero, rising to 180 feet and overlooking the city.

Not anticipating serious resistance, Marshal Bessières despatched General Lefebvre-Desnouettes with instructions to make a sweep down the Ebro valley and putting at his disposal 3,500 infantry, 1,000 cavalry and a battery of field artillery. This was shortly brought up to a strength of 6,000, when it was joined by another brigade and battery. The attempts of Palafox and his brother, the Marquis of Lazán, to hold up the advance were speedily crushed thanks to the overwhelming superiority of the French cavalry and artillery; and on 15 June 1808 Lefebvre appeared to the south of the city and decided upon an immediate frontal assault. In the light of similar attacks on cities elsewhere in Europe it was not an unduly rash decision; but Lefebvre had reckoned without the patriotic fervour of its inhabitants, who flocked to the walls and barricades. A simultaneous assault was made on the Portillo, Carmen and Santa Engracia gates, and at the latter a squadron of Polish lancers overran the battery defending the entrance and penetrated deep into the city, only to be decimated by a hail of bullets from the surrounding houses. At the end of the day Lefebvre withdrew, leaving 700 dead and a number of guns, and decided to postpone a further attempt pending the arrival of reinforcements.

Palafox was not himself in the city at the time of the first assault; as his brother later confessed in his memoirs, they 'had not believed that an open town defended by untrained peasants could defend itself'. Instead, he had ridden out to raise further levies; but his attempt to disrupt the French rear was summarily brought to nothing, when on the night of 23/24 June a mixed French and Polish force detached by Lefebvre fell upon his hastily assembled men and routed them. Having at last learned the lesson that his raw levies were no match for the French in the open field, Palafox, who had been wounded in the encounter, made a long detour with as many of his discouraged men as he could hold together and re-entered the city on 2 July by the bridge over the Ebro to the rear.

The second phase of the siege began with the arrival of some 3,500 French reinforcements under General Verdier, together with heavy siege guns earlier captured by trickery at Pamplona. Verdier took over command from Lefebvre-Desnouettes, and his first move was to occupy the hill of Monte Torrero and to install a battery of forty-six guns and mortars, which opened concentrated fire on the city and the old Moorish castle on the night of 30 June.

In the meantime, the defenders, encouraged by their earlier success, had banked up the walls with earth and sandbags, stockaded the gates and thrown barricades across the streets. Although the barrage caused enormous damage to buildings and opened fresh breaches in the walls, the population took refuge in the cellars and behind the stout walls of their churches, and their spirit was still high when, shortly after Palafox's return on the 2nd, Verdier launched six columns against the city. All were thrown back, the most desperate fighting taking place at the Portillo gate, where the gunners manning the small battery were shot down by musket fire. For a moment the defenders faltered, and then a young woman, Agustina Zaragoza, sprang forward, seized the lighted match from a dying artilleryman and discharged a round of canister point blank at the onrushing assault troops. In his account of the siege Palafox describes how her spirited action turned the tide. He commissioned her as a sub-lieutenant of artillery, and she later served with her battery in Andalusia. Sir Charles Vaughan met the 'Maid of Saragossa' and describes her as 'a handsome young woman of the lower class', while another contemporary English observer tells how he saw her at Seville, wearing 'a blue artillery tunic, with one epaulette, over a short skirt'. Goya's portrait shows her standing fusee in hand by the gun among the fallen artillerymen, one of whom, according to Palafox, was her lover.

The French lost 200 killed and 300 wounded in this second abortive attack, and Verdier now settled down to the systematic investment of the city by digging a series of trenches, or 'parallels', so as to bring his batteries close to the walls. The final assault began on 4 August with a murderous artillery barrage, which so shattered the walls that the infantry were at last able to capture the monastery of Santa Engracia and to penetrate the streets. At this point the French general sent in a messenger with a white flag to demand surrender; Palafox sent him back with the laconic reply '*Guerra a cuchillo*' ('War to the knife'). All through the afternoon the French fought their way forward, storming each house and barricade in turn with terrible losses on both sides, until they had driven a broad wedge as far as the Coso, the only wide street in the city; but they were still only half-way to the bridge across the Ebro, and as evening approached the attack lost impetus and the Spanish began to drive them back.

Both sides were by now exhausted; the French had lost 2,000 men in killed and wounded and the Saragossans probably about the same number. On the following day there was a lull inside the city; but Palafox had meanwhile received much-needed reinforcements from Catalonia, and in the evening news of the great French defeat at Bailén in Andalusia reached both sides. The heart had gone out of the attack; Verdier continued a sporadic bombardment, but on the 14th he began blowing up ammunition and spiking guns which he was unable to retrieve; and by 17 August his army was in full retreat on Tudela.

Over the two months of the siege French losses had amounted to 3,500 men. In all probability the Spanish had suffered even more, but the boost to morale was incalculable. The siege of Saragossa is one of those great romantic episodes, like the Cid's defence of Valencia against the Moors, which every Spanish child accepts as part of his heritage. Its historical significance is that it demonstrated to the hard-pressed Spaniards of the time that the Imperial armies, so formidable on the battlefield, when denied the freedom to manoeuvre could still be beaten—and by people who were not soldiers at all.

Marshal Moncey's expedition to Valencia, though in less dramatic fashion than the siege of Saragossa, spelt out the same message to both sides: that the Spanish regulars were no match for the French in open country, but that an aroused citizenry, fighting from the shelter of its walls and houses, was not to be cowed by conventional military methods.

One of the most senior and respected of French officers, Moncey began the 180-mile march from Madrid to Valencia on 4 June 1808 with an army of 9,000. Because of the impatience of Savary, who had replaced the ailing Murat, he took the shorter but more difficult northern route, so by luck rather than good management avoiding an army under the Count of Cervellón, which at the orders of the Valencian Junta was awaiting him at Almanza to his south. The excellent defensive positions of the precipitous defiles of Cabriel and Cabrillas were only weakly guarded, and by 26 June he had crossed the level *huerta* of Valencia with its scented orange groves and was in front of the city.

Having beaten back a sortie in strength, he now demanded its surrender. Valencia, like Saragossa, was a town of old walls and narrow streets; but it was protected by the River Guadalaviar to the north, and by opening up the irrigation canals and flooding the approaches, the defenders left open only a narrow sector to the south. Like Lefebvre-Desnouettes at Saragossa, Moncey launched a frontal assault, which the townspeople behind their earthworks and barricades beat back with heavy loss. The marshal then brought up his field artillery and attempted a second and even more disastrous attack, his retreating infantry being caught in destructive flanking fire on the open ground. '*On ne prend pas par collet une ville de quatre-vingt milles âmes*,' said Napoleon afterwards; and Moncey, belatedly aware of his danger, beat a prompt retreat towards Madrid. He was fortunate, in that Cervellón, always late and on the wrong spot, had meanwhile moved up to Cabriel and Cabrillas, leaving the escape route to the south wide open.

In accordance with Napoleon's overall plan of campaign, Duhesme in Barcelona had despatched a column towards Valencia on 4 June under General Chabran; it got no further than fifty miles down the coast road as far as Tarragona, when it was urgently recalled. Duhesme himself was in serious difficulties. All Catalonia was now aflame, with bands of armed peasantry, the so-called *somatenes* (from the Spanish, *somatén*, alarm bell) at large in the countryside. A second column under General Schwartz, destined to join Lefebvre-Desnouettes at Saragossa, had not even achieved its first objective of Lérida before being driven back in confusion to Barcelona. The *somatenes*, without the benefit of professional military leadership, had not as yet mastered the methods employed to such purpose by the guerrillas of later years; but Schwartz proved himself singularly unresourceful. Caught in a wide defile at Bruch in the mountains east of Barcelona, he formed his men into a large square with the cavalry and guns in the middle and began a slow retreat, thus offering a sitting target to the *somatenes* in the wooded heights on his flanks.

Duhesme, with his insufficient forces, shortly found himself with an even more pressing problem on his hands. One of the omissions of the original French advance into Catalonia had been to leave the garrison town of Gerona, astride the main road into France, in Spanish hands. With the *somatenes* active around Figueras and in the valleys of the Pyrenees further north, he now found that his communications had been cut and resolved that Gerona must be taken. Gerona was in fact no stronger than Saragossa or Valencia, but its small Irish garrison under Lieutentant-Colonels O'Donovan and La Valeta was determined and its citizenry equally resolute. After attempts to carry the gates by storm and to scale the walls under cover of a truce, Duhesme retreated in disorder to Barcelona.

With Perpignan across the border now threatened by the *somatenes*, Napoleon at last took notice of his pleas for reinforcements and despatched one of his aides-de-camp, General Reille, with orders to march south from Perpignan and join forces with Duhesme. Harassed from the sea by ships of the British fleet, which landed parties of marines to collaborate with the *somatenes* and to blow up the coast road, and threatened by the landing of a Spanish army from the Balearics, the combined forces of the two French generals proved entirely inadequate. A second siege of Gerona was an even more costly failure than the first; and towards the end of August 1808 Duhesme and Reille withdrew their forces to Barcelona. Napoleon had gravely underestimated the extent of Spanish resistance, and the situation was only to be restored after the arrival of massive numbers of seasoned French troops.

The most ambitious of the French operations, between them designed to bring Spanish resistance to an end in the summer of 1808, was the thrust south into Andalusia. Napoleon entrusted the expedition to General Dupont, a talented young officer who had won his spurs against the Prussians, but without experience of independent command prior to his arrival in Spain. The army of 13,000 with which he started from Toledo on 24 May was again unsuited to the magnitude of its task, comprising as it did only one battalion of French veterans, a mass of raw conscripts and such heterogeneous units as two detachments of the Paris Municipal Guard.

Dupont met with no resistance in the level uplands of La Mancha, nor even in the defiles of the Sierra Morena. Emerging into the Córdoban plain, he rapidly brushed aside the hastily organized opposition and on 7 June occupied the ancient capital of the Caliphate with the loss of only 32 dead and 87 wounded. There was therefore no excuse for the pillage, rape and murder, which continued unabated for two days. Córdoba was one of the richest cities of Spain; its churches and palaces were treasure houses of paintings, tapestries and metal-work; and the treasury alone was sacked of no less than ten million reals in coin. Officers and men alike took part in the systematic looting; and when the

French retreated nine days later they left with five hundred wagons piled high with the spoils. The atrocities set in train prompt Spanish reprisals: isolated parties of French wounded and foragers were set upon and tortured to death. General Foy, most reliable of French historians, in condemning the conduct of Dupont's army, goes on to relate how a French officer, Brigadier-General Rémé, was surprised and captured and then boiled alive. According to another account he was strapped down and sawn in two. In fact, the sack of Córdoba appears to have set the pattern for the brutalities perpetrated by both sides and so mercilessly depicted in Goya's *Desastres de la Guerra*.

By 16 June Dupont realized that all Andalusia was under arms and that his communications with Madrid were cut. He accordingly abandoned the idea of a further advance and retreated to the town of Andújar, short of the high mountain barrier of the Sierra Morena which lay between him and the capital. Here he injudiciously remained for a whole month awaiting reinforcements. The Seville Junta, under Francisco de Saavedra, made energetic use of this breathing space to reorganize its regular forces and to levy new recruits. By 11 July the Spanish commander-in-chief, General Castaños, had 33,000 troops at his disposal, including 2,600 cavalry, from which he formed four divisions, one under his own command and the others under Generals Reding, Coupigny, and Jones y La Peña. The French, in spite of Napoleon's disapproval, had meanwhile been twice reinforced from Madrid; but instead of concentrating the troops, which should have been more than a match for the ill-trained Spanish, Dupont made the fatal mistake of stationing his 20,000 men between three different towns: Andújar, where he was himself in command, and Bailén and La Carolina further north, but still to the south of the Sierra Morena.

The French flank was protected by the Guadalquivir; and a tentative thrust across the river by Reding east of Andújar led Dupont to the mistaken conclusion that the Spanish were cutting off his route of retreat through the Sierra Morena. He ordered up General Vedel with a strong force to liquidate this imagined threat; and Reding thereupon moved forward in strength across the river, driving a wedge between the two French armies. On 19 July Dupont began a hasty retreat in an attempt to join forces with Vedel, now pulling back across the mountains. Successive French attacks were beaten back by the Spanish divisions under

Reding and Coupigny drawn up in front of Bailén, and when La Peña descended on his baggage train and rearguard, Dupont sent his aide-de-camp to Reding, asking for terms.

Castaños drove a hard bargain. Dupont's surrounded army was to lay down its arms and even Vedel's division, now on the high road to Madrid, was required to turn back and surrender. It was agreed that all the disarmed French troops should be repatriated to Rochefort by sea. The Spanish were in no position to fulfil this last condition without the co-operation of Admiral Collingwood and the British navy. Grudging permission for the evacuation was obtained from London, so as to uphold the honour of Britain's Spanish allies; but in the event the Seville Junta and the Central Junta which succeeded it withheld permission for the return of any of the troops except Dupont and his staff. 'What right', wrote General Morla, the Captain General of Cadiz, to Dupont, 'have you to require the performance of these impossible conditions on behalf of an army which entered Spain under a pretence of alliance, and then imprisoned our King and princes, sacked his palaces, slew and robbed his subjects, wasted his provinces, and tore away his crown?' Many of the French prisoners were consigned to the Balearic Islands, where they subsequently died of cold and starvation. Dupont and his senior officers were more fortunate in being allowed to take with them part of their plunder, thus earning the bitter criticism of Napoleon, who accused them of more concern for their booty than their men.

The immediate result of the Battle of Bailén was the liquidation of a French army of some 18,000 and of the threat to southern Spain. It was going too far to describe Dupont's troops as 'the invincibles of Austerlitz and Friedland'—a claim still echoed by some Spanish historians today—but a recent British authority is equally wrong in dismissing the victory as 'a fluke'. All credit is due to the hastily trained Spanish levies in accomplishing what no other European nation had so far achieved since the Revolution: the destruction of an entire French army in open battle.

The repercussions of Dupont's disastrous defeat at Bailén were profound. In practical terms it led to the hasty retreat beyond the Ebro of Joseph Bonaparte and the 20,000 French troops remaining in Madrid. This left Marshal Junot, who had been ordered to go to Dupont's assistance, completely isolated in Portugal. Faced with a popular insurrection, he left only skeleton forces on the Spanish frontier to secure a possible line of retreat and withdrew the bulk of his troops to Lisbon. In the Spanish, their victory induced a heady mood of over-confidence and a belief that the French would soon be driven back across the Pyrenees. Instead of despatching Castaños with all speed after the retiring French, the intransigent Seville Junta found reasons for detaining their army in Andalusia and even contemplated sending it against Granada, whose Junta had refused to recognize Seville as the central authority for Andalusia and instead supported a Murcian proposal for forming a Central Junta. As reported by the historian Toreno, Castaños swept aside this divisive proposal with: 'Who is the man that dares bid the troops march without my leave? Away with all provincial differences: I am the general of the Spanish nation, I am in command of an honourable army, and we are not going to allow anyone to stir up civil war.'

During the months of August and September 1808, while the French were regrouping beyond the Ebro, the overriding preoccupation in Spain was with the formation of a central government. First in the field with its proposals was the discredited council of Castile, eager to resume power now that Joseph Bonaparte, whom it had come within an ace of recognizing, had fled the capital. Not unnaturally its approaches were scornfully rejected by the provincial Juntas. There remained three alternatives: to establish a regency, a proposal favoured among others by Palafox, Jovellanos and the Duke of Infantado; to convoke the Cortes; or to create a supreme Central Junta. It was felt by the local Juntas that it was they, as representing the popular will to resistance, who were responsible for the rebuff to the French. Not without a great deal of argument as to its powers and constitution, they therefore agreed to form a sovereign Central Junta, to which each of the local Juntas should send two representatives. In deference to the powerful Seville Junta it first met on 25 September 1808 in the royal palace of Aranjuez, rather than in Madrid. It numbered thirty-five delegates, of whom the majority were titled nobility, the balance being made up of jurists, clergy and the third estate; there was only one plebeian, Calvo de Rozas from Madrid.

From the outset it was criticized as being too numerous to act as an effective executive or Council of Regency, and not representative enough to take the place of the Cortes. Successive British ministers were particularly outspoken. Thus Charles Stuart wrote to Canning, regretting that its composition was not such as to inspire the courage or enthusiasm of those at its orders. Hookham Frere considered that its base should be broadened, while Richard Wellesley, embittered by its failure to ensure regular supplies to his brother, the future Duke of Wellington, later remonstrated with its secretary, Martín de Garay, and was partly instrumental in obtaining its replacement by a Council of Regency in January 1810. There was in fact a marked divergence of opinion between the British, who felt that the prime object of the Junta should be to secure the energetic prosecution of the fight against the French, and the Spanish, who remained preoccupied with its functions and programme as a new and revolutionary form of government.

In August 1808 the crying need, from the military point of view, was to appoint a commander-in-chief and to mount a concerted operation against the discouraged French. After his success at Bailén, Castaños was the obvious choice; but when a council of war finally met at Madrid on 5 September, attended by Castaños, Cuesta, General Llamas from Valencia and representatives of Blake and Palafox, it was dominated by personal and regional jealousies. Unabashed by his earlier defeats, Cuesta, who seems to have been the original Colonel Blimp and was shortly to be relieved of his command after his high-handed arrest of the delegates from his own Junta of León, claimed prededence. The meeting broke up with only a loose agreement for the convergence of the different Spanish armies on Vitoria. Even after the formation of the Central Junta at the end of September 1808, no provision was made for a unified command, and the generals acted on their own initiative with a minimum of consultation. The first fruits of this disorganization had been an abortive uprising in Biscay at the beginning of August, easily quelled by Bessières. It was a policy—or rather a lack of policy —which was soon to contribute to a series of shattering disasters for the Spanish armies in the field.

Meanwhile, events in Madrid were overshadowed by two new developments: the imminent arrival of Napoleon to take over personal command of the French armies and the intervention of Wellesley in Portugal.

Chapter 9

'A TIME TO STAND UP'

Now is the time to stand up boldly and fairly for the deliverance of Europe, and if the ministry will cooperate effectually with the Spanish patriots they shall receive from us cordial support. . . . Never was anything so brave, so noble, so generous as the conduct of the Spaniards: never was there a more important crisis than that which their patriotism has occasioned to the state of Europe. Instead of striking at the core of the evil, the Administrations of this country have hitherto gone on nibbling merely at the rind; filching sugar islands, but neglecting all that was dignified and consonant to the real interests of the country. Now is the moment to let the world know that we are resolved to stand up for the salvation of Europe . . .

RICHARD BRINSLEY SHERIDAN,
Leader of the Opposition,
in the House of Commons, 15 June 1808

Lord Portland's government was quick to grasp the possibilities of intervention in Spain and to implement its promise to the deputies from the Asturias. In this it had the full support of the Whig opposition, which had previously condemned aid for the 'effete despotisms of the Continent'; after a series of half-hearted and ineffectual expeditions abroad there was a general feeling in Britain that it was time to get to grips with Napoleon.

As commander of the British expeditionary force the Secretary of State for War, Castlereagh, chose the youngest lieutenant-general in the British army, Sir Arthur Wellesley (who is, of course, better known under the title of the Duke of Wellington, conferred on him later). It was an imaginative decision, since at the age of thirty-nine Wellesley had to his credit a series of brilliant victories in India, where the terrain and difficulties of supply resembled those in the Peninsula. At the time he was in Cork, mustering an army which was destined for South America to revenge a British defeat at Buenos Aires the previous summer. Once the decision was taken to send Wellesley's 9,000 men to the Peninsula, it was further decided to reinforce them with 5,000 from Gibraltar under Major-General Spencer, 3,000 from Madeira under Major-General Beresford and 10,000 under

Lieutenant-General Sir John Moore, to be recalled from an expedition to the Baltic.

It was largely thanks to Moore that in the quality of its fighting men, as well as numbers, the British army was better equipped to fight than at any time since the War of the Spanish Succession. The earlier campaigns of the Napoleonic War had stressed the need for an effective answer to the French *tirailleurs*. At Shorncliffe camp Moore had trained a Light Brigade, armed with the new and efficient Baker rifle instead of the old smooth bore musket, whose men were taught not only to manoeuvre rapidly and to take every advantage of tactical cover, but to rely on their own initiative and to support themselves in the field. It is nevertheless true that the army still suffered from the old and bad traditions of barbaric punishment for minor offences, incompetent officers, especially in the higher ranks, a lack of guns and cavalry, and grave deficiencies in the support services. Of this latter Wellesley wrote before leaving Ireland: 'I declare that I do not understand the principles on which our military establishments are formed, if, when large corps are sent out to perform important and difficult services, they are not to have with them those means of equipment which they require, such as horses to draw the artillery, and drivers attached to the commissariat.'

For all his reputation as a martinet, Wellesley was scrupulous in providing food and medical services for his men as far as was humanly possible—this at a time when one of his sergeants in the 7th Royal Fusiliers could write: 'When a man entered upon a soldier's life in 1806, he should have parted with half his stomach.' The same Sergeant John Spence Cooper gives such a vivid description in his *Rough Notes on Seven Campaigns* of the difficulties under which the British soldier fought that it is worth quoting at length:

> The dress of a soldier at that time was not for use, but show, like a child's doll in a toyshop.
> Take for example one of the 7th Fusiliers full dressed. On his head he wore a cap covered with heel-ball, polished like a mirror. On the cap, under a varnished rosette, stood a tuft of wool, six inches long, neatly trimmed. This weighty cap, or rather helmet, had nothing attached to prevent its falling off. When it did it took hours to repair the damage.
> All his hair, except for a little on the sides and front, was tightly bound round a piece of lead behind. The hair on the

sides was rubbed round till matted, then greased and powdered with flour. The whiskers were greased, set up, and also powdered.

About his neck he wore a stock of stiff leather four inches broad, well-varnished. This thing was a real nuisance.

Projecting two inches from his breast, he had a neatly crimped ruffle. On his shoulders there were two wings made of cloth and wool, neatly combed and trimmed. The wings were useful in keeping on the cross belts.

His jacket fitted far too tightly; his buttons were bright as silver; and the lace on his breast and cuffs was as white as pipe clay could make it.

His breeches were of white cloth, and reached a little below the knee; his long gaiters were black, and both breeches and gaiters were tight of course.

To bring all parts of his dress and accoutrements into close contact, there were loops, loops, loops; loops to the gaiters, loops to the cross belts; loops to the wings, etc., etc. Should he try to reach the ground it would have been fatal to some article of his set-off. Nothing could be contrived worse for real service.

Cooper further supplies a complete inventory of the articles carried by the infantryman on the march, see page 87.

It says a great deal for Sergeant Cooper's companions, drawn as they were from the roughest and most deprived sections of the community, that, uncomfortable, overladen, underfed and often having spent the night in the open on some bleak Spanish sierra, they should repeatedly have stood rock-firm against the most formidable troops in the world. At the Battle of Talavera the 7th Fusiliers went without food for forty-three hours.

Wellesley sailed from Cork ahead of the main body of his troops and arrived in Corunna on 20 July 1808. He soon discovered that, although the Galician Junta was eager for arms and money, it had set its face against the landing of a British army in Spain, no doubt suspicious about the presence of *any* foreign troops after the behaviour of her French 'allies'. Instead, the Junta reported to Wellesley on the uprising in northern Portugal and pressed for British intervention against Junot. He accordingly continued his journey to Oporto, which he reached on 24 July.

The city had risen in revolt a month before, thrown out the

1 Fusee and Bayonet	14 lb.
1 Pouch and Sixty Rounds of Ball, etc.	6
1 Canteen and Belt	1
1 Mess Tin	1
1 Knapsack Frame and Belts	3
1 Blanket	4
1 Great Coat	4
1 Dress Coat	3
1 White Jacket	0½
2 Shirts and 3 Breasts	2½
2 Pairs Shoes	3
1 Pair Trousers	2
1 Pair Gaiters	0¼
2 Pairs Stockings	1
4 Brushes, Button Stick, Comb	3
2 Cross Belts	1
Pen, Ink and Paper	0¼
Pipe Clay, Chalk, etc.	1
2 Tent Pegs	0½
	51 lb.
Extra Weight for Marching:	
Two Days' Beef and Three Days' Bread	5
Water in our Canteens	3
	59 lb.

French garrison and formed a Supreme Junta under its aged bishop, Dom Antonio de Castro. The Portuguese were desperately short of weapons and equipment, but had meanwhile been arming the peasantry with pikes and scythes, calling out the militia and reassembling units of the disbanded regulars. After Wellesley had further conferred with Admiral Cotton, whose fleet was blockading Lisbon and the Tagus, it was agreed that the British army should be put ashore at Mondego Bay some eighty miles north of Lisbon and the nearest point to the capital where troops could safely be landed without interference from the French. On 1 August, the day that Joseph Bonaparte evacuated Madrid, the British transports began disembarking their troops. The landings took place on an open beach in heavy surf and many of the boats were upturned, but the great bulk of the army and its equipment was safely put ashore. With the arrival at Mondego Bay a few days later of Spencer and his men from

Andalusia, Wellesley had at his disposal some 13,000 troops, reinforced by a further 2,000 Portuguese.

He had meanwhile received the unwelcome news from London that he was to be superseded in his command by two senior officers, Sir Hew Dalrymple, Governor of Gibraltar, and Sir Harry Burrard, an old Guards officer. Neither were soldiers of any great distinction or with Wellesley's own experience of handling a considerable army; and their appointments were made against Castlereagh's wishes and at the insistence of the War Office, which was unwilling to see eventual command of the forces in the Peninsula devolve on the underrated and unpopular Sir John Moore. In deferring to this decision, Wellesley wrote to his brother, William: 'I don't know what the Government proposes to do with me. I shall be the junior of all the Lieutenant-Generals, and of all the awkward situations in the world that which is most so is to serve in subordinate capacity in an army which one has commanded. However, I will do whatever they please.'

Without waiting for the arrival of his new superiors Wellesley began an advance on Lisbon, choosing the coast road so as to keep in contact with the British fleet and to minimize the threat to his flank from the French forces inland. Junot's first response was to despatch a force of 4,500 men under General Laborde to check the advance; but after heroic resistance they were dislodged and driven back from hilly positions at Roliça near the little walled town of Óbidos. With Lisbon on the verge of insurrection, Junot now found himself in an extremely difficult position and reluctantly decided to muster all the troops that he could spare from garrison duties so as to seek out and destroy the British army. Joining forces with General Loison and reinforced by the remnants of Laborde's defeated division, he succeeded in assembling 13,000 men and 23 guns and moved forward from his position at Torres Vedras.

Wellesley, too, was experiencing his own difficulties, since the new second-in-command, Sir Harry Burrard, had arrived in Maceira Bay and at once given orders to halt the British advance at Vimeiro pending the arrival of Sir John Moore and further reinforcements. It was therefore with something approaching elation that, during the last few hours of independent and unhampered command, he learned that the French were moving in to the attack on the morning of 21 August 1808. The battle followed a pattern that was often to be repeated. Regrouping his army to meet a threat to his left flank, Wellesley prepared for the main French attack by stationing his men in line just behind the crest of Vimeiro hill and throwing out a screen of riflemen in front of them to keep off the French *tirailleurs*. As Junot's densely packed columns now struggled towards the top of the hill, they were first met by concentrated artillery fire at short range. It was at Vimeiro that the British army first employed shrapnel—named after its inventor, Henry Shrapnel of the Royal Artillery—in its early form of a shell containing a large number of bullets and a bursting charge which sprayed them forward over a wide cone-shaped front. The destruction of the faltering columns was completed by a devastating flanking fire from the double row of musketeers, who had held their ground unscathed behind the ridge and finally swept the disorganized French downhill in a tumultuous bayonet charge.

The success at the centre was repeated on the left flank a mile to the east, and Wellesley, galloping along the ridge and surveying the wreck of Junot's army, was for immediate pursuit and a general advance on Lisbon. To his chagrin, General Burrard, who had hitherto stayed his leaden hand, absolutely declined to sanction any further move, saying that the army had done enough for one day and must await Moore's reinforcements now disembarking. On the next day, 22 August, Burrard was himself superseded by Sir Hew Dalrymple, who was ill disposed to Wellesley from the start—no doubt because he had been instructed by Castlereagh 'to make the most prominent use of him which the rules of the service would permit'. The stolid 'Dowager Dalrymple and Betty Burrard', as Wellesley scathingly referred to them in a letter to his brother, were spared the effort of further decisions by the arrival of an emissary from General Junot, the quick-minded and persuasive General Kellermann.

Junot at least was under no illusions as to his precarious position, but putting a bold face on matters, authorized Kellermann to offer the evacuation of all French troops from Portugal—provided they were conveyed in British ships to a French port on the Channel seaboard together with all their arms, equipment and baggage. This 'baggage' was later to be the cause of acrimonious dispute, since it was found to contain such items as priceless books from the Royal Library, church plate and a war chest to the tune of a million francs in gold bars. However, the ponderous Sir Hew was concerned only with securing the departure of the French army from Portugal; and since the military initiative had now been lost, Wellesley added his signature to those of his colleagues when the Convention of Sintra was finally signed on 30 August 1808. At the same time he had lost all confidence in his superiors and their ability to continue the war and at his own request sailed for England on 20 September.

Wellesley had by no means heard the last of the Convention and on his return home found himself at the centre of a storm of controversy. He wrote to his brother, the Marquis of Wellesley, on 5 October: 'I arrived here this day and don't know whether I am to be hanged, drawn and quartered, or roasted alive. However I shall not allow the mob of London to deprive me of my temper or my spirits; or the satisfaction which I feel in the consciousness that I acted right.'

Whatever the rights and wrongs of securing the French withdrawal from Portugal at the expense of evacuating their army, the Convention embodied clauses which were politically indefensible. The notorious Articles XVI and XVII provided for the British army to take under its protection both French subjects who had profiteered from Junot's presence in Lisbon and also Portuguese collaborators. These were decisions that should clearly not have been taken without the consent of the Oporto Junta. Dalrymple's pretext for failing to consult it was the somewhat feeble one that the Junta was not a legally constituted government; and he compounded this omission by reinstating the effete Council of Regency, although at Wellesley's insistence the doughty Bishop of Oporto was co-opted to it. The result, not unnaturally, was an immediate political storm in Portugal. The Convention further fell short in allowing Admiral Cotton to make his own terms with Siniavin, commander of the hostile Russian fleet trapped in the Tagus, and arranging for its sailors to be repatriated. Popular indignation in England was echoed in a petition presented to the King by the Corporation of London: 'The treaty is humiliating and degrading, because after a signal victory, by which the enemy appears to have been cut off from all means of succour or escape, we had the sad mortification of seeing the laurels so nobly acquired torn from the brows of our brave soldiers, and terms granted to the enemy disgraceful to the British name....'

Wellesley had some satisfaction in that Dalrymple and Burrard were immediately recalled and the command in the Peninsula given to Sir John Moore, but was outraged to learn that he himself was to appear before a Court of Inquiry in company with them. He defended himself with great spirit, attacking Dalrymple and Burrard for their timidity and lack of decision; and in the event all three generals were acquitted. In Wellesley's case the Court went further and added a rider to the effect that his whole conduct of the campaign was 'highly honourable and successful, and such as might have been expected from a distinguished officer'. Dalrymple was censured for his mishandling of 'those articles in the Convention in which stipulations were made affecting the interests of the Spanish and Portuguese nations', and the Government made no further use of his or Sir Harry Burrard's services in the field. Wellesley had to wait only four months, after the death of Sir John Moore at Corunna, before he was sent back to the Peninsula in undisputed command.

Chapter 10

NAPOLEON IN SPAIN

If public opinion in Britain was outraged by the Convention of Sintra, Napoleon was hardly less incensed; indeed, he is on record as saying that it was only the Court of Inquiry into the conduct of the English generals which saved him from sending Junot before a court martial. However, the surrender in Portugal was overshadowed by the news of the disaster at Bailén. 'Has there ever, since the world began,' he wrote in Bordeaux, 'been such a stupid, cowardly, idiotic business as this? . . . Dupont's own despatch shows that all that has occurred is the result of his own inconceivable folly. . . . The loss of 20,000 picked men [sic], will necessarily have the worst moral influence on the Spanish nation. . . .' To his brother, Joseph, he wrote: 'Dupont has dishonoured our flag. What incapacity, what cowardice! Those troops will be taken by the English. Events of such importance make it necessary for me to return to Paris. Germany, Poland, Italy, etc., all depend on one another. . . .'

Napoleon's fury was none the less because by now he must have realized that it was his own machinations at Bayonne and miscalculations as to the strength of Spanish resistance which were now threatening him with a war on two fronts. His first step was to send immediate reinforcements to northern Spain under Marshal Jourdan, who assumed general command when he arrived at Miranda de Ebro on 25 August 1808, pending the further arrival of much more massive bodies of veteran troops from Germany. In the meantime Napoleon endeavoured to secure his rear by cementing his alliance with the Czar of Russia, threatening the Austrians with dire repercussions in the event of any move against him and with an offer of peace to Britain—a theatrical move, recognized for what it was by Canning and promptly declined. In an order of the day dated 6 November 1808, the Emperor personally took over command of his armies in Spain.

Faced with some 300,000 troops including the flower of the

Grande Armée under such formidable commanders as Ney, Soult and Victor, the performance of the unco-ordinated Spanish armies was only what might be expected. More numerous, and much better led and equipped, the French were compactly massed behind the line of the Ebro and had the further advantage of short lines of communication. The Spaniards, on the other hand, were scattered along an extended perimeter without the benefit of unified command. Their strategy, such as it was, was to attack the French flanks; and for this purpose Blake massed his Army of Galicia in Biscay, while Castaños joined forces with Palafox to the east with the idea that the combined Armies of Andalusia and Aragon should roll back the French towards the Pyrenees. The fatal flaw in this scheme was that it left the whole centre of the front unprotected except for the small Army of the Extremadura under the Count of Belvedere. Thanks to the preoccupation of the Central Junta with constitutional matters and its failure to raise further troops on an adequate scale, Belvedere had only 11,000 men at his disposal; it had been hoped that these might be reinforced by the English from Portugal, but Sir John Moore was still more than a hundred miles away at Salamanca awaiting his artillery. The first reaction of the French was of caution; after the débâcle of Bailén King Joseph and Marshal Jourdan suspected a trap and failed to realize the complete inadequacy of the Spanish dispositions.

On taking over the supreme command, Napoleon at once took stock of the dangerous dispersion and overextension of the Spanish forces. He decided to play a waiting game, allowing the imprudent advance of Blake on his right and Castaños and Palafox on his left to continue still further before annihilating their armies and then smashing through the weakly held centre and advancing down the road to Madrid. Since his personal reputation was now at stake, he had taken care to assemble more than sufficient infantry, guns and cavalry to leave the outcome in any doubt.

In accordance with these plans Marshal Lefebvre, after a preliminary encounter at Zornoza on 31 October, routed Blake's Galician army at Espinosa in the mountainous Picos de Europa on 9 November. Blake himself escaped to Reinosa, further to the west. He had lost only 3,000 men, but two-thirds of his famished effectives melted away into the hills; they were later to fight to more purpose as irregulars.

Napoleon himself was meanwhile advancing on Burgos with some 70,000 troops under the command of Marshals Soult, Ney and Bessières. The Count of Belvedere, a young aristocrat without military experience who had taken over command of the Army of Extremadura only the day before, marched his 11,000 men out of the city on to open ground near the village of Gamonal, where they were promptly cut to pieces by a force of 5,000 French cavalry and fled in confusion, abandoning their guns and equipment. The French army thereupon occupied Burgos amidst the now familiar scenes of rape and pillage. Delaying his advance on Madrid for the next nine days, the Emperor next devoted himself to the destruction of the Spanish armies on his flanks. A column under Marshal Soult was despatched northwards to mop up the remnants of Blake's defeated army; without making contact with the elusive Blake, who had retired still further west into the Asturian mountains, it succeeded in capturing his baggage train and guns, together with a vast quantity of newly landed English stores, including 15,000 muskets, 35 field guns and a huge consignment of Cheshire cheese.

The remaining phase of the operation was the encirclement and destruction of the armies under Castaños and Palafox to the east. They were at the time confronted by Moncey's corps to the north of them. Napoleon decided that Marshal Lannes, though only recently recovered from an accident in which he had ridden his horse over a precipice, would be a more aggressive commander than the deliberate Moncey; and the change was therefore effected. Meanwhile Ney, with 9,000 troops, was despatched via Soria to take the Spanish in the rear.

Between them, Castaños and Palafox had about 40,000 men at their disposal, but many of the troops had marched from the south only in their light summer uniforms and were without greatcoats, and the army was ridden with dysentery. Castaños himself was ill when an envoy from the Central Junta, Francisco Palafox, a brother of Joseph, arrived with orders for an immediate offensive, which he issued on his own initiative. Castaños cannot have been reassured to learn on 18 November that he was being superseded, and when the Spanish army was attacked by Lannes at Tudela on the 23rd, it was in disarray with wide gaps between its different units. That disaster was not complete was because Ney, advancing by forced marches from the south, had been unable to reach Tudela in time—a deficiency for which he was later unfairly criticized on the score that he wasted time in the pillage of Soria. The Army of Aragon, which had borne the whole brunt of the French attack, was severely mauled, losing 4,000 men in killed and wounded. The only consolation for the Spanish was that the 20,000 strong Army of Andalusia, which General La Peña to his discredit had never fully committed, was able to make its escape and, uniting with other defeated units, to retire into New Castile to the south.

These operations marked the beginning of the dismal and all too frequent series of defeats which the regular Spanish armies were to suffer until the French were decisively beaten at the Battle of Vitoria almost five years later. The lack of success can be attributed to the same factors: bad generalship, the impetuous commitment of insufficient numbers of troops on unsuitable terrain, lack of guns and cavalry and the ill-equipment of soldiers who were often half starved. But if Napoleon's first operations had achieved their primary objectives and the road to Madrid was now wide open, in one respect they had signally failed. His aim was to *destroy* the opposing Spanish armies; they had not been destroyed, but dispersed; some of the troops were to find their way back to the ranks only to suffer further defeat, but others were to spring up like dragon's teeth and to swell the bands of irregulars. For all Napoleon's assertion that, 'Ever since he served at Toulon he knew them for the worst troops in Europe', or that, 'Nothing could be so bad as the Spaniards—they are mere rabble—6,000 French can beat 20,000 of them', in the last place he and his marshals were to find no answer against an enemy that simply melted into the landscape when attacked. By all the rules of the book the Spaniards should have submitted to their French masters once their armies were beaten and their cities occupied; but the Spaniards were not fighting a gentleman's war in approved eighteenth-century fashion, and the further the French extended themselves the more vulnerable were they to become.

Napoleon was meanwhile poised for the entry into Madrid and the reinstallation of his brother, Joseph, in the capital. The defences of the city were weak and a Junta of Defence was hastily organized to prepare for the attack. The most considerable body of troops at its disposal were nine battalions from Reding's division which had triumphed at Bailén; and these with other units, amounting in all to 12,000 men, were pushed forward under General San Juan in a forlorn attempt to hold the pass of Somosierra on the road from Burgos fifty miles to the north. San Juan posted the main body of his troops across the main road at the crest of the pass, without, however, securing the heights on either side. On making contact with the Spanish on 30 November 1808 with a vastly superior force, Napoleon at once sent forward his *tirailleurs* to outflank the position, but impatient of the result and with his usual scorn for the Spanish army, simultaneously launched a frontal attack with some hundred Polish lancers. Riding up to the muzzles of the guns with the greatest gallantry, they were shot to pieces; but this Spanish success was short-lived, and despite San Juan's efforts to rally his men, they were soon in precipitate flight. The retreat only stopped at Talavera, south-east of Madrid, where the unfortunate San Juan was set on by his own mutinous troops, shot while trying to save himself, and hung from an elm tree.

The Junta of Defence had pinned its hopes on holding the pass of Somosierra and was well aware that the city, with its open spaces and wide avenues, was indefensible; but the citizenry, with fresh memories of the heroic stand at Saragossa, was in fighting spirit. With Napoleon almost at the gates, hasty and amateurish efforts were therefore made to throw up barricades, and muskets were served out from the arsenal. Feelings ran so high that when it was discovered that some of the cartridges contained sand instead of gunpowder, an enraged mob seized the Marquis of Perales, charged with distributing ammunition, and beat him to death. It seems that he paid with his life for the peculation of some sub-contractor of Godoy's and that his murderers were in fact headed by a disappointed ex-mistress.

All this sound and fury availed nothing. On 2 December 1808, the anniversary of the Battle of Austerlitz, Napoleon arrived in front of the city and demanded its immediate surrender. His envoy was mobbed and only extricated with difficulty, and the Junta declared that 'the people of Madrid were resolved to bury themselves under the ruins of their houses rather than to permit the French troops to enter their city.' Napoleon retaliated by a cannonade of the gates, in which the splintering paving stones of the improvised barricades did great execution among the defenders, and by seizing the commanding heights of the Retiro. From here it was simple work for his battalions to sweep down

1. Queen María Luisa of Spain. Portrait by Goya. By courtesy of the Museo del Prado (Foto Oronoz)

2. King Ferdinand VII of Spain. Portrait by Goya. By courtesy of the Museo del Prado (Foto Oronoz)

3. The women of Saragossa man the guns. Engraving from *Luchas políticas del siglo XIX*. By courtesy of the Museo Romantico, Madrid (Foto Oronoz)

4. José Palafox. Portrait by Goya. By courtesy of the Museo del Prado (Foto Oronoz)

5. Soldiers on the March. Cartoon by Thomas Rowlandson. By courtesy of the British Museum

6. The harbour of Corunna and the explosion of 13 January 1809. Watercolour by Sir Robert Ker Porter. By courtesy of the British Museum

NI ES CABALLO, NI YEGUA, NI POLLINO EN EL QUE VA MONTADO, QUE ES PEPINO

7. Pepe Botella. Contemporary cartoon of Joseph Bonaparte. By courtesy of the Museo Municipal, Madrid (Foto Oronoz)

8. Napoleon. Contemporary Spanish cartoon. By courtesy of the Museo Municipal, Madrid (Foto Oronoz)

9. The Duke of Wellington. Engraving by Forster from a portrait by Gérard. By courtesy of the Museo Municipal, Madrid (Foto Oronoz).

10. Spanish guerrillas casting bullets in the Sierra Tardienta. Detail from a painting by Goya. By courtesy of the Patrimonio Nacional (Foto Oronoz)

11. *Madre Infeliz*. Etching from Goya's *Disasters of the War*. By courtesy of the British Museum

12. The convocation of the Cortes of Cadiz in 1810. Lithograph by Salmon y Capuz from a painting by Casado. By courtesy of the Museo Romántico, Madrid

into the broad avenue of the Prado. On 4 December the Junta recognized that further resistance was useless and capitulated.

A French officer has described the scene as the occupying troops entered the city: 'A melancholy silence had succeeded the noisy and tumultuous agitation which had reigned only the day before, both within and without the walls of the capital. The streets were deserted, and in the public places, even the numerous shops for eatables had not reopened. The water carriers were the only inhabitants who had not interrupted their customary employ. They walked along, calling, with the slow nasal accent of their native mountains of Galicia, *Quien quiere agua?* Nobody appearing to buy, the *aguador* from time to time ruefully answered himself, *Dios que la da*, and began his cry again.

'As we advanced towards the centre of Madrid, we saw a few groups of Spaniards standing upright, wrapped in their great cloaks. They looked at us with a melancholy and dejected air. When they discovered among our ranks any horse we might have taken, and ridden by one of our hussars, they immediately knew him by his paces. This roused them from their apathy, and they exclaimed to each other, *Este caballo es español*; as if to reproach them for belonging to us.'

Napoleon's prime object was to gain acceptance for the renewed rule of King Joseph, and in view of the passive attitude of the inhabitants he was careful to keep the occupying troops to a minimum and to restrain them from their customary violence. Only those Spaniards whom he regarded as the ringleaders of resistance were punished by imprisonment or deportation to France; other members of the Junta, like General Morla, were induced to swear allegiance to Joseph.

For the next three weeks the Emperor established himself at Chamartin outside the city and occupied himself with drawing up administrative reforms. Some, like the abolition of the Inquisition, were liberal in tenor and designed as a sop to the Spanish; but neither they, forcibly deprived of their liberty, nor Joseph, as their titular sovereign, were disposed to accept them. In fact, Joseph, who now, as later, took his responsibilities seriously, formally protested and asked to abdicate. This, Napoleon refused to countenance, and in bullying the notables of the city to sign a petition for the return 'of that sovereign who unites so much kindness of heart with such an interest in the welfare of his subjects, and whose presence will be their joy', his real object was to ensure that the inhabitants were in a properly submissive frame of mind before his brother's formal re-entry in January.

He was also, of course, active in making plans for the complete subjugation of the Peninsula. Apart from throwing out a protective screen around Madrid, it would seem that he was weighing up the advantages of two schemes: either to commit the mass of his troops to a southward thrust under Victor towards Seville or to send them west with Marshal Lefebvre to Lisbon. At the time he was under the impression that the British under Moore were in retreat through Portugal, and the Madrid *Gazette* carried a statement on 12 December that 'the English are in full flight towards Lisbon, and if they do not make good speed the French may enter the capital before them'. It therefore seems fairly certain that he was on the point of despatching Lefebvre to speed their departure, when he learned that, instead of retreating from Salamanca, Moore had broken into Old Castile and was challenging Marshal Soult. He at once abandoned all other plans and marched north with 50,000 men to aid Soult in the accomplishment of a plan even nearer his heart: the encirclement and destruction of the British army.

Sir John Moore took over command in Portugal on 6 October 1808 after the recall of Sir Hew Dalrymple and Sir Harry Burrard. The Government had earlier promised Sir Hew large reinforcements and urged him to advance into Spain, but the slow-moving Dalrymple had done nothing but enter into inconclusive negotiations with the Central Junta about the plan of campaign. Before leaving Portugal Wellesley wrote to Moore pledging him his support and also to Castlereagh, suggesting that the most effective way in which the British could intervene in Spain would be by marching north and striking at the French flank, thus disrupting communications between Madrid and the French troops massed behind the Ebro. This was in effect what Moore decided to do, with the further object of reinforcing the Spanish south of the river.

Unfortunately he was in possession of only the scantiest information about the state of the roads from Lisbon to Salamanca, which was his first objective. Dalrymple's earlier enquiries from the Junta about routes and supplies had proved entirely fruitless, and Moore was now informed by Portuguese officers that the direct route via Coimbra, Celorico and the frontier fort of

Almeida was impracticable for artillery. He therefore made the disastrous mistake of himself proceeding by Coimbra, but sending six of his seven batteries of artillery, supported by his only two cavalry regiments, by an enormous detour through Elvas far to the south and then in a great loop through Talavera and the Escorial, close to the Spanish capital: the mileages were 250 via Coimbra and 380 by Elvas. The first units of the main column, which had left Lisbon on 11 October, entered Salamanca on 13 November, but the guns and cavalry were not to appear until 2 December—by which time the Spanish armies on the Ebro had been shattered and Napoleon was entering Madrid. In the meantime Moore had discovered that the Coimbra road was perfectly suitable for artillery. It was a costly blunder for which Moore himself must bear part of the blame, since he might easily have verified that General Loison had earlier taken guns to Almeida from Lisbon along this selfsame road.

The British build-up was further delayed by the late arrival of the promised reinforcements from England. The bulk of a division of 12,000 fresh troops under Sir David Baird arrived off Corunna on 13 October 1808, only to be refused permission to land by the Junta of Galicia. This was the result of a disagreement between the British government and the Central Junta, which emerges very clearly in Lady Holland's *Journal*—and the Hollands, who had obtained a passage to Corunna on the British frigate *Amazon*, arriving on 5 October and thereafter spending ten weeks with the British expeditionary force in the north before embarking on a hazardous overland journey to Lisbon and the south, were in the best position to see both sides of the argument:

> The substance of Jovellanos's conversation with me when he spoke in the most open and frank manner possible, was as follows:
>
> I. An application was made to the English Govt. to furnish military support to Gen. Blake. Through Mr. Stuart [the British envoy to the Junta], a promise of 10,000 men was made to them, who were to be landed at Santander to cooperate with Blake, then at Reinosa. Orders accordingly were issued by the Ministry of War that every preparation should be made for the reception of this force. To the great astonishment of the Supreme Junta, the Governor of Coruña announced the arrival of the English army in that harbour

demanding cantonments about Ferrol, which request the Governor did not think was consistent with his duty to comply with until he knew what were the intentions of his Govt. with respect to that armament.

II. They have received from Apodaca [the Spanish Ambassador in London] *las quejas* or griefs which the Eng. Govt. has against them. I could only collect three, but rather think there is a fourth which has escaped my memory. 1st, the delay in allowing Baird's army to land and the want of alacrity to supply and further them on their march. 2ndly, the reserve and want of confidence in the Spanish. 3rdly, their requiring the English generals to be subordinate to the Spanish generals.

A factor that undoubtedly weighed heavily with the British government was the risk of landing a large force at Santander, which was in imminent danger of falling to the French; while on their side the Junta of Galicia was obviously loath to make provisions for the feeding and transport of such a large army in a region already denuded of supplies by General Blake. The upshot was that the Governor made no speed to acquaint the Central Junta of the situation, with the result that the landings were not completed until 4 November, when it was already too late for the troops to play any part in the crucial battles further south.

Having arrived at Salamanca, Moore settled down to wait for his artillery, unable to move forward without it, increasingly aware of the Spanish defeats and the nearness of the French, and debating with himself the necessity of an undignified retreat into Portugal, because he was deeply conscious that the army with which he had been entrusted was not simply '*a* British army, but *the* British army'. What added to his frustration was the continual arrival of messages and delegates from the Central Junta urging immediate action and bringing over-optimistic and misleading reports as to the military situation and the state of the Spanish armies. The mutual lack of confidence is vividly illustrated by a letter written by one of his officers, the brilliant cavalry commander, Lord Henry Paget, some weeks later. As will be evident from its tone, Lord Holland, to whom it was addressed, was one of the few Englishmen to speak up for the Central Junta.

MY DEAR LORD,—I am in a violent rage with you. You are the most prejudiced man alive. You talk to a parcel of people snug upon the sea coast [at Cadiz] and who, knowing your enthusiasm for the Spanish cause, flatter *your misconceptions* of the state of this country, and from the language of such people you form your judgement of the dispositions of the Spanish nation. '*Tis one not worth saving*. Such ignorance, such deceit, such apathy, such pusillanimity, such cruelty, was never both united. There is not one army that has fought at all. There is not one general who has exerted himself, there is not one province that has made any sacrifice whatever. There is but one town in Spain that has shown an atom of energy [Saragossa]. We are treated like enemies. The houses are shut against us. The resources of the country are withheld from us; we are roving about the country in search of Quixotic adventures to save our own honour, whilst there is not a Spaniard who does not skulk and shrink within himself at the very name of a Frenchman. . . .

This must be balanced by a further entry in Lady Holland's *Journal*, in which Jovellanos gives *his* impression of Moore: 'He complained of Moore's whole conduct, and his offensive treatment of the persons sent from the Junta. Escalante, when the first retreat was known, was deputed, and found him sulky and repulsive at Salamanca. In reply to the arguments urged to induce him to advance, he made no further reply than that, "Mon parti est pris, mon parti est pris; Romana has only 5,000 men. I have ordered rations at Ciudad Rodrigo for ye 10th of Dec., and mon parti est pris." Escalante, disgusted at his reserve and haughtiness of manner, quitted him, finding it hopeless to make any impression upon such an obdurate character. . . .'

After the news of the Spanish defeat at Tudela Moore had in fact ordered a general retreat on 28 November, and this provoked a violent reaction, not only from the Junta, but also from its new British envoy, Hookham Frere, who wrote on 9 December: 'If the British army had been sent abroad for the express object of doing the utmost possible mischief to the cause of Spain, short of actually firing on Spanish troops, they would have most completely fulfilled their purpose by carrying out exactly the measures which they had taken.'

Fortunately, for his own reputation and that of his country, Moore countermanded his order. He was belatedly joined by General Hope and the artillery on 2 December 1808 and shortly afterwards received news, apparently reliable, that Madrid was to be defended as stubbornly as Saragossa. It had, in fact, already fallen by the time the despatch reached him, but having at last reached his decision Moore decided to press his attack on the French lines of communication and wrote to Castlereagh on 10 December that if Fortune 'smiles we may do something good: if not, we shall still I hope have the merit of having done all that we could. The army, for its numbers, is excellent, and is (I am confident) quite determined to do its duty.'

He accordingly gave orders for his own forces and those of Baird to the north to converge on Valladolid. However, by the greatest good luck, there now fell into his hands an intercepted French despatch. Apart from giving detailed information about overall French strategy in the Peninsula, it contained the interesting news that Napoleon believed him to be in full retreat on Portugal and had ordered Marshal Soult to pursue the Spanish army of the north into the mountains of Galicia. It was evident that Soult, with some 15,000 men, would be almost entirely isolated from the bulk of the French forces. On the strength of this, Moore redirected his march northwards to seek out the French force. A junction was effected at Mayorga with Baird's column from Corunna; and on 21 December the British cavalry under Lord Henry Paget fought a brilliant action with Soult's advance guard near Sahagun. Moore was poised for a general attack, when news reached him that Napoleon was in hot pursuit from Madrid; he at once ordered his disappointed troops to retreat towards the north-west.

Napoleon was now under the misapprehension that Moore was near Valladolid, and his object was to press forward along the main road to Benavente and so to cut off the escape line to the north and west. It seems that, for his part, Moore was under no illusions as to the danger of his own manoeuvre and that it was deliberately undertaken to draw off French forces from Portugal and the south. As early as 6 December he had written to Baird: 'I mean to proceed bridle in hand, and if the bubble bursts, we shall have to make a run for it.' As matters turned out, he never came under any threat from Napoleon's army. By the time the Emperor reached the Guadarrama mountains north of Madrid his column was engulfed in a swirling blizzard; his guns became stuck in the snow and were only extricated by unhorsing his cavalry, trampling down a track and laboriously hauling the guns across the pass with double teams. Napoleon, in fact, only proceeded as far as Astorga, long after Moore had passed through the place on his way to Corunna. Here, on 1 January 1809, he received disturbing despatches from Paris and left the pursuit to Soult's reinforced army, while he himself made plans to return to France.

Moore was meanwhile urging his flagging troops along the wild and mountainous roads towards Corunna, while his rearguard under General Edward Paget blew up bridges in its wake and held off the incessant harrying attacks of the French cavalry close behind. Discipline in the ranks was beginning to fail, as 'T.S.' [Thomas Pococke] of the 71st Highlanders recounts. 'Our sufferings were so great, that many of our troops lost all their natural activity and spirits, and became savage in their dispositions. The idea of running away from an enemy we had beat so easily at Vimiero, without even firing a shot, was too galling to their feelings. Each spoke to his fellow, even in common conversation, with bitterness; rage flashing from their eyes, even on the most trifling occasions of disagreement. The poor Spaniards had little to expect from men such as these, who blamed them for their inactivity. Every man found at home, was looked upon as a traitor to his country. . . .' Lady Holland, reinforcing this, reports that, 'There are many letters from Galicia complaining of the atrocities committed by the English, and in one of them is this expression, "*Terror enfurecido de nuestros aliados*" (rampant terror of our allies), who ravaged towns and villages and even surpassed some of the French in some of their excesses.'

The army was held together only by the superb bearing of the Light Brigade under Robert Craufurd, of the Guards Brigade and of Paget's division. Having struggled forward as far as Astorga, the demoralized troops had hopes that Moore would make common cause with a 5,000-strong Spanish army under the Marquis of La Romana and turn to face the French; but although there were ample supplies in the town and the position was strong, Moore's only consideration seems to have been to extricate his army and evacuate it from Corunna.

Some of the worst scenes of the retreat occurred at the villages of Villafranca and Bembibre. At the first, hundreds of men broke into the local wine store, and many of the drunken redcoats were still there when the French cavalry rode in, 'slashing among them as a schoolboy does among thistles'. Bembibre was an important supply base, and again the troops ran wild, breaking open barrels of rum, pillaging the stores, breaking into private houses and terrorizing the inhabitants.

The worst deprivations of this unhappy army occurred on the last stages of the retreat near Lugo. Dr. Adam Neale writes in his *Spanish Campaign of 1808*: 'All that has hitherto been suffered by our troops was but a prelude to this time of horrors. It had still been attempted to carry forward our sick and wounded: here (on Monte Cebrero) the beasts which dragged them failed, and they were left in their wagons, to perish among the snow. As we looked round on gaining the highest point of these slippery precipices, and observed the rear of the army winding along the narrow road, we could see the whole track marked out by our own wretched people, who lay expiring from fatigue and the severity of the cold—while their uniforms reddened in spots the white surface of the ground. . . . But too frequently their dying groans were mingled with imprecations upon the General, who chose rather to let them die like beasts than to take their chance on the field of battle. That no degree of horror might be wanting, this unfortunate army was accompanied by many women and children, of whom some were frozen to death on the abandoned baggage-wagons, some died of fatigue and cold, while their infants were seen vainly sucking their clay-cold breasts.'

The army reached Betanzos, twelve miles east of Corunna on the coast, on 11 January 1809. With the goal now in sight and thanks to milder weather and supplies of food sent out from Corunna, spirits revived somewhat; but Moore was put out to find that his transports were rounding Cape Finisterre from Vigo and not yet at anchor. He therefore spent the next few days destroying the great supply dumps in the city and blowing up ammunition—no less than 4,000 barrels of gunpowder intended for the Junta of Galicia were destroyed in this way, shattering half the windows in Corunna. On the 14th the ships at last appeared, and embarkation of guns, cavalry and wounded was begun. Three hundred of the sick were too ill to travel and were left in hospitals, and 2,000 of the horses were in such sorry state that they were shot and flung into the bay. Moore left himself with only sufficient artillery to hold off Soult, with whom he now realized that he would have to fight a pitched battle to gain time for the embarkation to be completed.

Five thousand of his troops had been lost during the terrible retreat, and allowing for those already embarked he was left with 15,000 men to face the French. The bulk of these, refreshed by the four days' rest and issued with new muskets from the store at Corunna, he disposed on a ridge two miles outside the walls of the city, with further units under Paget and Major-General Alexander Fraser held further back to ward off any flanking movement.

Soult's army, like the British, had suffered severe losses during its progress through the snow-covered mountains and probably numbered some 20,000, including 4,500 cavalry; but it was in worse shape than Moore's since it had had no time to rest. Nevertheless Soult felt that superiority of numbers gave him the advantage. He spent most of 16 January dragging his artillery up the Penascedo heights facing the British positions and it was not until late in the day, when Moore was on the point of withdrawing and resuming his embarkation, that the attack was launched.

The fiercest fighting took place around the village of Elvina, where the French made determined attempts to turn the right of the British line and to advance across lower ground towards the city. Baird, who was in command at this point, suffered a severe wound to his arm, and his place was taken by Moore in person. While directing operations against the village he was struck by a cannon ball and dashed from his horse. His left shoulder and arm were terribly injured and he was carried mortally wounded to the rear, but not before he had gasped out a message for Hope to take command and continue the fight. Several times he bade his bearers turn him to see the now retreating French, and when they tried to ease him by unstrapping his sword he said 'in his usual tone and with a very distinct voice, "It is well as it is. I had rather that it should go out of the field with me." ' Moore retained consciousness to the last and died in the knowledge that the battle had been won. 'I hope', he managed to say, 'the people of England will be satisfied, I hope my country will do me justice.'

Moore had made grave mistakes, of which the principal was the diversion of his artillery. This left him powerless to take action at the crucial point when the French were breaking out from behind the Ebro and laid him open to charges of inactivity and cowardice by his Spanish allies, with whom he was consistently offhand and arrogant. It would seem that the latter stages of his retreat were conducted with needless haste, causing appalling losses and hardship, and that both for the morale of his men and to gain time he would have done better to turn and engage Soult's advance guard in a number of the strong defensive positions along the route. The main body of the French infantry was always far to his rear. Nevertheless, as he wrote to Castlereagh from Astorga, 'As a diversion the movement has answered completely.' By diverting a mass of French troops to the far north-west corner of the Peninsula, he certainly held up operations in Portugal and the south by many months; and it is doubtful whether with a force of some 30,000 he could have intervened effectively in central Spain against armies which outnumbered him by ten to one. At his own request he was buried in the ramparts of Corunna shortly before the final evacuation of the British army:

> *We buried him darkly at dead of night,*
> *The sods with our bayonets turning,*
> *By the struggling moonbeam's misty light*
> *And the lanthorn dimly burning....*
>
> *Lightly they'll talk of the spirit that's gone,*
> *And o'er his cold ashes upbraid him—*
> *But little he'll reck, if they let him sleep on*
> *In the grave where a Briton has laid him....*

From 'The Burial of Sir John Moore after Corunna' by CHARLES WOLFE

Chapter 11

'PEPE BOTELLA'

Ni es caballo, ni yegua, ni pollino en el que va montado, que es pepino.
  Botellas, copas, pepino,
  Son los titulos José
  Con que le honra de contino
  España, advirtiendo que
  Tu suerte fué qual con-vino.
It is not horse, mare or ass on which he is mounted, but a cucumber.
  Bottles, glasses, cucumber,
  are the titles, Joseph, with
  which Spain honours you; and
  like wine you will soon be
  finished.

Legend of a contemporary Spanish cartoon

Don José, by the grace of God, King of Castile, of Aragon, of the Two Sicilies, of Jerusalem, of Navarre, of Granada, of Toledo, of Valencia, of Galicia, of Majorca, of Minorca, of Seville, of Sardinia, of Corsica, of Córdoba, of Murcia, of Santiago, of the Algarves, of Algeciras, of Gibraltar, of the Canary Islands, of the East and West Indies, of the Ocean Islands; Archduke of Austria; Duke of Burgundy, of Brabant, of Milan; Count of Hapsburg, Tyrol and Barcelona; Sire of Biscay and of Molina: such were the self-assumed titles of Joseph Bonaparte. In Spain he was more briefly known as 'Pepe (or Tio) Botella'— 'Uncle Bottle'.

Joseph Bonaparte, the titular ruler of Spain during the five years of the French occupation, was not a drunkard, although popular resentment often led to his being depicted in his cups. A typical lampoon of the period shows him slumped over his desk and is further entitled 'The King of the Cups in his office, working for the happiness of Spain'. Napoleon was well aware of his weakness for titles and crisply bade him divest himself of all except 'Joseph Napoleon, King of Spain and the Indies'. Of all the parties to the Treaty of Bayonne, Joseph and his Spanish supporters, the *afrancesados*, took it most seriously. He did, in fact, genuinely try to rule as an independent king of Spain, working for the benefit of *all* his subjects; but the assignment was an impossible one from the outset, given the implacable opposition of Spaniards in unoccupied parts of the country and the imperialistic ambitions of his brother.

The position of the *afrancesados* has been much misrepresented and it is a great oversimplification to describe them, as has been done, as 'the timid, the misguided, the conformists by nature who took the French side against the patriots'. In the first place, the word is sometimes used to embrace all the Spanish liberals of the period imbued with the ideas of the *Encyclopédie* and Age of Enlightenment—such as the members of the Cadiz Cortes who drew up the famous Constitution of 1812. After the restoration of Ferdinand VII in 1814 and during the monarchist revival which ensued, repressive measures against the liberals made little if any distinction between the former supporters of Joseph Bonaparte and the authors of the Constitution. Again, the great bulk of so-called *afrancesados* are better described as *juramentados*, of whom the French ambassador, La Forest, wrote: 'All this considerable and influential section of the populace [comprising the minor government employees], has simply followed the instinct of self-preservation and has shown no greater enthusiasm for the new regime than the old.' The position of these bureaucrats was spelt out in Joseph's decree of October 1808 issued from Vitoria: 'Office-holders of whatever category who enjoy salaries or pensions paid from the public funds must subscribe to the oath of loyalty as laid down by the Constitution and will cease to draw this salary or pension if there is no record in the appropriate secretariat of their having taken the oath.'

A very similar state of affairs obtained during the Civil War of 1936–9, when Spaniards had little choice but to fight for General Franco or the Republicans according to where they lived—so that members of the same family could find themselves on opposite sides. In territory firmly held by the French most of the upper and professional classes became *afrancesados*: when Soult made his headquarters in Seville after the Andalusian campaign of 1810, former 'patriots' transferred their allegiance *en bloc*, and he was able to find recruits for his army even among the *juramentados* and peasantry.

There were thus three main parties in Spain: the Absolutists, who numbered most of the generals, like Cuesta, La Romana and

Palafox, and believed implicitly in the restoration of Ferdinand VII, the revival of the old regime and the maintenance of the Roman Catholic Church with all its rights and privileges; the liberals, who saw a need for reform, but only under Spanish auspices; and the *afrancesados*, who felt that many of these same reforms might best be carried out by co-operating with Joseph Bonaparte. The mass of the common people were motivated simply by hatred for the invader and unswerving loyalty to the 'Desired One', Ferdinand VII.

The most dedicated of the *afrancesados* were those like Joseph's prime minister, Azanza, who had been at Bayonne and agreed to return with him to Spain and to take part in his government. It is clear from their many pronouncements that they quite genuinely believed in the urgent need for reform, but thought that it must be carried out within the framework of a constitutional monarchy—whether it was that of the Bourbons or of Joseph Bonaparte was of secondary importance. The other alternative, as they saw it, was a state of anarchy. Thus, on the one hand, Llorente wrote: 'The persons and families of kings change from one day to another; the country remains. A sovereign deserves loyalty only when he exercises sovereignty', while on the other, Azanza stated his conviction that, 'Anarchy is the greatest punishment which God inflicts on the community; it leads to licence and libertinism, plunder, burning, destruction and every sort of disorder.'

The *afrancesados* were also convinced of the uselessness of continuing the struggle against France, as emerges from the *Memoria* of Azanza and O'Farrill, the most lucid exposition of the *afrancesado* position: 'In that critical situation [after the Battle of Bailén] there were only two alternatives: one offered Spain the preservation of her independence and integrity, a constitutional king supported by a neighbouring and formidable power, the reform of all that were generally regarded as abuses by the nation, and the guarantee of the most tangible rights for people united in our society. The other could only offer the dream of restoring our monarch by force of arms; and the war could bring the nation no benefit commensurate with the enormous sacrifices, requiring perseverance and sufferings impossible to calculate, and involving a revolution.'

Another consideration was that a prolonged war would so weaken Spain as to lead to the loss of the Americas. In the event, this fear was justified—although it was, in any case, only a matter of time before the American possessions broke away from the mother country. Where the *afrancesados* must most be blamed was in accepting Napoleon's assurances at face value and in believing, as they evidently did, that he would allow Spain any real degree of independence. Misguided and fruitless as their efforts proved to be, Marshal Suchet was probably doing them justice when he said: 'Conscious of the situation of the country, they accepted the honourable task of just and moderate mediation between the inhabitants and the soldiers and of protecting the interests of their compatriots with a perseverance that has never been disputed.'

This perseverance first displayed itself in broadcasting pamphlets to the unoccupied parts of the country and in efforts to make contact with the Spanish commanders in the field and the Juntas. A determined attempt was made to negotiate with the Central Junta; and the Marquis of Urquijo composed a letter which was carried to General Cuesta in Mérida in April of 1809 by one, Joaquín María Sotelo, of whom La Forest said cynically: 'He has so many faults that he must be pardoned for them—if only because they allow him free access to the enemy.' Cuesta duly conveyed the letter to the Junta, who refused to answer it; and after two further unavailing attempts to open negotiations the envoy returned empty-handed to Madrid.

Apart from the decrees issued by Napoleon in December 1808, abolishing feudal rights and also directed against the Inquisition and the monasteries, Joseph's government instituted a series of political and social reforms which were of more interest as a declaration of intent than for any lasting benefit they conferred. The country was redivided into civil and military districts, schools were to be created on the model of the French lycées and in the judicial field steps were taken towards introducing the Napoleonic Code. The National Debt was to be abolished—an empty gesture, because there were no funds available for implementing the decision. In this, as in so many ways, Joseph was hamstrung by a chronic lack of finance. Having, for example, decided on an ambitious rebuilding programme in Madrid, he demolished a large number of houses without any means of replacing them.

The financial problem was critical from the first moment that he entered Spain in the mistaken belief, shared by the Emperor, that it was a rich country nurtured by the gold and silver of the Americas. His first recourse was to redouble taxation in the limited area of the country in French control, with such crippling results that when Wellington eventually entered Madrid he was greeted with cries of 'Long live the peseta loaf!' During the five years of Joseph's rule he bombarded his brother with appeals for money, of which the following extracts, all written within a space of days in 1808, are typical:

July 11th: 'What I know, is the great necessity that I have for money; we possess only poor provinces; nothing comes into the Treasury. With money it would be possible to bring up to strength the regiments that still remain in Madrid.'

July 13th: 'I repeat to Your Majesty that you cannot make too many sacrifices to pacify Spain: what is necessary are troops and money.'

July 18th: '*La besoigne taillée est très grande; pour en sortir avec honneur il faut des moyens immenses.*'

None of these, or subsequent agonized appeals, were ever answered, since Napoleon stood firm on his proposition that 'War should feed war'. The position has been well put by Miguel Artola Gallego in Volume XXVI of the *Historia de España*: 'And here emerges the first of the inherent contradictions of *afrancesado* politics. While necessity obliged the *afrancesados* to look to France, their ideas did not allow them to accept French dictation in the country's affairs. Their policy was to founder, among other reasons, because they wished to be anti-French, while at the same time using the Empire's soldiers and money. Napoleon, on his side, saw the situation in a very different light. Since it was his troops which maintained the government, he considered it to be on the same footing as the various armies commanded by his marshals. Hence there emerged two clear-cut and antagonistic viewpoints: that of the *afrancesados*, who demanded overall power for Joseph and his Spanish ministers; and Napoleon's, which was that control should be shared between his army commanders, of whom Joseph was only one more.'

As time went on and the French armies spread out over Spain, their marshals—Soult, Ney, Suchet and the rest—created for themselves viceroyalties, seizing the treasures of the cities for their personal benefit and applying the revenues and the produce from the land to the maintenance of the troops of their commands. Little or nothing found its way back to Madrid, and when Joseph complained, he was ignored. After Marshal Ney had raided Avila, supposedly under Joseph's own control, the King wrote to Paris that 'the Emperor cannot desire that his own brother—however unworthy—should be openly humiliated and insulted'. Napoleon's only reply was to transfer the control of Avila to the Army of Portugal.

This was, in fact, part of a deliberate policy of decentralization. Already in February 1810 he had set up separate governments in Catalonia, Aragon, Navarre and Biscay, explaining his reasons in a letter to his chief-of-staff, the Prince of Neufchâtel: 'I can no longer stand the enormous expense of my army of Spain. I intend the administration of the conquered provinces to be in future in the hands of the military commandants, in order that all their resources may be applied to maintaining the armies. In future I shall be able to send only two millions monthly to pay the troops around Madrid.' When the Army of Portugal was organized under Marshal Masséna in April, it was made completely independent of the Madrid government, and in naming Soult commander in Andalusia, Napoleon made it very clear that he was a viceroy in his own right: 'I need not remind you of the respect which you owe to the King. You must act in concert with his ministers, although in reality you are general-in-chief.'

Joseph and his *afrancesado* ministers were at one in seeing a threat to Spanish integrity and affected to ignore the decrees, but by 8 August 1810 the financial situation was so critical and he so keenly resented the lack of any real authority that he addressed a *cri de coeur* to his brother:

> ... In the present state of affairs in Spain the commander-in-chief in a province is its king. All its resources become inadequate, because what are called the wants of the army are indefinite, and the general increases them as he sees the means of supplying them. Thus the provinces commanded by generals who are not under my orders are nothing to me. In Andalusia alone I hoped to find a few resources, after having assigned to the army what was supposed to be sufficient, if Your Majesty continues to send two millions every month. But to give the command of the troops to a general [Soult] who does not recognize my authority, is to give him the administration and government of the country. ... I am here

surrounded by the ruins of a great nation. I have a guard, I have depots, I have hospitals, a garrison, a household, a ministry, a privy-council, refugees from all the other provinces, etc., etc. Even if my honour, if the sentiment of what is due to me allowed me to maintain so humiliating a position, this state of things could not last two months. For, in fact, if the army of Andalusia is taken from me, what shall I be? The porter of the hospitals of Madrid and of the depots of the army, and the jailor of the prisoners?

Joseph goes on to threaten abdication unless Napoleon can grant him real authority over the marshals and dispel rumours about a partition of the country.

The Emperor could agree to neither of these things, both because he had little opinion of Joseph as a soldier and wished to issue direct orders to his marshals from France and because at that very moment he was planning to annex most of Spain north of the Ebro. To reinforce his letters, Joseph had already sent Azanza, newly created Duke of Santa Fe, as Ambassador Extraordinary to Paris; his wife, Queen Julia, was intervening with the Emperor as an unofficial ambassador; and on 7 August he despatched a further legate in the person of the Marquis of Almenara. The full extent of Napoleon's plans emerged at a meeting early in September 1810 between the two ambassadors and the foreign minister, Champagny, who made the French position very clear. Joseph's government had been unable to unite the country along the lines envisaged at Bayonne; the Constitution was therefore suspended and 'Spain belongs to the Emperor by right of conquest'. To safeguard the French presence in Spain, he therefore intended to annex the provinces of Catalonia, Aragon, Navarre and Biscay, ceding Joseph most of Portugal in return. On hearing of this Joseph was near desperation: 'What would the inhabitants of the counties round London say if they were menaced with being declared no longer English? What would the people of Provence or Languedoc say if they were told that they were no longer to be Frenchmen? My only chance here is to be authorized to announce that the promise that Spain should not be dismembered will be kept. If that is granted, and the generals who have misbehaved are recalled to France, all may be repaired. If not, the only honourable course for me is to retire into private life, as my conscience bids me, and honour demands.'

The Paris meetings broke up inconclusively, with Napoleon

agreeing to suspend his ukase, provided the *afrancesado* government could prevail on the refugee authorities in Cadiz to recognize Joseph as king and honour the Bayonne Constitution. A letter to the Cortes described by La Forest, the French ambassador in Madrid, as 'a composition as feeble and lacking in dignity as its predecessors', was drafted but never despatched owing to Joseph's last-minute doubts. And in the event Napoleon never carried out his threat, since he had decided that annexation was not feasible until the English had been driven out of Portugal.

Although he could not foresee it during the winter of 1810–11, Joseph's face was to be saved by Wellington's stand on the lines of Torres Vedras and the subsequent disastrous defeat of Masséna and his Army of Portugal. Meanwhile the King sold his plate to meet expenses and clung on to Madrid in fear of being overrun by Blake's Army of Murcia or the increasingly active guerrillas. 'At every moment of the day and night', he wrote, 'I must be ready to mount horse to defend my life against the exasperated insurgents who surround Madrid: this city is one of the outposts.'

On 29 March 1811 a letter arrived from Paris with the news that Napoleon's second wife, Marie Louise of Austria, had given birth to a son; and on the pretext of offering his congratulations Joseph decided to leave for Paris so as to make a last personal appeal to his brother. The Emperor received his unwelcome visitor on 16 May and at a meeting lasting six hours and described by a contemporary as '*très orageuse*' heard his brother out. Soon afterwards, without answering the petition, he left for Cherbourg in company with the Empress, indicating that 'the King can leave when he pleases, without awaiting my return'. At the same time, through his chief-of-staff, General Berthier, the Duke of Neufchâtel, he did make some concessions to bolster his brother's prestige: judgement in the law courts was to be delivered in the name of the King; in addition to a direct monthly grant of a million francs, Joseph was also to receive a quarter of the revenues levied by various of the armies in the occupied areas; and he obtained direct control of the Army of the Centre, while the Army of the North was to be commanded by a marshal acceptable to him. But Napoleon refused to make his brother commander-in-chief—not wanting to 'have a marshal at Madrid who would want all the glory along with all the responsibility'—

and instead issued a rather vague instruction that the commanders in the field were to consult with him and keep him informed of their movements.

It was only in March 1812, on the eve of his invasion of Russia, that Napoleon decided that it would be impossible for him to direct the campaign in the Peninsula from the other side of Europe and ordered Berthier to 'send an extraordinary express this evening to inform the King of Spain that I entrust to him the command of all my Spanish armies, and that Marshal Jourdan will perform the duties of chief-of-staff'. The order was a great fillip to the *afrancesados*, whose credibility, such as it was, had been still further undermined by the planned annexation of the north; but Joseph himself was dispirited and worn out by the constant rebuffs at the hands of his brother and the marshals. He had no clear picture of the military situation; the marshals, having for so long enjoyed complete authority, were not disposed to obey instructions from Madrid and on one pretext or another—delay in hearing of the change in command, the impracticality of Joseph's orders or the rapidly changing position in the field—often disobeyed them. Marshal Jourdan, regarded as out-of-date by his colleagues, in fact drew up a realistic assessment of the overall position and rightly concluded that the only hope of defeating Wellington was to evacuate Andalusia and to concentrate the French armies. This solution was naturally unacceptable to Marshal Soult and was vetoed by Napoleon himself, whose final instructions to Joseph and his chief-of-staff before leaving for Russia were to *'conserver les conquêtes et les étendre successivement'*.

Napoleon had once angrily asked how it was possible that 'forty thousand English should disrupt all the affairs of Spain'. With the vastly larger French armies dispersed across the country under self-willed commanders, tied down in garrison duties and harried by the Spanish irregulars, it was to prove not only possible, but inevitable. Marshal Marmont, at least, was aware of the dangers and was not simply being wise after the event when he wrote in his *Mémoires*: 'Having deliberately created this resistance, which was to be fatal, Napoleon did nothing to overcome it. On the contrary, he seems to have gone out of his way to reduce the possibilities of victory. The excessive division of commands, which he would never renounce, the rivalries of all sorts which he never wished to check, his absence from a place where only he could prevail, his habitual refusal to send help and money, his constant obstinacy in closing his eyes to the truth, and lastly, his mania for directing from France operations against a nation which he never tried to study or understand made up the gamut of ills to which the best armies in Europe were finally to succumb.'

Chapter 12

RETURN OF AN IRON MAN

After the death of Sir John Moore and the evacuation of the British army from Corunna in January 1809, it was mid February before Marshal Soult was able to deploy his forces for the invasion of Portugal. His colleague Ney was from the first sceptical about the feasibility of the project and there was little enthusiasm in the ranks, since many of Soult's men were drawn from Junot's defeated army and knew only too well of the ferocity of the Portuguese partisans and their habit of murdering and mutilating prisoners and stragglers. Nevertheless, Soult was under strict orders from the Emperor, so that while Ney was left with the equally thorny task of subduing Galicia, Soult attempted to ferry his men into Portugal across the mouth of the Minho river. The small craft met with heavy fire from the Portuguese on the opposite bank, and Soult was constrained to march upstream to the nearest practicable ford at Orense, an operation which was carried out under constant harassment from the Galician guerrillas and at the cost of leaving his heavy artillery at the fortress of Tuy on the coast. Once across the border, his 22,000 men were able to advance more rapidly, but lost all contact with the other French forces in the Peninsula. Months were to go by before he received despatches from any outside source.

Soult's first target was Oporto, and the only force that lay in his way was an undisciplined mass of 12,000 men under General Francisco Silveira, the military governor of Trás-os-Montes. The majority were raw levies of the local *ordenanza*, of whom, 6,000 possessed no firearms. Such British troops as remained in the country—some 10,000 men under Sir John Cradock—lay far south around Lisbon, thanks to the timidity of a commander whose only concern was to be in a position to evacuate them on the threat of a French advance. Against the orders of Silveira, a large body of his levies insisted on making a stand in the indefensible town of Chaves, whereupon he withdrew to the south, leaving open the road to Braga. The only resistance was from the peasantry, who, as one of Soult's aides-de-camp describes, fought as determinedly as the *guerrilleros* across the border: 'If only these brave and devoted fellows had possessed competent leaders, we should have been forced to give up the expedition, or else we should never have got out of the country. But their resistance was individual: each man died defending his hamlet and his home, and a single battalion of our advanced guards easily cleared the way for us. I saw during these days young girls in the fighting line, firing on us, and meeting their death without recoiling a step. The priests had told them that they were martyrs, and that all who died defending their country went straight to paradise. In these petty combats, which lasted day after day, we frequently found, among the enemy's dead, monks in their robes, their crucifixes still clasped in their hands. . . .'

A few miles east of Braga the French found their way barred by a motley and ill-armed force of some 25,000 men, who had taken up positions in the hills flanking the road. Their commander, General Bernado Freire, had so little control over his unruly levies that he abandoned his command and was murdered in Braga by a party of the *ordenanza*. Soult thereupon launched a frontal attack and had little trouble in smashing through the Portuguese lines and continuing his advance on Oporto.

With more energy than wisdom the bustling Bishop of Oporto had organized a *levée en masse* in the city. Its only lasting fruits were the institution of a small, but well-trained Lusitanian Legion under the resourceful Sir Robert Wilson; but Wilson had tired of the Bishop's domestic quarrels and feuds with the Regency and taken off his 1,500 men towards Almeida on the frontier. Meanwhile the city had been turned into a fortified camp with barricades in the streets and a line of fortifications crowning the hills to its immediate north. The defenders, including 9,000 armed citizenry, numbered some 30,000, but were ill trained and unable to make effective use of the 200 assorted guns which studded the heights. On 29 March Soult again mounted a frontal attack and his troops were soon driving the Portuguese down the precipitous streets towards the River Douro at the bottom. Here there occurred one of the most horrible episodes in a war of horrors. The city proper was connected to the suburb of Vila Nova de Gaia, with its quays and Port Lodges, by a single pontoon bridge across the Douro. Some thousand refugees and defeated troops had safely crossed when, to prevent pursuit by the French, a Portuguese officer ordered the drawbridge connecting the central pontoons to be raised. Herded on by musket fire from the rear, a great horde of men, women and children kept pouring on to the bridge and were forced forward into the water. After a time the whole forty-foot gap became a solid mass of drowning humanity. Elsewhere in the city, the usual scenes of rape and pillage had succeeded its capture; but at the bridge the French soldiers were so sickened by the catastrophe that they gave over shooting and set about clearing the bridgehead and rescuing survivors. Soult reported only 80 dead and 350 wounded, but between the drowned and killed Portuguese losses, including non-combatants, amounted to some 8,000.

It was Napoleon's intention that, after the occupation of Oporto, Soult should push south on Lisbon; but the Duke of Dalmatia now found himself completely isolated, with insufficient troops to renew his advance and entirely in the dark as to the movements of the nearest French armies. He therefore limited himself to sending out columns under Heudelet and Loison to seek news of Ney in Galicia and Lapisse in Salamanca. It had been envisaged that Lapisse with his 9,000 men should join forces with him, but Sir Robert Wilson had so skilfully deployed his small Lusitanian Legion around Almeida that the French general was under the impression that he was faced by a large British army and accordingly moved off south to the Extremadura; and Loison, in the event, never got further than Amarante, thirty miles east of Oporto, where he was held up by the Portuguese under Silveira.

Heudelet succeeded in evacuating the garrison left at Tuy, but learned that Ney was far too occupied in Galicia to lend any assistance. It seems that Soult meanwhile occupied himself with day-dreams about establishing himself as independent king of Portugal. A document to this effect, issued by his chief-of-staff, while assuring the army that no disloyalty to the Emperor was intended, made his ambitions so clear that Napoleon was later to write that, 'He is astounded to find the chief of the staff suggesting to the generals that the Marshal should be requested to take up the reigns of government, and assume the attributes of supreme authority. If he had assumed sovereign power on his own responsibility, it would have been a crime, clear *lèse-majesté*, an attack on the imperial authority. . . .' Intriguing reached such proportions that a group of disgruntled French officers were shortly to approach Wellesley with the suggestion that he should take advantage of Soult's pretensions to help foment a revolt in the occupying army.

It was on 22 April 1809 that Wellesley returned to Portugal to take over command of the British forces. After the return to England of Sir John Moore's dilapidated army, enthusiasm for continuing the war had waned and it required considerable resolution on Castlereagh's part to reinforce Cradock's 10,000 men in Lisbon, rather than recall them; but the Secretary of State for War had the greatest trust in Wellesley, who had prepared for him a memorandum recommending that 'the Portuguese military establishment ought to be revived, and that in addition to those troops His Majesty ought to employ about 20,000 British troops, including about 4,000 cavalry. My opinion was that, even if Spain should have been conquered, the French would not be able to overrun Portugal with a smaller force than 100,000 men. As long as the contest may continue in Spain, this force, if it could be placed in a state of activity, would be highly useful to the Spaniards, and might eventually decide the contest.'

Few generals indeed have ever looked ahead with such accuracy, and in view of Moore's gloomy predictions about the impossibility of defending Portugal and considering that there were some 300,000 French troops in the Peninsula at the time, Wellesley's decision to resume the fight on such terms was daring as well as courageous. In itself it would seem to give the lie to the criticisms, still voiced in France and Spain, that he was an overcautious general. Wellington had his faults as a tactician, probably the most serious being a failure to exploit a victory and a disinclination to make full use of his cavalry in pursuing and scattering a defeated army. He has, for example, been criticized for his somewhat indecisive action after the Battle of Arapiles in 1812, when Marmont's shattered forces were allowed to regroup on Burgos, where their resistance a few months later caused a general withdrawal into Portugal. But considering the run of Wellington's victories in the Peninsula, unmatched by any other commander and often won in the face of heavy odds, his treatment at the hands of foreign historians is frequently grudging to a degree.

His sternest critic was, of course, Napoleon, who remarked to

Soult on the field of Waterloo: '*Et Moi, je vous dis que Wellington est un mauvais géneral, et que les Anglais sont de mauvaises troupes.*' Nearer the truth was the Emperor's earlier judgement on the French army defeated at Talavera—'that as long as they continue to attack good troops, like the English, in good positions, without reconnoitring and ascertaining whether these positions can be carried, my men will be led to destruction, and to no good purpose.' General Foy, while lauding to the skies the marshals 'of our army of glorious memory', which 'had occasion to form officers and generals sufficient in number to supply all the armies of the world', was of opinion that 'there were twenty officers (and to mention only some of those who served in this war, Picton, Craufurd, and Sir George Murray), any one of whom would have commanded with as much, and perhaps more ability and success than Wellington'. But for Foy the acme of good generalship was attack and the winning of battles with éclat. Although he is uneasily aware of the dubious morality of overrunning and pillaging another's country, for him, as for Napoleon's other commanders, the successful prosecution of a war is a glorious end in itself; and another passage from his *History of the War in the Peninsula* goes far to explain his strictures on a general who regarded the Peninsular campaign as more than an opportunity for the display of military pyrotechnics: 'War is looked upon by the English in a narrow point of view; the bulk of the nation possesses the instinctive qualities for it, such as exalted courage and contempt of death; but men of cultivated minds see nothing in it but a regular employment of physical force and material means. In vain would you tell them, that the genius of destruction has also his sublime revelations, and that he awakens a power of thought superior to that which presides at the creation of poetry and philosophy; still less would you persuade them that the highest part of the art, strategy, is philanthropic in its developments. . . . It may also be said that Fortune has been pleased to justify the prejudice we have alluded to, by elevating generals of ordinary abilities to the skies.'

It is hardly surprising that both Wellington and his Spanish allies failed to grasp the philanthropic aspects of a strategy based on 'living off the land', widespread pillage and violence to civilians; and in his complacent belief that the French had brought the science and art of war to their highest peak, Foy was unable to see that Wellington's strategy of 'indirect approach' was a great deal better suited to the Peninsula than that of Napoleon and his marshals. Again, to imply that Wellington was a 'lucky general' verges on the ridiculous—witness the list of accidents, disappointments and orders disobeyed by his allies quoted by Sir Charles Oman—and it is perhaps Oman who delivers the sanest judgement: 'In short, he was a safe general, not a cautious one.'

Much of the contemporary Spanish impatience with what was considered excessive deliberation arose from the fact that Wellington had promised his government to fight the war with 30,000 British troops; if he had chanced his modest forces in some rash and ill-judged move, as did the Spanish generals with monotonous regularity, the only result could have been the total withdrawal of the British presence in the Peninsula. The Spaniards, always overconfident after any success, felt that the victorious Duke kept holding back and might have saved thousands of Spanish lives if he had pressed forward more precipitately. But during the earlier years of the campaign Wellington's last object was to concentrate the various French armies and to fight a pitched battle against overwhelming odds. This was exactly what the French wished and what Napoleon hoped to achieve by despatching the great Army of Portugal against him under Masséna. It was only by diversionary tactics which kept the French dispersed over the whole Peninsula that he enabled the Spanish guerrillas to play a role more important than any set battles in winning the war.

Wellington's austere character and style were in any case not such as to appeal to his hot-blooded allies. Even with his compatriots he was distant, autocratic, unwilling to allow scope for individual initiative and savage with those who failed to carry out his orders to the letter. When he appeared among his troops on the battlefield—and he was generally to be found at the point of greatest danger—a slight, wiry man with prominent nose and cold grey eyes, habitually dressed in a plain blue frock coat and a cocked hat without feathers, he inspired the deepest confidence, rather than love or affection. Of his staff he once said, 'When I give an order to an officer of the line it is, I venture to say, a hundred to one against its being done at all.' On a personal level he was equally biting. When, for example, a brigade commander came to him and mentioned that he was suffering from rheumatism, without hearing him out Wellington snapped back:

'and you must go to England to get cured of it. By all means. Go there immediately.'

On the subject of the rank and file he was even more scathing, and remarks like that to Lord Stanhope have passed into history: 'They are the scum of the earth; English soldiers are fellows who have enlisted for drink. That is the plain fact—they have *all* enlisted for drink.' Although he went out of his way to provide for the provisioning and medical care of his men as far as lay in his power, he rarely if ever appealed to their patriotism or better feelings, and was a firm believer in the most savage punishment even for minor offences. Thus a half-starving soldier caught sticking a pig or stealing a chicken might be hanged or condemned to hundreds of strokes of the lash, an ordeal which left some of its victims permanently crippled.

Wellington's biographers, like Elizabeth Longford and Arthur Bryant, tell of a more human side to his character; but it is plain that a man with such an unbending sense of discipline and one who demanded that every last order be obeyed to the letter could have little use for the lax Spanish army or a Junta which was often unable to fulfil its promises of food and transport. Wellington's strategy of scorched earth and strategic retreat was well adapted to military realities and resulted as he had planned, in the over-extension of the French armies, but it was carried out at the expense of enormous suffering to the Spanish and Portuguese inhabitants of the occupied territories. The Spanish authorities hankered for more spectacular and decisive confrontation; and always, at the back of their minds, was the spectre that the British, with their line of retreat assured by the presence of the navy at Lisbon, might abandon the Peninsula to its fate. Given, on the one hand, a Spanish impatience for quick results which led the Junta to launch its offensives without adequate foresight or preparation and, on the other, Wellington's cool assessment of practicalities, it is hardly surprising that misunderstandings should have arisen. If promised supplies for the British army were not forthcoming, it must often have been because, in the denuded state of the country, they simply did not exist.

Within two days of landing in Lisbon, Wellesley had made plans for driving the French out of Portugal in accordance with his promise to Castlereagh. What made this feasible was that the only French armies within striking distance were widely separated and operating largely in the dark: to the south, Marshal Victor lay at Mérida, but was faced by a Spanish army under General Cuesta, who had rallied his forces after a disastrous defeat at Medillín a month before; to the north, Soult with 23,000 men was still at Oporto; and between them, but out of effective touch with either, General Lapisse was in occupation of Ciudad Rodrigo with a further army of 6,000.

Wellesley had learned a good deal about the dispersal of Soult's forces and the disquiet among senior officers about the Marshal's ambition of carving out an independent principality through the secret visit of a French dissident, Captain Argenton. He therefore decided to despatch a containing force under General Mackenzie to safeguard Lisbon against a possible advance by Victor, and himself marched rapidly north on Oporto with a mixed army of 25,000 British and 16,000 Portuguese. These were troops which had in the interim been trained by General Beresford with officers seconded from the British army, and although Wellesley still considered that they 'cut a bad figure', they were greatly superior to any that the Portuguese Regency had previously been able to put into the field and were to acquit themselves well.

On 6 May 1809, a day before the general advance from Coimbra, General Beresford was despatched inland to Lamego with 6,000 men so as to protect the army's right flank and, joining forces with General Silveira, to prevent a French retreat along the northern bank of the Douro. Wellesley, with the main force, now moved rapidly forward and, after sharp encounters with advanced elements of Soult's army to the south of the Douro, swept aside resistance at the mouth of the River Vouga and in rugged country above Grijon, reaching Vila Nova, directly across the River Douro from Oporto, on the evening of the 11th. He was encouraged to note that the 16th Portuguese regiment, which numbered students from Coimbra University, gave a good account of itself in this fighting and wrote to General Mackenzie: 'You are in error in supposing that these troops will not fight; one battalion has behaved remarkably well under my own eyes.'

Soult, behind the broad Douro, felt that there was no immediate danger and contented himself with blowing up the pontoon bridge and either destroying or removing to the north bank all the boats on the river. His expectation was that Wellesley might in due course bring up the fleet of fishing boats earlier employed in crossing the Vouga and use them to ferry his troops across the estuary to the south of the city; and it was therefore in this quarter that he concentrated most of his men.

However, Wellesley, reconnoitring the position from the heights further upstream next morning, realized that the gardens and houses of the inland eastern suburb were virtually unguarded. By good fortune a Portuguese refugee, a barber by trade, was now brought to his headquarters. He had crossed the river in a skiff and reported that four large wine barges were lying stranded on the shore opposite. Above them lay a deserted seminary, a massive building with a high wall, also unguarded and an ideal bridgehead. The bulk of the British troops had now moved up to Vila Nova and were lying concealed in its gardens and wooded heights. With characteristic decision Wellesley ordered an immediate crossing of the river. Having quietly moved up three batteries of guns to cover the approaches to the seminary from the opposite bank, he ferried a strong detachment of the Buffs across the river, thirty at a time in each of the four barges. It was a full hour before the French discovered what was going on; and by this time the Buffs were firmly established in the seminary.

The Duke of Dalmatia, who had spent the night making arrangements for an ordered retreat, was still in bed when the news reached him. He at once ordered a massive counter-attack to drive the English into the river; but successive waves of troops were decimated by the concentrated barrage from the guns across the river and the fire of the thousand infantry now solidly established behind the stout walls of the seminary. In a desperate effort to retrieve the situation Soult called up the brigade guarding the quays, upon which the citizenry poured down to the river and began ferrying every available boat to the opposite side. A new wave of British troops now crossed over and stormed through the city, taking the besiegers of the seminary in the rear. Soult, realizing that the game was up, ordered an immediate retreat, and in the utmost confusion the French army poured out of the city along the road east towards Amarante. British losses amounted to only twenty-three dead and ninety-eight wounded, while the French left some 300 killed and 1,500 sick and wounded in the hospitals of Oporto. Their disaster might have been even greater if General Murray had employed his small force, ferried across the river further up, to fall upon the disorganized rearguard.

Soult was yet to drain his bitter cup. He had started for Amarante in the full expectation that General Loison had secured his line of retreat by clearing the main road to Spain through Vila Real; but at half past one on the morning of 13 May he was woken to be told that Loison had been repulsed by the Portuguese under Silveira and that Beresford's force lay across the road between Amarante and his own retreating army. Caught between Beresford to the east, Wellesley to the west and the Douro to the south, Soult reached the unpalatable decision that the only way to save his mauled army was to jettison everything that could not be carried in knapsacks or on horseback and to strike north for Galicia by the bridle paths of the savage Serra de Catalina. The destruction was enormous: guns were immobilized by being discharged mouth to mouth; baggage and loot were abandoned; powder wagons were blown up; and even the silver coin from the army's war chest was scattered broadside.

By these Draconian measures Soult succeeded in eluding his pursuers. For nine days, amidst the driving rain, his bedraggled host faced hardships equalling those of Sir John Moore's army in the retreat to Corunna; and in some ways its plight was worse, since stragglers were lucky if they were killed outright by the merciless Portuguese peasants without being nailed to a barn door or obscenely mutilated. Wellesley has been criticized for failing to press on with more speed from Oporto; but, as he wrote in a despatch to Castlereagh, 'It is obvious that if an army throws away all its cannon, equipment, and baggage, and everything that can strengthen it and enable it to act together as a body; and if it abandons all those who are entitled to its protection, but add to its weight and impede its progress, it must be able to march on roads on which it cannot be followed, with any prospect of being overtaken, by an army which has not made the same sacrifices.' Soult's famished and exhausted column finally limped into Orense on 19 May 1809; it had lost 2,000 of its strength on the way.

Elsewhere in Galicia his colleague, Marshal Ney, had been endeavouring to carry out his instructions with mixed fortunes. Napoleon's orders were to 'organize Galicia, make examples, for severe examples are much more effective than garrisons', to 'leave the policing of the country to the Spanish authorities' and finally to 'use the months of March and April, when there is nothing to fear on the Galician coasts, for an expedition to conquer the Asturias'. With the force of 17,000 at his disposal, the task was clearly beyond Ney's means and once again illustrates the Emperor's failure to grasp the realities of the situation in Spain. Ney nevertheless made a determined effort to comply, and in concert with General Bonnet, moving west from Santander, and General Kellermann, who had been sent to his assistance from Madrid by King Joseph, mounted a three-pronged attack on the Asturias. It was partially successful, in that the capital, Oviedo, and the principal port of Gijón were temporarily occupied and the Army of Asturias under General Ballesteros was mauled—though not decisively defeated. However, the Marquis of La Romana wisely confined his Army of Galicia to harassing tactics and could not be tempted into set battle; and the month-long French occupation of the province was achieved by depleting the garrisons in Galicia to such an extent that Santiago was captured by the Spanish and Lugo was only saved from a similar fate by the unexpected arrival of Soult's 2nd Corps from Portugal.

When Ney and Soult met in Lugo on 30 May 1809, accrimonious arguments at once broke out between the two marshals, vividly illustrating the justice of Marmont's criticism of Napoleon for failing to establish an overall command. Soult felt that Ney was not doing enough to help him re-equip his own battered army; but the crux of their disagreement was over future strategy. Ney insisted that the two armies should join forces to subdue Galicia in accordance with the Emperor's instructions; Soult, on the other hand, had little inclination to remain in this remote corner of Spain and was for marching south to León to help in expelling the British army from the Peninsula. As Marshal Jourdan later remarked to King Joseph, 'he could not keep his eye off Portugal'. In the end, Soult grudgingly agreed to take part in a combined movement to trap the Marquis of La Romana in the southern corner of Galicia—but not, it seems, before the hot-tempered Ney had drawn his sword upon him.

The operation was a complete failure: Ney was checked south of Santiago by the stubborn opposition of the 'Division of the Miño' under the Count of Noroña, and Soult failed to deliver the planned flank attack, instead leaving Ney to his own resources and marching south as, perhaps, he had always intended. In letters to Napoleon and King Joseph justifying his action he cites lack of men and money and adds: 'This province is always in a state of upheaval. La Romana's threats of death and burning; the executions that he orders; the devastation caused by frequent troop movements; the ruin of most of the inhabitants; the money poured in by the English; the straits of the French generals, who, lacking means, often cannot pay their emissaries; all these things daily increase the number of our enemies with the result that a war in this murderous country is infinitely disagreeable and without forseeable end.'

The result of Soult's defection was that Ney found himself obliged to evacuate the whole province at the end of June. As Oman shrewdly remarks, 'The attempt to subdue the province had only been made because Moore had drawn after him to Corunna the armies of Soult and Ney; and since they were on the spot, the temptation to use them was too great to be withstood. This is but one more instance of the way in which the famous march to Sahagun had disarranged all the Emperor's original plans for the conquest of the Peninsula.' The French had no more been able to subdue Galicia than the Moors before them, and it was to remain free for the rest of the war.

Chapter 13

CATALONIA AND BEYOND

If, between them, the British and their Portuguese and Spanish allies had been able to clear the French from Portugal and the far north-west of Spain by the early summer of 1809, the position in the east and centre of Spain was much less favourable. The renewed French offensive in Aragon, Catalonia and the Levante, while achieving great gains and at the same time tying down large numbers of French troops, was in many ways a war apart. Soult was right in thinking that the decisive battles would be fought along the Portuguese border; and before returning to them it seems appropriate to describe the campaign at the other side of the Peninsula as a whole.

The general to whom Napoleon entrusted 25,000 fresh troops, many Italian and drawn from his 7th Corps, was Gouvion St. Cyr, a fine soldier, but notoriously selfish and morose, and as unpopular with his colleagues and subordinates as with the Emperor himself. Not for nothing was he nicknamed '*le hibou*': at the siege of Gerona and elsewhere his self-centred attitude and refusal to co-operate was to lead to delays and frustrations in the field.

As the prime objective Napoleon charged him with the relief of Barcelona: 'If you were to lose this place, I should not be able to recapture it with twenty-five thousand men.' Before advancing into Catalonia St. Cyr had first to secure his communications with France, which were threatened by the fortresses of Gerona, astride the main road inland, and Rosas, on the alternative route by the coast. Duhesme's earlier siege of Gerona had proved so prolonged and so unsuccessful that St. Cyr decided to tackle the lesser obstacle of Rosas, for which purpose he detached 12,000 men under General Reille. Against them were ranged only 3,000 Spanish troops, some of them new levies and *miqueletes* (irregulars) commanded by Colonel Pedro O'Daly, one of the heroes of Gerona.

When Reille began his attack on 8 November 1808, it seemed

that the ramshackle citadel and the outlying fort of La Trinidad could not hold out for more than a few days; but this was to reckon without the intervention of the British navy and in particular of the fiery Lord Cochrane in his frigate the *Impérieuse*. For cool and insolent daring Cochrane's defence of Fort Trinidad must be reckoned one of the outstanding combined operations of the war and has been vividly recorded by Captain Marryat, who served under Cochrane as a midshipman at Rosas, in his novel *Frank Mildmay*.

Cochrane had been given a roving commission by Admiral Collingwood to harry the Mediterranean coasts of France and French-occupied Spain and had already created havoc by his systematic raids on French semaphore stations as far afield as Marseilles, and the disruption, in co-operation with the Catalan *miqueletes*, of French support columns moving along the coast road to Barcelona. When the *Impérieuse* anchored off Rosas on 20 November the defenders were in a bad way despite covering fire and the landing of marines from British warships already on the spot. As Cochrane reports in his *Autobiography of a Seaman*: 'The practice of the French when breaching the walls of Rosas, was beautiful. So skilfully was their artillery conducted, that, to use a schoolboy similitude, every discharge "ruled a straight line" along the lower part of the walls; this being repeated till the upper portion was without support, as a matter of course, the whole fell in the ditch, forming a breach of easy ascent.' If O'Daly in the citadel was hard pressed, the position of the garrison at Fort Trinidad seemed even worse, since the French had battered a breach in the main tower. Captain Bennet of the *Fame* had seconded twenty-five of his marines to help in its defence; these, he now decided to withdraw, but not before Cochrane had obtained permission to replace them with sailors from the *Impérieuse*, giving as his reasons that, 'The occupation of Catalonia, in short, turned on two points: 1st, whether the Junta of Gerona supplied adequate reinforcement; and, 2ndly, whether I could hold Fort Trinidad till it arrived.'

Cochrane had the edge over his superior in having examined the fort in person and discovered that the French artillery was placed on a height so far above that it could not hole the tower less than sixty feet above the ground. He therefore 'got together all the timber at hand, and constructed a huge wooden case, exactly resembling the hopper of a mill—the upper part being kept well greased with cook's slush from the *Impérieuse*, so that to retain a hold upon it was impossible. Down this, with the slightest pressure from behind, the storming party must have fallen to a depth of fifty feet, and all they could have done, if not killed, would have been to remain prisoners at the bottom of the bomb proof.' When the French launched an all-out attack on the fort on 30 November with some 1,200 men they fought shy of Cochrane's mantrap and were repulsed with heavy loss. Cochrane himself had earlier been 'struck by a stone splinter in the face; the splinter flattening my nose and then penetrating my mouth. By the skill of our excellent doctor, Mr. Guthrie, my nose was after a time rendered serviceable.'

The stubborn defence of Rosas was in the end unavailing because of the late despatch of a Spanish relief force and its inability to fight its way through to the citadel; Cochrane evacuated his men to the *Impérieuse* on 5 December 1808, placing a delayed action charge to blow up the fort; and O'Daly and his garrison were left with no alternative but to surrender. Between them they had, however, held up the French advance for a month; and Cochrane, who had a firm grasp of the effectiveness of harassing tactics and the worth of the Spanish irregulars, was later to write 'that during our operations against the French on the Spanish coast, I had seen so much of them as to convince me, that if with a single frigate I could paralyse the movements of their armies in the Mediterranean—with three or four ships it would not be difficult so to spread terror on their Atlantic shores, as to render it impossible for them to send an army into Western Spain. . . . Had this permission been granted, I do not hesitate to stake my professional reputation *that neither the Peninsular War, nor its enormous cost to the nation, from 1809 onwards, would ever have been heard of.* . . . By members not aware of this power of harassing an enemy's coast by means of a few frigates, the ministry was greatly blamed for not having sent a military force to Catalonia, instead of despatching the very inadequate force under Sir John Moore to the western shores of the Peninsula. That this latter step was a great mistake, likely only to end in disaster, is now admitted. . . .'

Cochrane overstated his case and later fell foul of the Admiralty over his outspoken criticisms of naval operations. Napoleon, at least, recognized him as a kindred spirit; and the unconventional Cochrane was long afterwards, on his way to assume command of the Chilean navy, to hatch a scheme which would have secured Napoleon's release from St. Helena and installed him as Emperor of South America.

With Rosas in his hands St. Cyr pushed forward towards Barcelona and, having defeated General Reding at Cardadeu on the outskirts, entered the city and relieved Duhesme's beleagured garrison on 17 December 1808. A further series of Spanish defeats, in the last of which, at Valls, General Reding was killed, resulted in General Blake taking over command of the Spanish Army of Aragon. There was also a change in the French high command: having ordered the capture of Gerona, so as to strengthen communications with France, in May 1809 Napoleon replaced St. Cyr by the elderly Marshal Augereau, and Reille by General Verdier. St. Cyr felt that he had been unfairly treated by the Emperor, who had quite unrealistically demanded the simultaneous sieges of Tarragona, Tortosa and Gerona; and when Augereau proved unable to take over for the foreseeable future because of a crippling attack of gout, immediate friction developed between St. Cyr and Verdier over the measures for reducing Gerona.

Meanwhile the French had been engaged in another costly and exhausting siege further west in Aragon. After his defeat at the Battle of Tudela in November 1808, Joseph Palafox was left with a month's respite to organize the defences of Saragossa against the renewed attack which he realized to be imminent. For this purpose he mustered some 35,000 troops and set to work 60,000 enthusiastic labourers to construct a system of formidable and well-planned defence works. Nor did he overlook the provisioning of the city—a weak point in the defence of other strongholds; when Saragossa finally fell, there remained ample supplies of wheat, maize, oil, salt fish, wine and fodder. The spirit of the inhabitants was high after their previous triumph— to the point of embarrassment for their commander, since the people had been brought to such a pitch of patriotic excitement by their priests and popular demagogues that they were prone to engage in witch-hunts on the least suspicion of faint-heartedness or treachery. The only criticism that can be made of Palafox's arrangements was that he had assembled *too many* troops within the city and that it would have been more effective to assign a part of his forces for harassing operations outside the perimeter.

The siege began on 20 December 1808, with the deployment

of some 45,000 troops under Marshals Mortier and Moncey, lavishly equipped with heavy siege artillery and including 3,000 sappers. It took this formidable force a month to penetrate the outer works; and the second part of the siege, which lasted from 16 January to 20 February, when the city fell, was occupied with breaking through the walls and in street fighting every bit as bitter as during the first siege. So as to reduce his casualties, Marshal Lannes, who took over the final phase of the operations, mined and blew up the houses block by block, their ruins forming advanced positions for a further advance. As the defenders were pressed in and confined to their cellars under the incessant French bombardment, fevers, dysentery and typhus broke out among them; and it was disease, even more than the death of San Genis, the chief engineer, the illness of Palafox himself or the loss of the powder factory, which compelled the surrender of the city by the chagrined and desperate Junta, to which Palafox had handed over authority on his sickbed.

A French officer has left vivid testimony as to the state of mind of the disease-ridden garrison when they finally filed out: 'Their clothes were torn and dirty; everything about them bore witness to terrible misery. But in spite of their livid faces, blackened with powder and scarred with rage and grief, they bore themselves with dignity and pride. The bright coloured sashes, the large round hats surmounted by a few cock's feathers which shaded their foreheads, the brown cloaks or *ponchos* flung over their varied costumes, lent a certain picturesqueness to their tattered garb. When the moment came for them to pile their arms and deliver up their flags, many of them gave violent expression to their despair. Their eyes gleamed with rage, and their savage looks seemed to say that they had counted our ranks, and deeply regretted having surrendered to such a small army of enemies.' Palafox, now desperately ill, was first threatened with death and later transferred to France and kept in close confinement at the prison of Vincennes.

Saragossa had cost the French some 10,000 troops and the defenders the appalling figure of 54,000 souls; the siege of Gerona was to prove even more costly and prolonged for the invaders. It began on 24 May 1809, with Verdier in charge of the actual assault and St. Cyr holding a line further back with the object of keeping off General Blake and his Army of Aragon. Nevertheless, Blake succeeded in breaking through and reinforcing the garrison on 4 September. The Spanish commander, Mariano Álvarez de Castro, conducted the defence with such spirit, making sorties to destroy the siege works and inflicting heavy casualties on the enemy, that Verdier threw in his hand at the end of September after a bitter quarrel with St. Cyr and retired to Perpignan.

Operations were continued by St. Cyr until he was at long last replaced by Marshal Augereau in October. After the failure of further renewed attempts by Blake to relieve the fortress, the garrison was in desperate straits by November as a result of illness and starvation. Álvarez himself was feverish and prostrated by dysentery, but to one of his officers who suggested retiring he snapped 'to the cemetery', and to another who complained of the depletion of supplies, 'When the last food is gone we will start eating the cowards, beginning with you.' But the outcome was now inevitable; and when Álvarez finally lapsed into delirium, his second-in-command surrendered to Augereau on 11 December 1809. Like Lannes at Saragossa, Augereau treated the gallant garrison with the utmost brutality. The stricken Álvarez was moved from one prison to another until he died in a dungeon at Figueras. It was widely rumoured in Spain that he had been poisoned. Augereau's retaliation, if unpardonable, may be explained on the score that the six months' defence of Gerona had cost the French army in Catalonia the best part of the campaigning season of 1809.

General Blake had meanwhile been making determined efforts to restore the position in Aragon, but after a preliminary success at Alcañiz, his army was routed by General Suchet at Belchite near Saragossa in June 1809; and with his disappearance from the scene the French devoted the campaign of 1810 to the union of their forces in Aragon and Catalonia. A preliminary thrust southwards towards Valencia, undertaken by Suchet at the express orders of King Joseph, proved over-ambitious, and in accordance with instructions from Napoleon Suchet retraced his steps and embarked upon the siege of Lérida, a key point in the marches between Aragon and Catalonia.

The only meagre success which Augereau was able to report during the spring of 1810 was the capture of the hill fortress of Hostalrich, a supply base for the Spanish during the siege of Gerona. Napoleon, out of patience with the tardy moves of the elderly marshal, recalled him to Paris in disgrace and yet again appointed a new commander in Catalonia, Étienne Macdonald, Duke of Tarentum.

Suchet was about to begin the siege of Lérida on 13 April 1810 when he received news that a force under the fiery General O'Donnell, of mixed Irish and Spanish descent, was on its way to relieve the city. After inflicting a sharp defeat on the 8,000 Spaniards, Suchet started operations in earnest on the 29th and by 13 May his troops had penetrated the streets; but the citadel crowning the hill on which the town is built remained intact. There now followed what Oman has described as on the whole 'the greatest atrocity perpetrated by any combatant, French, Spanish, or English, during the whole Peninsular War. . . . The act places that polished writer and administrator Louis-Gabriel Suchet on the moral level of a king of Dahomey.'

In the words of Suchet's own *Mémoires*, 'the troops, by a simultaneous movement towards the centre, and a well-sustained fire of musketry, endeavoured to drive the garrison and the inhabitants from street to street and house to house, towards the elevated part of the town and towards the castle. . . . Pursued by our soldiers, they hastened to reach the enclosure and to shut themselves up in it, the governor not having had time to order their being driven back, or courage to enforce such an order. Our mortars and howitzers never ceased firing the whole of the night nor during the morning of the following day. Each bomb being aimed at the narrow space in which this crowd had taken refuge, fell upon groups of soldiers and unarmed men all huddled together, and spread destruction and disorder among them. It was natural that the efforts of the governor and of the most determined men should be checked by the presence of the women, the children, the aged men, and the unarmed peasantry, who suddenly fell from the height of popular phrensy into discouragement and a dread of death. These measures were attended with as prompt and decisive an effect as general Suchet had anticipated.' Himmler could hardly have spoken with more pride of his extermination camps.

The following year, 1811, saw the progressive fall of all the remaining cities and strongpoints in Catalonia and Aragon: Tortosa was captured by Suchet in January and Tarragona in June; and although the *miqueletes* achieved an important success by the recapture of the immensely important fortress of Figueras in April, it yielded again to Macdonald in August after a prolonged and bitterly contested siege. Miguel Artola Gallego, writing in Vol. XXVI of the *Historia de España*, has well summed up the reasons for these Spanish reverses: 'The crushing defeats of the Spanish regulars during the fourteen months preceding the loss of Tarragona are the result of a strategy devoted to the retention of cities and strongpoints and based on the deceptive security of walls and fortresses. The immobilization of large numbers of effectives in one place and in a posture of forced inactivity, without any guarantee of help from outside, left all the strategic initiative to the French. Popular support, one of the decisive factors of the Spanish resistance, could hardly benefit a garrison cooped up in a fortress, as long as the French, thanks to Spanish inactivity, enjoyed complete superiority in men and guns in each place where they decided to give battle.' The Spanish were to achieve ultimate success only by a reversal of roles, when they left the French to tie up their effectives in the occupation of cities and fortresses and themselves spread out into the surrounding countryside, harrying supply lines, disrupting communications and attacking the French piecemeal where they were weakest.

After the recapture of Figueras and the re-establishment of a solid line of communication with France, Napoleon, on 25 August 1811, sent urgent orders to Suchet for the conquest of the last of the great cities in eastern Spain, Valencia: 'Everything leads me to believe that Valencia is in a state of panic, and that, when Murviedro [Sagunto] has been taken and a battle in the open field has been won, that city will surrender. . . . I must inform you that, in every case, it is the imperative order of the Emperor that your headquarters are to be on Valencian territory on or about September 15th, and as far forward towards the city as possible.'

Leaving some 30,000 troops to hold down the country to his rear, Suchet began his advance to the south on 15 September with an army of 26,000, despatched by three separate routes. His troops met no serious opposition; and by the 23rd he had successfully concentrated them opposite Sagunto, the only considerable fortress blocking the approach to Valencia itself. The little town of Sagunto or Murviedro, the Saguntum of the Romans and scene of fierce fighting during the Third Punic War, is surmounted by a steep outcrop of rock. The citadel which crowns it had fallen into disrepair since Moorish times, but during the preceding year the Junta of Valencia had taken steps to restore it by dismantling the Roman theatre beneath—then one of the finest in Europe—and building up the curtain wall with great blocks of stone from the ravished terraces. The works were not complete when Suchet made his sudden appearance; but General Blake, now Spanish commander-in-chief charged with the defence of Valencia, had equipped it with 17 guns and drafted into it a brigade of some 2,500 men under the command of Colonel Luis Andriani. Such was the natural strength of the position on its rocky height that an attempt to rush the fortress with scaling ladders was beaten off with heavy losses, and Suchet had no alternative but to contain his impatience and to wait until 16 October for the arrival of his siege train.

Blake had meanwhile been biding his time in Valencia and strengthening its defences while he waited for reinforcements from Murcia further south. He was detested by the Junta and inhabitants of the city; and on his side entertained the liveliest apprehensions about the fighting qualities of his Valencian levies. His only effective move was to send messages to the guerrilla leaders *El Empecinado* and Mina, asking them to harass the French rear in Old Castile and Aragon. This they did to such effect that *El Empecinado* gained temporary possession of the town of Calatayud, killing many of the garrison, taking 560 prisoners and diverting large French forces before retiring into the hills. Mina, for his part, descended on Aragon with 4,000 men, wiped out a column of 800 Italians near Ayerbe and then succeeded in marching his 600 prisoners across the whole of French-occupied northern Spain before delivering them to the British frigate *Isis* on the coast of Biscay.

Although these daring exploits embarrassed the French, they did not divert Suchet from his main object; and with the walls of Sagunto now crumbling under his heavy artillery, the state of public opinion was such as to compel Blake to move forward and seek open confrontation with the French army. The battle took place on 25 October 1811 on ground chosen by Suchet, a narrow coastal plain to the south of Sagunto. Blake's army, including the newly arrived Murcian troops under General Mahy, amounted to 28,000 and outnumbered the French by two to one; but his lack of confidence in the Valencians proved only too well founded. Despite great local superiority in numbers, the left wing, composed of Valencians and Murcians, almost at once turned tail in panic-stricken rout—Mahy was later to remark to Blake: 'I must tell you, with my usual bluntness, that you had better sell the horses of this cavalry, and draft the men into the infantry. I could not have believed in the possibility of such conduct, if I had not seen it with my own eyes take place and cost us so much.' Blake's own two seasoned 'Expeditionary Divisions' on the left, although somewhat outnumbered, fought with courage and determination and staged a breakthrough which was nearly disastrous for the French. Suchet retrieved the situation only by throwing in his last reserves; and the Spanish army retreated in disorder on Valencia. The Governor of Sagunto, who had watched the whole encounter from the vantage point of the castle, surrendered next morning.

Although Blake's army had been defeated, its casualties had not been high, and before attacking the strong defensive positions along the Guadalaviar river covering Valencia, Suchet decided to appeal for reinforcements to Napoleon. The Emperor's decision to transfer troops from the Army of Portugal proved to be one of the most disastrous of the whole war. His exact instructions were that Marshal Marmont should detach sufficient men as to provide, together with a smaller force from King Joseph, a total of 12,000 and that he should find an additional 3,000 to safeguard the column's communications with its base in New Castile. The expeditionary force moved off towards the end of December 1811 under General Montbrun. Both Marmont and Napoleon had supposed that Wellington was in no position to advance out of Portugal; but the depletion of Marmont's army allowed him to strike at Ciudad Rodrigo and so to undertake his offensive of 1812 which was to result in the evacuation of Andalusia and to initiate a general French retreat towards the north.

In the event, Suchet came to the conclusion that Blake and his army were so demoralized as for there to be no need to wait for the reinforcements. The defences of Valencia extended along the line of the Guadalaviar river from the sea to the village of Manises eight miles west of the city, taking in part of the ancient walls, which had been strengthened and backed up by gun emplacements. Suchet's plan aimed at nothing less than the complete encirclement of the Spanish army. A strong flanking force was to turn the defences west of Manises and to link up south of the city with another column thrusting between Valencia and the sea, while much smaller French detachments attacked the centre of the line. Given the strength of the defences, which should have more than made up for a French superiority in numbers, it was a bold concept and was carried out with almost complete success, only some 5,000 or 6,000 of Blake's regulars under Mahy and Obispo eluding encirclement and straggling south. Blake made the fundamental mistake of placing his weakest Valencian and Murcian troops at the western extremity of the line, and was not even aware that it had been turned until the French under Harispe, Musnier and Reille were pouring across the Guadalaviar in strength. His reaction to this disastrous news, as described by an eyewitness, was that 'he looked like a man of stone, when any remark was addressed to him he made no reply, and he could make no decision'. Abandoning the outer defences, he withdrew his army inside the city and, after a belated and ill-judged attempt to break out to the north, surrendered on terms dictated to him by Suchet on 8 January 1812. He had passed his last days in Valencia like a man hypnotized, and such was his unpopularity with the inhabitants that he gave himself up to the French without waiting for the formal surrender or their entry into the city.

One concession that Blake had obtained from Suchet was 'that there will be no reprisal against those who in the past took an active part in the war or the revolution'. This was cynically disregarded by Suchet, who later admitted that he had only agreed to it 'to get things over quickly'. Apart from the murder and brutal treatment of prisoners, hundreds of 'suspects' were summarily shot and hundreds more priests and students marched off and imprisoned in France. On Napoleon's orders Suchet proceeded to levy, over and above ordinary taxes, the huge 'war contribution' of 200,000,000 reals (or £2,800,000) and further despoiled the cathedral of its silver apostles; these and other treasures were sent to France. During the seventeen months that he ruled Valencia, Suchet behaved as an independent viceroy, administering 'justice' in the name of Napoleon rather than King Joseph and consistently snubbing the King in his appeals for money or troops. According to his own *Mémoires* he was a magnanimous and benevolent ruler who earned the respect of his subjects; Spanish sources tell a very different story of violence, murder and oppression. For these services he was the only

French general to earn his marshal's baton in the Peninsula and was also created Duke of Albufera, after the name of the lagoon to the south of the city, where fighting had taken place during its capture.

Montbrun, who had arrived in the Levante with 10,000 men too late to take part in the siege of Valencia, decided on his own initiative to march against Alicante. Lacking a siege train, he was easily repulsed; and this adventure only resulted in delaying the much-needed return of the troops to the Army of Portugal. Another expedition into Murcia under Pierre Soult, brother of the marshal, achieved only transitory success; and the recall by Napoleon of the Imperial Guard and other substantial units for his Russian campaign put an end to any further gains in the east of Spain.

Chapter 14

SOUTH TO CADIZ

When Napoleon set off in pursuit of Sir John Moore in December 1808 the forces which he left around Madrid were insufficient for a further advance into Andalusia and barely enough for the defence of the capital. During this respite at the turn of the year the Duke of Infantado, who had succeeded to the command of the Spanish Army of the Centre, was able to reassemble the remnants of the troops beaten at Tudela and amounting to some 21,000 at Cuenca to the south-east of Madrid. Having rested and re-equipped his men as far as the depleted resources of the poverty-stricken province would allow, he decided to take advantage of the French involvement with Moore in the north to strike at the capital. Unfortunately, the operation was badly planned and half hearted; and on 13 January 1809 the advance guard under General Venegas was routed by Marshal Victor at Uclés, the scene of a previous Spanish disaster at the hands of the Moors, while Infantado himself hung back in the rear. As a result, the Central Junta deprived Infantado of his command, and King Joseph was at last safe to make his formal re-entry into Madrid amidst empty pomp and along streets lined by French bayonets.

Victor was now free to carry out instructions left by Napoleon before his departure for France on 17 January 1809, which envisaged a pincer movement on Lisbon, Soult striking from the north and Victor from the east. It was not, however, until March that he was able to mount an offensive against the Army of the Extremadura which blocked his advance into Portugal and which the Junta had entrusted to the aged and intransigent General Cuesta.

The Junta, after the defeats on the Ebro in the autumn of 1808, the recapture of Madrid by the French and an enforced decampment from Aranjuez to Seville, had been passing through a difficult and chaotic period. To add to its troubles, disagreement had broken out with the British government over a suggestion for British troops to be landed at Cadiz, a plan originally mooted by Hookham Frere, only to be turned down—probably because the Spaniards harboured a suspicion that the city might become another Gibraltar. Unfortunately, with unwonted zeal, which he might better have displayed in Portugal, Sir John Cradock despatched the force in advance of orders, with the result that the transports and their troops lay idle for a month in the Bay of Cadiz and were finally returned to Lisbon, with ruffled feelings on both sides. If British troops were unwelcome in Cadiz, a great stream of British arms and equipment went far to restoring the beaten armies; and equally welcome was a massive contribution of £2,800,000 in specie received from the colonies in South America, which had declared themselves loyal to Ferdinand VII. That the Junta applied part of these resources to re-equipping an army for Cuesta in spite of his resounding defeats at Cabezon and Río Seco was because, whatever his deficiencies as a soldier, his patriotism was above suspicion. Amidst the general disillusionment that followed the wreck of the Spanish armies in the north, even Blake and Castaños were accused of being in the pay of the French!

The confrontation between Cuesta's reorganized Army of the Extremadura and Marshal Victor took place at Medellín near the Portuguese border on 29 March 1809. Victor's army of 18,000 was outnumbered by some 6,000 Spanish infantry, but possessed a superiority in cavalry and guns which was to prove decisive. Drawing up his troops in a compact arc to the south of Medellín with the broad River Guadiana to his rear, Victor prepared to receive the Spanish attack, which was delivered along a great curving front four miles long, with the object of turning the French flanks. In the face of a determined Spanish onslaught, 'We retired slowly and in good order,' as de Rocca of the 2nd Hussars wrote in his *Mémoires*, 'every moment facing about, and presenting a front to the enemy. The cannon balls ploughed up the earth around us, but we were not dismayed. The Spaniards now shouted to us that they would give no quarter. We replied to them only by keeping our ranks unbroken.' When Victor had been pressed back to the point where he had decided he must make a stand, 'Our hussars, who had hitherto preserved the strictest silence, now drowned the sound of the trumpet as they moved onwards by a single and terrible shout of joy and fury. The Spanish lancers were seized with terror; they turned their horses at the distance of half pistol-shot, and overthrew in their flight their own cavalry.' Cuesta himself was overridden and dismounted by his own horsemen and was with difficulty extricated. After this setback on their left, 'The Spanish infantry seemed shaken by the flight of their cavalry, and our dragoons made a brilliant and fortunate charge. In an instant the army that was before us disappeared, and the enemy vanished like clouds driven by the wind.... Our soldiers, who had seen themselves threatened with certain death, gave no quarter at first. The infantry followed the cavalry at a distance, and despatched the wounded with the bayonet.'

In the ensuing rout no less than 10,000 Spanish troops were lost, three-quarters of them killed. But perhaps the most remarkable aspect of the defeat was the speed with which the Spanish recovered. Two days before, the remnants of Infantado's army under General Cartaojal had been scattered to the winds at Ciudad Real south of Madrid, yet Marshal Jourdan could write: 'In any other country of Europe the gaining of two such successes as Medellín and Ciudad Real would have reduced the countryside to submission, and have enabled the victorious armies to press forward to new conquests. In Spain the reverse was the case: the greater the disaster suffered by the national troops, the more willing were the population to take to arms.' The most succinct postscript is de Rocca's: 'The Roman senate, after the defeat at Cannae, thanked Varus because he had not despaired of the salvation of Rome. The supreme junta of Seville, with a like magnanimity, declared by a public ordinance, that Cuesta and his army had deserved well of their country, and awarded to them the same recompense as if they had been victorious.... A fortnight after the Battle of Medellín, the Spanish army recovered from its losses, and, with a force of 30,000 men, had occupied the passes of the mountains in our front. General Sebastiani [the victor of Ciudad Real] did not advance farther into La Mancha than Mudella, and our corps remained quartered between the Tagus and Guadiana. We dared not advance very far from the latter river, lest our only communication with Madrid, by the bridge of Almarez, should be cut off by the new bodies of Spaniards, which were ready to form in our rear. Nor had we yet heard of Marshal Soult's army, which was to have entered Portugal, and with which we were to co-operate.'

While Victor hesitated near the Portuguese border, waiting for news from Soult, Wellesley was already marching south for Abrantes, which he reached on 8 June, a few days ahead of his army. Now that he had liquidated the French threat to Lisbon from the north he was eager to get to grips with Victor's 1st Corps and had already written to Cuesta with proposals for a co-ordinated attack. Had the generals seen eye to eye from the beginning, the Battle of Talavera, instead of resulting in a tactical success with little advantage to the allies, might well have been decisive and would certainly have prevented the French occupation of Andalusia. It has been the subject of so much mutual and heated recrimination on the part of English and Spanish historians that it is perhaps as well to explain the political background, the difficulties of logistics and the personal rivalries which bedevilled the operation from the start.

In spite of the Junta's support for Cuesta, there was a strong faction which was intriguing for his removal. Why, if Infantado had been disgraced after Uclés and Cartaojal after Ciudad Real, should Cuesta be left with his command? His opponents had secured the appointment of one of the old general's bitterest rivals, Venegas, to replace Cartaojal in La Mancha; and it was Venegas's deliberate refusal to obey orders which more than any other factor resulted in the French escaping complete disaster. But Cuesta regarded Wellesley himself as an even more formidable rival. Hookham Frere had unofficially, but assiduously, been floating the idea that no one else was so suited for the position of commander-in-chief. It was not until after the victory of Arapiles that Wellington was to be accorded this honour; meanwhile Frere's activities must certainly have been reported to Cuesta. It was therefore not simply national pride or an innate stubbornness, but personal jealousy, which motivated the repeated, 'No, no, no,' which Cuesta, through his interpreter and chief-of-staff, General O'Donaju, kept posing to Wellesley's suggestions at their first meeting.

If Cuesta has been accused by British historians of being stiff-necked and obdurate, the complaint of the Spaniards is that Wellesley was slow in moving and let the opportunity of crushing Marshal Victor slip through his fingers. Unlike the French, whose avowed policy was to live off the country, the British army paid for its food and transport; and, as Wellesley wrote to John Villiers, he was desperately short of ready cash—'We are terribly distressed for money. . . . I suspect the Ministers in

England are very indifferent to our operations in this country', or again, 'the ball is at my feet, and I hope I shall have strength enough to give it a good kick: I should begin immediately but I cannot venture to stir without money'. Even when supplies could be paid for they were scarce or unobtainable; and Wellesley was so driven to distraction by the Junta's over-enthusiastic promises that he could write at one point: 'If the people of Spain are unable or unwilling to supply what the army requires, I am afraid that they must do without its services.' To be fair to the Junta, the region had been denuded of supplies by the French and Spanish armies; and the proof of this is Victor's letter of 25 June to King Joseph:

> The position is desperate. The 1st Corps is on the eve of dissolution: the men are dropping down from mere starvation. I have nothing, absolutely nothing, to give them. They are in a state of despair. . . . I am forced to fall back on Talavera, where there are more resources to be found. We must have prompt succour, but where can it be found?

Wellesley and Cuesta met face to face on the night of 10 June 1809 at the Spanish headquarters near the bridge of Almaraz on the Tagus. Despite the lateness of the hour they at once proceeded to a review of the Spanish army; by the lurid torchlight, the troops in their motley uniforms presented a strange sight, British observers being more impressed with the spirit of the rank and file than the bearing of their officers. Cuesta himself, after his accident at Medellín, was conveyed thither in an antique coach drawn by nine mules and during the inspection could barely be supported on his horse by two pages. Next day, after four hours of argument, an overall plan of campaign was finally settled. In broad outline, the main force of 20,000 British and 36,000 Spanish was to mount a frontal attack at Talavera on the 35,000 French, with which it was estimated that Victor and King Joseph, drawing on his reserves at Madrid, could oppose them. A small force of 3,500, part Spanish and part Portuguese, under Sir Robert Wilson, was to cover the left flank; and, much more important, the 23,000 troops of the Army of La Mancha under Venegas were to advance on Madrid, thus occupying Sebastiani and his 17,000 men and if possible seizing the capital.

Both sides were to a great extent operating in the dark. The allies were not to know that on 1 July Soult had received despatches from Napoleon, issued as so often in complete ignorance of the current situation, ordering him to combine the armies of Ney and Mortier with his own for 'beating, hunting down and throwing the British army into the sea'. In the belief that Wellesley was still in the north, Soult was making plans for concentrating his 60,000 men at Salamanca and advancing into Portugal, when on 22 July King Joseph at last received news of the British presence near the Tagus and realized that their objective was Madrid. An urgent message arrived too late for Soult to lend assistance in the now imminent battle; but he at once changed the direction of his march southwards to Placencia, so as to threaten the allied flank.

The preliminaries to the Battle of Talavera only underlined the discord between Wellesley and Cuesta. Their two armies made junction at Oropesa on 21 July, and it was agreed that an attack should be made on Victor on the 23rd before he could receive reinforcements. Wellesley waited in vain for the Spanish, and when on the 24th, with Victor now in full retreat towards Madrid, Cuesta insisted on pursuing him, Wellesley in turn refused to move. Venegas had meanwhile, in downright disobedience of orders, failed to carry out the diversionary attack towards Madrid; Sebastiani had therefore been able to link forces with King Joseph; and Victor had retired only to join them. In the face of a combined French army of 46,000 Cuesta's troops were soon streaming back down the road to Talavera; and the story goes that, such was the friction between the two generals, Wellesley actually had to go down on his knees before the stubborn old Spaniard would agree to withdraw his army to a safe position across the Tagus. On the evening of the 27th Wellesley himself came within inches of being captured while reconnoitring the situation of a British detachment, which had been thrown out to safeguard the Spanish retreat.

It was on this same night that the French, pursuing their advantage, began the attack. The armies faced one another along a line some three miles wide, extending northwards from the town of Talavera on the Tagus to the spurs of the mountainous Sierra de Segurilla. Between them lay a stream described by Sergeant Cooper of the 7th Royal Fusiliers as 'a small rivulet dry in many places, but where there were pools, black, ugly-looking snakes were plentiful'. Wellesley had little confidence in the ability of the Army of the Extremadura to manoeuvre, and by agreement with Cuesta it was posted in a strong defensive position among the vineyards and gardens immediately north of Talavera. The British were extended across open country, the key position being the low hill with the ill-omened name of Medellín to the left of the British line. The scene on the evening of 27 July 1809 has been described by Lord Munster: 'The men, as they formed and faced the enemy, looked pale, but the officers riding along their line, only two deep, on which all our hopes depended, observed that they appeared not less tranquil than determined. In the meantime the departing sun showed by his rays the immense masses moving towards us, and the last glimmering of light proved their direction to be across our front, towards the left. The darkness, only broken in upon by the bursting shells and the flashes of the French guns, closed quickly upon us, and it was the opinion of many that the enemy would rest till the morning.'

This expectation was not to be fulfilled. The first occurrence of the night was a furious fusillade from jumpy Spanish troops on the right, who mistakenly imagined the French to be advancing on them. Of this Wellesley remarked tersely to a liaison officer: 'If they will but fire as well tomorrow, the day is our own; but as there seems nobody to fire at just now, I wish you would stop it.' It was followed by a precipitous stampede through the British encampment to the rear; and Cuesta promptly sent his cavalry to round up the demoralized levies and ordered the execution of two hundred of them, a figure subsequently reduced to forty at Wellesley's intercession. The Spaniards were in fact so strongly entrenched that the French made no serious attempt to displace them; what little part they later played in the battle in holding their positions was carried out well and with determination, and Cuesta, forgetting past differences, was to despatch reinforcements when it seemed that there was a danger of the French breaking through the British line.

The impetuous Marshal Victor did not wait for daybreak, but launched a surprise attack that same night against the Cerro de Medellín. Owing to a misunderstanding about the positioning of the defenders, the French succeeded in gaining the top of the hill and overwhelming a force of the King's German Legion, before the prompt intervention of General Hill drove them back after fierce hand-to-hand fighting. The main attack developed next morning with some 40,000 French troops concentrated against the 20,000 redcoats thinly deployed along the British section of the line. It was column against line, and, as at Vimeiro, the French almost reached the crest of the hill, only to be driven back in confusion by a withering crossfire.

The sun was already high when a truce was called at eight o'clock in the morning and soldiers from both sides went down to the 'snake-pools' of the Portina for water. Meanwhile an acrimonious argument was taking place on the hill of Cascajal opposite. After their resounding repulse King Joseph and Marshal Jourdan were for breaking off the engagement, but Victor kept repeating that if a further assault by the whole of the French forces did not smash Wellesley's army, '*il faudrait renoncer à faire la guerre.*' He had his way, and in quick succession two formidable attacks in massed column were launched against the entire British line. Both were held; but after the second, a brigade of Guards and two of the German Legion over-impetuously charged the retreating columns and were shattered by fresh French troops to the rear. A great hole was torn in the centre of the thin British line; and for half an hour it seemed as if Sebastiani's 15,000 infantry and 7,000 cavalry might punch their way through. Wellesley saved the day by throwing in the last of his scanty reserves; and by late afternoon King Joseph, to Victor's disgust, ordered a general retreat towards Madrid.

Wellesley was shortly to be rewarded for his victory by a peerage; but surveying the corpse-strewn battlefield, over which, to add to the horrors, fire had broken out in the dry grass, he can have felt little elation. The casualties on both sides had been appalling: the British lost 5,000 in killed and wounded and the French over 7,000; Cuesta, who was not involved in the main engagement, lost some 500 men. Pursuit was for the moment out of the question, although Wellesley's first intention was to push forward with his army 'as soon as it shall be a little rested and refreshed after two days of the hardest fighting that I have ever been a party to. We shall certainly move forward towards Madrid, if not interrupted by some accident on our flank.'

When, on 3 August, Cuesta forwarded him a captured French despatch with the information that Soult was threatening his flank, not with 15,000 men as had been supposed, but 50,000, it became clear that the only option was to withdraw. Both the Spanish and British armies beat a hasty retreat over the Tagus at Arzobispo. Cuesta was shortly to suffer a paralytic stroke as a delayed result of his injuries incurred at Medellín and to resign his command; Wellesley withdrew south towards Portugal and then camped some twenty miles south of Almaraz, where he posted a detachment of Robert Crawfurd's Light Brigade to prevent the passage of the French across this last bridge across the Tagus.

Through his brother, the Marquis of Wellesley, who had replaced Frere as the British legate to the Seville Junta, he was bombarded with pleas to remain in Spain and continue the fight. Thus the Marquis writes on 22 August:

> Don Martin de Garay [the Junta's secretary] declared to me with expressions of the deepest sorrow and terror that if your army should quit Spain, at this critical moment, inevitable and immediate ruin must ensue to his government, to whatever provinces remain under its authority, to the cause of Spain itself, and to every interest connected with the alliance so happily established between Great Britain and the Spanish nation. . . .

What perhaps clinched Wellesley's belief in the impossibility of useful co-operation with the remaining Spanish armies, over and above the unfulfilled promises of the Junta in supplying food and transport, was the defeat in La Mancha of General Venegas, who had wrecked his plans at Talavera.

That Soult had not pressed home an attack on Wellesley and pursued him into Portugal was because King Joseph was determined to make an end of Venegas and the threat to Madrid. For this purpose he recalled Victor's 1st Corps from Talavera, ordering Marshal Mortier to take his place and so seriously depleting the number of troops at Soult's disposal. Meanwhile Venegas, who had so mulishly refused to move when it was imperative, threw caution to the winds and, abandoning the passes of the Sierra Morena and the defence of Andalusia, began a rash advance towards Toledo with his 23,000 men and was soundly trounced at Almonacid to the south of the city by a rather smaller force under General Sebastiani on 11 August 1809.

Wellesley now saw no further reason to remain at Almaraz and retired to Badajoz, just within the Spanish border, as the first stage of a planned withdrawal on Lisbon. Now that Napoleon at the other side of Europe had brought his Austrian campaign to a successful conclusion, there was nothing to prevent his pouring fresh troops into Spain; and, given the poor state of the Spanish armies, the small British force in the Peninsula could do little to defend Andalusia. Wellesley, with his usual clear-sightedness, realized that even the defence of Portugal was now problematical: 'the whole country is frontier' and it would therefore be necessary 'to confine himself to preserving what is most important—the capital'. While he set about fortifying the lines of Torres Vedras his army was not, in fact, to fire another shot in anger for a full five months. It was a decision bitterly criticized, at the time and since, both in England and Spain. Thus Miguel Artola Gallego writes in the *Historia de España*: 'Wellesley, whatever the capacity for strategy attributed to him, saw the war from a professional standpoint which ignored the revolutionary theory of permanent war espoused by the Spaniards. When the Central Junta proposed a renewed advance on the capital, the English commander roundly refused to lend any support to a new offensive.' This, at least, seems wide of the mark. Wellington had more use for the Spanish guerrillas than the regulars; what he refused to do until given overall command was to co-operate with generals who, if left to themselves, regularly sacrificed raw troops in headstrong frontal attacks on a greatly superior opponent.

Juan Carlos Areizaga, to whom the Junta gave the command of the Army of the Centre in place of Venegas, was exactly such a general. His appointment over the head of the Marquis of La Romana, one of the few Spanish leaders to have grasped the strategy of dispersal, as his campaigning in Galicia proved, is evidence enough that Sr Artola is mistaken in thinking that the Junta had by now understood the principles of '*la guerra permanente*'. On the contrary, to bolster its waning prestige, the Junta ordered an all-out attack which was once and for all to drive the French from the country. This was to be delivered by the Army of the Centre, which had been re-equipped and brought up to the strength of 50,000, while smaller forces under the Dukes of Albuquerque and del Parque were to make diversionary attacks in the Extremadura and Old Castile, so as to draw away French troops from Madrid.

Albuquerque and del Parque acquitted themselves well; in fact del Parque, with his Army of the Left drawn mainly from Blake's old Army of Galicia, inflicted a swingeing defeat on the French at Tamames and was for short periods able to occupy the neighbouring city of Salamanca. On the other hand, General Areizaga, descending from the heights of the Sierra Morena on 3 November 1809, was unable to take advantage of his temporary superiority in numbers. His only hope of success was to surprise the French and to defeat their forces in detail. After a rapid advance to La Guardia near Aranjuez, Areizaga lost confidence and halted for three days, so enabling Soult to concentrate his troops under Victor and Sebastiani. First throwing forward General Lacy with his advance guard, Areizaga later began an abrupt retreat and was pursued by the French, advancing across the Tagus, and brought to battle on 19 November 1809 near the town of Ocaña. The battle was the scene of the largest cavalry clash of the war and ended in the utter rout of the army on which the Junta had pinned its hopes: 4,000 Spanish were killed or wounded and 14,000 taken prisoner, against French losses of 2,000.

As Wellington, who had paid a brief visit to Seville and advised against the plan, had foreseen, the whole of Andalusia was now left defenceless; and the disaster spelt the end of the discredited Central Junta. Pending the election of a representative Cortes, an executive committee, of which La Romana was a member, was set up to raise funds and recruit more troops. Married men and novices in holy orders were conscripted; churches were required to contribute plate not actually needed for the communion, and private citizens table silver; while gangs of peasants, under the direction of army engineers, laboured to fortify the passes of the Sierra Moreno. The committee's activities were hampered by the intrigues of the dissident Conde de Montijo and Francis Palafox, brother of the defender of Saragossa; and, in any case, the two months' respite before the French resumed the offensive was all too short.

That Joseph waited so long was because the activity of del Parque and also the guerrillas in Old Castile threatened his lines of communication; but by the beginning of December 1809 thousands of reinforcements from Germany were beginning to roll across the Pyrenees. In the meantime Marshal Jourdan had resigned as chief-of-staff; he was later to write: 'The English army being now the only organized force in a state to face the imperial troops, and its presence in the Peninsula being the thing that sustained the Spanish government and gave confidence to the Spanish people, I imagine that we ought to have set ourselves to destroy that army, rather than to have disseminated our troops in garrisoning the whole surface of Spain.' However, it seems that Joseph was less interested in Portugal than his own kingdom of Spain and had set his heart on the conquest of its richest province. He succeeded in winning over Jourdan's successor, Marshal Soult; and all that remained was to receive Napoleon's assent. In fact, the orders from the Emperor never came, so that it was of their own volition that the two moved out of Madrid on 7 January 1810.

Their 40,000 men were faced by some 23,000 Spanish, hopelessly extended over a front of 150 miles, so that the defence was doomed from the start. The first plan of campaign envisaged a wide flanking movement, with Valencia and the Extremadura as the first objectives; but this was abandoned in favour of a direct advance on Seville. For this purpose the French army was split into two columns, one aiming for Almadén and Córdoba and the other for the passes of the Sierra Morena and La Carolina further east. Neither had much difficulty in rolling back Areizaga's dispersed and scanty troops, and the army was reunited on 22 January at Andújar, near the scene of Dupont's earlier débâcle. From here Sebastiani was despatched towards Granada with 10,000 men, while Joseph and Soult took the road to Córdoba and Seville.

Córdoba fell without a fight on the 24th; and Seville was in a state of mounting chaos. Within hours of sending to the Duke of Alburquerque to march to its aid, the Junta decamped for Cadiz on the 23rd, where its twenty-three members abdicated on 29 January, handing over all authority to a Regency charged with summoning the planned Cortes. Alburquerque, realizing that Seville was lost, wisely ignored his orders and instead made for Cadiz with his Army of the Extremadura. Meanwhile Seville fell into the hands of an excited mob, and a revolutionary 'Supreme National Junta', numbering Palafox, Montijo, the Marquis of La Romana, General Eguía and Francisco Saavedra, assumed brief power before its members too took flight, abandoning the panic-stricken inhabitants and disorganized soldiery without warning. Indeed, it seems that King Joseph's entry on 1 February 1810 was a matter of relief to many of the citizens, out of all patience with mob law and the intrigues and manoeuvrings of the Juntas. Nothing had been done to destroy the arsenals, the largest in Spain; and vast quantities of munitions, as well as tobacco to the value of £1,000,000 fell into the hands of the invaders.

Losing no time, Joseph and Soult now despatched Victor to take Cadiz. Although he covered the eighty-three miles in four days, he arrived just too late, on 5 February, to intercept Alburquerque's 12,000 troops, who had entered the place two days before, blowing up behind them the only bridge over the wide salt-water channel of the Río Santi Petri, which lies between the mainland and the Isla de León, an island of some size with which the city proper is connected on the seaward side by a narrow sand spit. Here the rot stopped. Because of the 300-yard-wide channel, Cadiz has never been captured except from the sea. Victor lacked boats; and even with them a successful assault would have been impossible, since the channel was covered by artillery, and the presence of gunboats in the inner harbour and larger units of the Spanish and British navies further out and in the Mediterranean ruled out any seaborne attack, now and in the future. Joseph wrote to his brother, proposing that a squadron be despatched from Toulon; but Napoleon was only too well aware of the realities of the naval position in the Mediterranean. Despite a French blockade lasting for years, Cadiz held out without difficulty until the end of the war and was to provide a last retreat for the Regency and the Cortes which succeeded it, and also a base for raids along the coast undertaken with the British navy. In their hour of peril the Spanish forgot their earlier fears about the landing of British troops, and 3,500 men under General William Stewart arrived in February 1810 to reinforce the Spanish garrison.

Meanwhile, all the rest of Andalusia lay open to the ravages of Soult, the connoisseur of other people's paintings, and Sebastiani, the plunderer of churches. By the end of February Sebastiani had successively occupied Jaén, Granada and Málaga, so making possible a triumphal tour of Andalusia by King Joseph before his return to Madrid at the end of March. Soult made his headquarters at Seville, where, as at Oporto earlier, he soon began to operate more as a viceroy than a military commander—behaviour which marked the end of his brief honeymoon with Joseph during the spring offensive.

Sweeping as the French victory had been, their hold on Andalusia was never more than tenuous and confined to the larger cities and towns; and the military outcome was to tie down yet larger numbers of troops. In Cadiz, the Regency soon found that the 18,000 Spanish and 8,000 British troops concentrated there by May were more than enough for the city's defence and began despatching seaborne expeditions in strength to the Niebla to the west and along the coast to the east. Blake, taking over the command of such troops of Areizaga's Army of the Centre as survived, and the Marquis of La Romana in the Extremadura, conducted operations which, if not overtly successful, at least diverted men whom Soult could ill spare; and even more damaging was the constant activity of the guerrillas in the mountainous country around Ronda and Granada. No sooner had Sebastiani attacked Murcia—actually bursting into the cathedral during mass to seize the plate and jewels—than he was compelled to evacuate the city and province because the mountaineers of the Alpujarras, the scourge of the *Reyes Católicos* at the time of the Moriscos, had risen in revolt, while Málaga had been reoccupied by the *serranos*.

In set encounters the French under Sebastiani, Victor and Mortier kept scoring tactical successes, like the defeat of Blake at Baza or the rout of Lord Blayney's amphibious expedition at Fuengirola; but the net result was that by the end of 1810 Soult's command of Andalusia was no more secure than at the beginning of the year, and he was powerless to give the effective aid so urgently required by Masséna in Portugal.

Chapter 15

THE LEOPARD AT BAY

After the Pyrrhic victory of Talavera and the arrival in England of thousands of fever-stricken survivors from the ill-fated Walcheren expedition, the Tory government was in disarray in September 1809 and faced with mounting criticism of its conduct of the war. Wellington's staunch supporter, Castlereagh, quarrelled violently with the foreign secretary, Canning, and fought a duel with him; both then resigned, together with the prime minister, Lord Portland. Although Portland's successor, Spencer Perceval, was to prove more resolute than there was reason to anticipate, the auguries were not good; and, for the Whigs, Lord Grey declared that, 'I am convinced that in six weeks' time, there will not remain a single British soldier in the Peninsula except as a prisoner.'

Meanwhile, Wellington remained convinced that with the small British and Portuguese forces under his command he could, if unable to intervene in Spain, repulse an attack on Portugal by a French army of anything less than 100,000. It was now clear that, in the wake of Wagram, an attack in force was imminent; and all the indications were that Napoleon would lead it in person. Portugal was, after all, Britain's oldest ally, and the first commitment was to her defence, so that, steeling his heart against the pleas of the Spanish Junta, Wellington systematically withdrew his troops on Lisbon during the autumn of 1809. His further plans embraced the continued reorganization of the Portuguese army and the *levée en masse* of the irregulars, or *ordenanza*; the devastation of the countryside in the path of the invader; and the construction of immensely strong lines of fortification in the 'Lisbon Peninsula' to the north of the capital.

As early as 10 September Wellington paid an unofficial visit to Lisbon and spent the next weeks in company with his chief engineer, Colonel Richard Fletcher, surveying the rough hill country around the town of Torres Vedras. The celebrated Lines comprised not one, but three separate defensive systems stretching some thirty miles from the natural barrier of the sea on the west to that of the Tagus inland. In the greatest secrecy, for this was essential to his plan, 10,000 peasants were employed to build forts and gun emplacements, dig ditches, construct lateral roads and 'scarp' the forward slopes of hills by removing earth and so making them more precipitous. Trees were cut down and their trunks employed for facing the earthworks, while the brushwood was used for outlying defences in the style of the barbed-wire entanglements of later wars. Since Wellington could not be certain of the enemy's line of approach—though he rightly foresaw that it would be from the north—extensive defence works were also constructed elsewhere. In typically thorough fashion he supervised the work in person. His answer to queries was always the same: 'I will get upon my Horse and take a look; and then tell you.'

Napoleon had already dictated a minute to his Minister of War on 7 October, ordering 100,000 troops, including the Old Guard, to Spain, and on 3 December 1809 made clear his intention of leading them, when he declared: 'The moment he displays himself beyond the Pyrenees the Leopard [his nickname for the British army] will seek the Ocean to avoid shame, defeat and death.' Very shortly afterwards he changed his mind about going to Spain in person, when the question arose of his divorce from Josephine and marriage to Marie Louise of Austria. The massive reinforcement went ahead, but on 17 April 1810 André Masséna, Duke of Rivoli and Prince of Essling, was named commander of the new Army of Portugal.

Masséna, though past his prime at the age of fifty-two and a thoroughly unlikable character, who, on the evidence of one of his subordinates, 'plundered like a *condottiere* of the Middle Ages', was still one of France's most formidable soldiers. Although he could say of himself to his staff, 'Gentlemen, I am here contrary to my own wish; I begin to find myself too old and too weary to go on active service', and Foy could write, 'He is no longer the Masséna of the flashing eye, the mobile face, and the alert figure I knew in 1799', for Wellington he was the one French marshal who could keep him awake at night. Napoleon was later to reproach Masséna for his lack of success with the bitter taunt, 'Well, Prince Essling, so you're no longer Masséna'; but the fault in the last place was his own, for the 70,000 troops with which the French entered Portugal were insufficient, as Wellington had foreseen, and without overall command in the Peninsula such as the Emperor would himself have exercised, Masséna had no authority to call on his colleagues in Spain for support on the required scale.

Operations were already well under way when Masséna arrived in Salamanca on 28 May 1810 to take up his command. In complete ignorance of what was afoot at Torres Vedras, Napoleon informed him that 'the army of General Wellington is composed of no more than 24,000 British and Germans, and his Portuguese are only 25,000 strong. . . . He need not hurry, but can go methodically to work.'

The first task was the reduction of the twin forts of Ciudad Rodrigo and Almeida on the opposite sides of the frontier. Ney's onslaught on Ciudad Rodrigo and its gallant defence by the septuagenarian governor, General Herresi, provoked an immediate demand both in England and Spain for the British army to move forward and raise the siege; but Wellington, heavily outnumbered on the ground, held back at Celorico, forty miles to the west inside Portugal, determined to play his waiting game. When the fortress fell on 10 July the expenditure of ammunition and supplies had been such as to hold up a further French advance until the 21st; Ney then began sweeping back General Craufurd's Light Division towards Almeida. In a brisk encounter on the River Coa Craufurd was all but overwhelmed and averted disaster only by a brilliantly executed withdrawal, when he turned the tables on the pursuing French as they struggled to cross the narrow bridge. The siege of Almeida, a much stronger fortress than Ciudad Rodrigo, began on 26 August; and Wellington was in hopes that it might hold up any further French advance until the end of September. It was not to be: a chance shot ignited a train of powder from a faulty keg; the fire ran back into the magazine; and the castle, in which it was located, the adjoining cathedral and the whole centre of the town rose into the sky. The British governor, General Cox, yielding to the discouraged survivors of the Portuguese garrison, was forced to surrender the following day.

It was only when Masséna resumed his advance towards Coimbra that he began to feel the full effects of Wellington's scorched earth policy and was soon to write to the Emperor: 'Sir, all our marches are across a desert; not a soul to be seen anywhere; everything is abandoned.' It was, in fact, a device practised by the Portuguese long before Wellington's time and could only have been carried out with the devoted co-operation of the peasants, who hid their supplies, destroyed their crops and drove away their flocks in the face of the advancing host; the behaviour of the wealthier townspeople was, understandably, less than whole-hearted.

Masséna's losses at Ciudad Rodrigo and Almeida and the need to garrison the fortresses compelled him to pull in 20,000 men under General Reynier, poised for a flanking attack on Castel Branco further south; and it was with a force of 65,000 that he moved in on Wellington along the Mondego river, harassed by the *ordenanza* and the Portuguese militia under Colonel Trant. Thanks to the lack of accurate information and the poor quality of his maps, which dated from 1778—they were later captured at Vitoria—he chose to advance along the abominable tracks to the north of the river instead of by the better road to the south. Wellington, who had been preparing to face him on hilly ground to the south-east of Coimbra, therefore took up position on the equally defensible ridge of Buçaco further north.

It seems likely that he would have preferred to retreat all the way to his prepared Lines at Torres Vedras; but public opinion both in England and Portugal now demanded a stand-up encounter. At home, patience was running out over the apparently endless retreat of the British army; and without disclosing his plans to the French and revealing the existence of the Lines, Wellington could not divulge his overall strategy. It was still harder for the Portuguese to accept the wholesale destruction of their countryside and to provide for the mounting thousands of refugees. Even the Regency, which had agreed the plan for defending Lisbon, voiced its doubts. It was now dominated by the influential Sousa family, who had little personal liking for Wellington, and the equally turbulent Bishop of Oporto, who had begun to question the effectiveness of physical destruction in checking the French; and they were evidently suspicious that his ultimate intention was to evacuate his army by sea. A remark from one of his later despatches vividly expresses his real feelings at the time: 'I don't know how the bloodthirsty people in England will like what I have been doing lately and am doing now but I am convinced I am right.'

Since political expediency dictated that Masséna must be fought and defeated before the withdrawal behind the prepared lines, Wellington chose his own ground with typical care. The ridge of Busaco (or more properly Buçaco), which barred the direct line of advance to Coimbra, is a rocky granite-strewn outcrop, dotted with clumps of pine trees and overgrown with broom, erica and ferns. It is now the site of a National Park; and the convent on the heights to the north, where Wellington established his headquarters, was later rebuilt as a royal hunting lodge and is now a luxurious hotel, decorated with tiled friezes depicting scenes from the battle. The ridge runs for nine miles from north to south, an extended front to be defended adequately by the 51,000 men, 25,000 of them Portuguese, of Wellington's army. But he had at once taken note of a rough track running almost the whole length of the heights behind the crest, thus enabling reinforcements to be rushed from one part of the line to another.

Masséna had never been in action against British troops and was contemptuous of their quality. He therefore decided on a frontal attack, to be delivered by two massed columns preceded by the usual screen of *voltigeurs*. Reynier was to storm the central and lower part of the ridge, to pierce the British line and then to outflank it. Ney's instructions were to wait until Reynier had reached the crest and then to launch his columns against the convent on the British left.

On 27 September 1810, under cover of the early morning mist, Reynier's two divisions toiled up the steep hillside. The sun broke through before one of the divisions under General Heudelet had reached the summit, and it was sent reeling back by concentrated artillery fire. The other division, under General Merle, succeeded in reaching a small plateau at the crest and was reforming its eleven battalions, when they were taken in the flank by the Connaught Rangers, charging from along the crest. 'Instantly a shout, loud and protracted rends the air, and the head of the enemy's column is annihilated by tremendous volleys', and although outnumbering the British by eleven battalions to four, 'The hapless shattered mass staggers, breaks, turns, and rushes down the steep like an avalanche, while bullet, ball and shell plunge into the fugitive crowd.' With the repulse of another attack by General Foy, Reynier had shot his bolt. Ney fared no better on the French right. The first of his columns had come within twenty yards of the summit, when Craufurd, waving on his men from behind the crest, called, 'Now 52nd, revenge the death of Sir John Moore!' The head of the French columns crumbled beneath a hail of fire at point-blank range; and the battalions in the front carried back with them those in the centre and at the rear and were sent hurtling down the hill. Ney attempted an attack with a further eleven battalions to his left; but by 11 a.m. it was all over. The French had suffered 4,500 casualties against 1,252, equally divided between British and the Portuguese, who had fought effectively and with courage.

Although balked of his prey, Masséna was convinced that the end was now in sight and marched into Coimbra on 1 October, hard on the heels of the retreating British and Portuguese. In spite of orders to evacuate the city, most of the 40,000 inhabitants had hung on, hoping against hope that the French would be thrown back at Buçaco. A pitiful exodus now began, and when the 8th Corps entered the place they found it deserted. For the first two days of October the half-starved French troops gave themselves over to looting the empty houses, plundering the University and churches and gorging themselves on provisions abandoned by Wellington's commissariat. The advance was resumed on the 3rd; and since Masséna had decided that he needed every available man, only a token garrison of a single company of marines remained to guard the 4,000 wounded and sick whom he left in the Convent of Santa Clara. A few days later Colonel Trant, who had been shadowing the French rearguard with some thousand Portuguese militia, swept into the place and brushed aside resistance. To his credit, he did his best to protect the prisoners against the fury of his own men; and the great majority were safely escorted to Oporto.

With two days' start on its pursuers, Wellington's army had meanwhile been conducting an orderly retreat down roads clogged with refugees towards the Lines of Torres Vedras. As the French army followed, the *ordenanza* closed in behind, cutting off all communication with Spain. So complete was their stranglehold that from 18 September to 15 November the garrisons at Almeida and Ciudad Rodrigo received no single message from Masséna; various aides-de-camp and Portuguese renegades sent with despatches were captured or killed; and Napoleon himself was dependent on what he read in the English newspapers.

The first British troops reached the Lines on 8 October 1810 and, while the onset of the autumn rains hampered the pursuit, began taking up their allotted positions during the next few days.

Masséna had sent forward cavalry under General Montbrun ahead of his main force; and it was he, on 10 October, who was the first Frenchman to receive news of the existence of the Lines from a captured British patrol. The following morning he rode forward towards the village of Sobral on a knoll in front of the defensive positions proper and took in the scarped hillsides and embrasures extending into the distance on either side. In Rocca's words, the French army was now face to face with its fate: 'Before them was a wall of brass; behind them the region of famine.'

Only on 14 October did Masséna himself come forward to Sobral. There, as his aide-de-camp relates, 'instead of the "undulating accessible plateau" that we had been told to expect, we saw steeply scarped mountains and deep ravines, a road passage only a few paces broad, and on each side walls of rock crowned with everything that could be accomplished in the way of field fortifications garnished with artillery'. Riding eastwards and close to the Lines at Monte Agraça, Masséna raised his marshal's hat, as a warning shot was fired, and retreated with his escort. It hardly required a council of war that same night to decide that a frontal attack would have been even more disastrous than the assault on Buçaco.

Wellington, on his side, noted with characteristic understatement that 'he thought his arrangements had now made the position tolerably secure'. The defences themselves were garrisoned by 20,000 second-line troops, the whole of his field army being kept in reserve in case the French columns should break through. He would have welcomed nothing better than an outright attack, but after some skirmishing around the outpost of Sobral, Masséna, unwilling to admit defeat and abandon the attempt on Lisbon, settled down in front of the Lines to await reinforcements. He maintained this position for exactly one month, and then, as a thick fog rolled back on the morning of 15 November, the British outposts discovered that the French sentries had been replaced by straw dummies topped with old shakos.

Masséna's losses, in battle and from illness, malnutrition and desertions, especially among Junot's conscripts in open encampments around Sobral, had been such as to reduce his army from the 65,000 men with whom he had set out from Almeida to about 50,000. He therefore decided to concentrate his troops in the so-called Plain of Golegão between Santarém and the Zezere river, where provisions were more plentiful. Already, on 31 October 1810, he had despatched General Foy with a battalion of infantry and a detachment of cavalry to cut his way through to Ciudad Rodrigo and from there to proceed with all haste to Paris and impress upon the Emperor the absolute necessity for strong reinforcements. After a searching cross-examination, Napoleon delivered himself of the opinion that Masséna should continue to blockade the Lines and also cross the Tagus into the Alentejo—this was, in fact, a move envisaged by Masséna and anticipated by Wellington, but which had proved impossible for the lack of pontoons and bridging equipment. Meanwhile Napoleon confirmed that orders had already been sent to Drouet at Valladolid and Soult in Andalusia to march to the aid of the Army of Portugal, but added cynically to Foy: '*Je donne l'ordre. L'executera-t-on? De si loin obéit qui veut.*' Drouet was the first to accede, and he joined Masséna on 26 December with 6,000 men —a force entirely inadequate to retrieve the deteriorating position of the Army of Portugal, which remained pinned down in its cantonments around Santarém under the surveillance of Wellington and the Portuguese partisans and reduced to a brutal and hand-to-mouth search for provisions.

Soult, for his part, had no intention of abandoning the fleshpots of Andalusia. To have amassed an army strong enough to march on Abrantes would have meant withdrawing the garrisons from Seville and the other large cities and leaving the province to the mercies of the guerrillas and raiding parties from Cadiz. Instead, he set himself the limited objective of capturing the frontier forts of the Extremadura, of which the most important was Badajoz, and set out in early January 1811 with 20,000 men, including a siege train and large numbers of engineers.

Wellington countered by releasing the Marquis of La Romana and 14,000 Spanish troops from garrison duties in the Lines and around Lisbon; but before the Marquis could start he died suddenly of a heart attack. Although he had been nicknamed the *Marques de las Romerías* ('the Marquis of the Pilgrimages') because of his caution and many retreats, he was perhaps the best Spanish general and the only one to be implicitly trusted by Wellington. His death was a disaster, in that General Mendizábal, who had been given temporary command by the Regency pending the arrival of Castaños, recklessly threw away the army in a pitched battle outside Badajoz, where he was routed. Worse was to follow after the French succeeded in breaching the citadel, when the governor, José Imaz, although in receipt of semaphore messages from Elvas that a large Anglo-Portuguese force was on its way and after delivering himself of the opinion 'that I think we should defend the place with valour and constancy', surrendered without a fight on 10 March 1811. By now Soult was in a fever to return to Andalusia, since only two days later he received news of a French reverse near Cadiz. Leaving Marshal Mortier with a garrison of 11,000 to hold Badajoz, he marched hurriedly back to Seville.

The news which had so much alarmed him was of the Battle of Barrosa. On hearing of Soult's departure for the Extremadura, the Regency in Cadiz had broached the subject of an attack on Marshal Victor, so as to raise the siege. It was agreed with General Graham and Admiral Sir Richard Keats, commanding the British forces, that this should take the form of a sortie on the French lines by Spanish troops under General Zayas, while at the same time a mixed Spanish and British force was landed further down the coast at Tarifa to take Victor in the rear. Unwisely in the event, Graham relinquished command of the seaborne expedition to General La Peña, who had so disgracefully abandoned Castaños at the Battle of Tudela during the early years of the war. Zayas succeeded in throwing a pontoon bridge across the channel of Santi Petri and establishing a bridgehead, but was contained by Victor, who, getting wind of the attack on his rear, marched swiftly to meet it and took up strong positions on the Barrosa ridge flanking the allied advance. La Peña, true to his earlier form, remained on a beach by the coast with his 9,500 Spaniards, leaving the uphill battle on the ridge to Graham and his 4,900 British and 300 Portuguese. After a bloody encounter on 5 March 1811, of which Graham had rather the better, the French were driven off; but Graham, in disgust, re-embarked his troops for Cadiz, refusing to have any further dealings with his Spanish colleague. If the sortie, which might well have relieved Cadiz, ended inconclusively, it did at least speed Soult's return from Badajoz.

Soult's intervention in the Extremadura and the capture of Badajoz did nothing to influence the main course of events in Portugal; already, on 5 March, Masséna had begun a general retreat northwards towards Spain. Wellington had underestimated the time that the Army of Portugal could survive in the devastated territories; but during the early months of 1811 provisions were procured only by what the French called *la chasse aux hommes*, unwary Portuguese peasants being pursued by foraging parties and either threatened at musket point or tortured until they revealed hidden stores of food.

After Foy's return from Paris, and having waited in vain for the appearance of Mortier in the Alentejo, Masséna called a meeting of his generals on 19 February. Marshal Ney was for a bold strike across the Tagus, but was overridden by Masséna and the others; and orders for the retreat were issued on 3 March. With Trant and the Portuguese partisans on his northern flank along the Mondego river and Wellington pressing hard to his rear, Masséna was unable to take the road through Coimbra and was compelled to go by the track to Celorico and Almeida through the barren mountains of Central Portugal. In exaggerated form all the horrors of the earlier retreats of Sir John Moore to Corunna and of Soult to Galicia were repeated.

The advancing British were at first sorry for the plight of the French stragglers, whom they found by the roadside, dead of hunger or illness or murdered by the partisans, but such feelings paled in the face of the atrocities committed by the French themselves. Thus Donaldson of the 94th writes of a village near Leiria: 'I never before witnessed such destruction: floors torn up, beds cut in pieces, their contents thrown about intermixed with kitchen utensils, broken mirrors, china etc. . . . we found a door leading to a chamber apart from the chapel. It was quite dark, so I took up a burning piece of wood to inspect it. It was full of half-consumed human bodies, some lying, others kneeling or leaning against the walls. . . . The expression of their scorched faces was horrible beyond description. In a bag lying at the upper end of the apartment was the dead body of a young child, who had been strangled: the cord used was still tight about its little neck.'

After a series of sharp rearguard actions Masséna reached Celorico on 22 March, with a clear road open to his bases at Almeida and Ciudad Rodrigo. Here, pride prevented him from retreating tamely by the route he had taken into Portugal, and he decided to lunge at Placencia, over the Spanish border to the south. Ney, whose men had borne the brunt of the rearguard actions, pungently opposed this wild plan and flatly refused to obey orders. Though forthwith superseded, he was entirely right in his predictions; and a week later Masséna was again in full retreat. After a sharp brush at Sabugal on the River Coa with Wellington's advance guard, which might have proved disastrous for Reynier's 2nd Corps but for the incompetence of General Sir William Erskine, the demoralized Army of Portugal finally began crossing the Spanish frontier on 5 April 1811. The ill-fated campaign had cost the French army some 25,000 men, 5,872 horses, its baggage train and munitions, and all but 36 of its wagons. The strategy of scorched earth and planned retreat had been triumphantly vindicated, but at the cost of even crueller civilian casualties: behind the Lines of Torres Vedras alone, no less than 50,000 refugees perished of hunger and exposure during the winter of 1810/11.

On 10 April 1811 Wellington announced that, 'The Portuguese are informed that the cruel enemy ... have been obliged to evacuate, after suffering great losses, and have retired across the Agueda. The inhabitants of the country are therefore at liberty to return to their homes.' Nevertheless the French still retained a toe-hold in Portugal at Almeida; and a British advance into Spain was blocked by their possession of the border fortresses of Badajoz and Ciudad Rodrigo. Leaving Sir Brent Spencer to invest Almeida, Wellington now made a whirlwind visit to the south to confer with General Beresford over plans for the recapture of Badajoz; they were to come to nothing for the lack of an adequate siege train, and meanwhile Wellington posted back to the north, on hearing from Spencer that Masséna had already succeeded in reorganizing his army and was advancing on Almeida with a force of 42,000 infantry, 4,500 cavalry and 38 guns. It was the formidable old marshal's last fling, and the 34,000 Anglo-Portuguese stood in much need of their commander, of whom Captain Kincaid of the Rifle Brigade said at the time: 'We would rather see his long nose in the fight than a reinforcement of ten thousand men any day.'

Wellington's prime object was to prevent the relief of Almeida and its fortress. Making the best use of the ground, he therefore deployed his troops on a rugged ridge rising behind the village of Fuentes de Oñoro, east of Almeida and in the line of Masséna's advance. The weakness of the position was the rolling plateau to the right of his line, allowing scope for a flanking movement by the cavalry, in which the French were much superior. It was here, on the morning of 5 May 1811, that the battle entered its critical phase. Only by forming squares in the face of a dashing and sustained attack by Montbrun's dragoons was Craufurd's Light Division, with help from regiments of British dragoons and German hussars, able to retreat across open ground with parade-ground precision and to form a new line forming a right angle on the rocky heights. About midday, with the flanking movement repulsed, Masséna threw the full weight of his attack into the village and against the front of the line. After desperate hand-to-hand fighting the onslaught finally crumbled against a wild charge led by the Connaught Rangers; and at two o'clock the French withdrew, leaving the narrow streets choked with corpses: their own, Scots, Irish and English.

It had been a near thing, the closest that Wellington came to defeat in the Peninsula. 'If Boney had been there,' he later told his brother, 'we should have been beat.' Losses were almost equal; but with Masséna in full retreat, the road to Portugal still open and Almeida unrelieved, he could claim it as a victory. One crumb of comfort remained to Masséna before he was suspended from his command and recalled to Paris. At dead of night General Brennier succeeded in blowing up the fortress of Almeida and cutting his way with his small garrison through the British lines. Of this Wellington wrote bitterly: 'I begin to be of the opinion that there is nothing so stupid as "a gallant officer". They [the blockading force] had about 13,000 men to watch 1,400, and on the night of the 10th, to the infinite surprise of the enemy they allowed the garrison to slip through their fingers and escape.... There they were, sleeping in their spurs even, but the French got off.'

1811 was to see one more major encounter in the frontier region, in terms of carnage the bloodiest of the whole war, and of which Wellington was to write, 'Another such battle would ruin us.' When Soult heard of Beresford's attack on Badajoz, he decided that he must march to its relief. Under pressure from Napoleon to abandon most of Andalusia, he again decided to cling on to his viceroyalty, and such was his difficulty in mustering the 25,000 troops with which he set out for the Extremadura on 10 May that the scanty garrisons in Seville and Córdoba were under orders to retire into their citadels if pressed by the Spanish irregulars.

In accordance with the strategy laid down by Wellington during his flying visit in April, Beresford concentrated his forces, British, Spanish and Portuguese, near the village of Albuera, east of Badajoz. The gentle slopes on either side of the stream across which the armies faced one another on 16 May 1811, gave no very definite advantage to either side—except that the movements of the French were partially screened by clumps of olive trees. Beresford had expected the main attack to be made on the village itself; but, in fact, it developed on his right flank, held by 12,000 Spaniards commanded by General Blake.

To set the record straight, the greatly outnumbered battalions under General Zayas, which bore the brunt of the first attack, fought with great courage. As Wellington later commented, 'The Spanish troops behaved admirably, I understand. They stood like stocks while both parties were firing into them. . . .' The trouble came because of Blake's inability to manoeuvre. A flank attack by Colborne's brigade threw the advancing French columns into confusion; but the Buffs, in the smoke of battle and during a sudden rainstorm, failed to notice the approach of 800 Polish lancers to their rear and were cut to pieces, losing some 1,200 out of 1,600 effectives in the space of five minutes. Beresford now brought up General Hoghton's brigade to relieve the Spaniards; but it was a line of 1,900 men two deep against 8,000 twelve deep on a narrow front. In a fearful exchange of fire, the British, without giving way, died where they stood. It was here that the 57th, under Colonel Inglis, earned their title of the Diehards. It seems that both Soult and Beresford were appalled by the unparalleled carnage, and that Beresford in particular was so numbed as to be incapable of decisive action. In this critical juncture, at the suggestion of Henry Hardinge, attached to the Portuguese forces, General Lowry Cole took it upon himself to throw his 4th Division against the French flank. Advancing uphill in open country, his own flank gallantly secured against the French cavalry by four battalions of Portuguese infantry, he swept the French up the hillside and over the ridge, where they finally broke and fled.

The battle had been won and Soult compelled to retreat into Andalusia, but only at the cost of enormous losses on both sides. The allies lost 5,900 men out of 35,000, and the British infantry 4,400 out of 6,500; Soult's casualties were about 7,000 out of 24,000. When Wellington arrived shortly afterwards and read

Beresford's despatch, he remarked: 'He could not stand the slaughter about him and the vast responsibility: the letter was quite in a desponding tone. It was brought to me by Arbuthnot while I was at dinner at Elvas, and I said, "This won't do: write me down a victory." ' And as a victory it was accordingly reported to the government at home.

Although Soult had withdrawn and Wellington took over the siege of Badajoz in person, it proved impossible to reduce the fortress, both for want of suitable artillery and lack of expertise on the part of his engineers. Meanwhile the young and energetic Marshal Marmont, who had taken over from Masséna, marched south to Soult's aid; and confronted by a combined force of 60,000, Wellington retreated westwards into the hills, where the French were unwilling to risk another Buçaco. Hostilities now shifted to the north. Wellington, reinforced from England, had set his sights on Ciudad Rodrigo. Here again, he was for the time being balked, since Marmont was equally alive to the importance of controlling this gateway to northern Spain and joined forces with Marshal Bessières's Army of the North to revictual the fortress. The year ended in stalemate, with Wellington biding his time and withdrawing to cantonments at Sabugal over the Portuguese frontier.

In this saga of marches and countermarches, of the clash of the reds with the blues, of battles won by a daring decision or a stoic resolve to stand and die, and of a campaign which turned on the stark logic of hunger, less than justice has been done to a more insidious and daily drain on the manpower and resources of the French army. Defeat in Portugal began in the Pyrenees and northern Spain.

Chapter 16

THE GUERRILLAS

If these men had known to fight as well as to die, we should not so easily have passed the Pyrenees. But they learned it at last.

From *History of the War of the French in Spain* by M. DE ROCCA, 1815

The guerrillas, who from the other side of the Peninsula contributed to Masséna's débâcle in Portugal, did not begin to play a decisive part in the war until after the defeat of the regular Spanish armies in the French counter-offensive of 1808; thereafter, many of the troops who had dispersed into the mountains were to rally under leaders, some like themselves ex-regulars, and to set the pattern for a new form of warfare. They proved that, in suitable broken terrain and with civilian co-operation, men who are fighting for survival on their own soil can be more than a match for a vastly superior regular army. In Vietnam, Africa, the Middle East and South America the guerrillas of today have fought, and are fighting, rightly or wrongly according to one's political standpoint, for a variety of causes; they owe their methods to the *guerrilleros* of the Peninsular War.

Few accounts of the Spanish guerrillas can be as vivid or as impartial as that of an officer in the French hussars, M. de Rocca, who was himself engaged in day-to-day operations against them and spent the latter days of the war as a prisoner in England, where he had ample time to reflect on the implications of the French invasion. No apology is therefore made for quoting from his *History of the War in Spain* at some length: 'As the Spanish armies had gradually been destroyed, the communications between the provincial juntas and the supreme Central Junta had been cut off; each, therefore, applied all its resources to the local defence of the district under its jurisdiction. Such of the inhabitants as had till then suffered with patience, daily expecting their deliverance after every pitched battle, now began to think of seeking for themselves individually the means of shaking off the yoke which oppressed them. Every province, every town, every individual felt more strongly every day the necessity of resisting the common enemy. The national hatred which existed against the French had produced a sort of unity in the undirected efforts of the people, and to regular warfare had succeeded a system of war in detail, a species of organized disorder which suited the fierce spirit of the Spanish nation exactly, as well as the unhappy circumstances in which it was placed.

'That part of Spain occupied by the French was soon filled with partisans and guerrillas, some of them regular soldiers from the broken armies, and others the inhabitants both of mountain and valley; clergy, husbandmen, students, shepherds even had become active and enterprising leaders. . . . And one might say of the Spaniards, that if at first they had been easily overcome, it was almost impossible to subdue them.

'When we marched from one province to another, the partisans immediately re-organized the country we had abandoned in the name of Fernando VII, as if we were never to go back, and punished very severely every one who had shewn any kind of zeal for the French. Thus the terror of our arms gave us no influence around us. As the enemy was spread out over the whole country, the different points that the French occupied were all more or less threatened; their victorious troops, dispersed in order to maintain their conquests, found themselves, from Irún to Cadiz, in a state of continual blockade; and they were not in reality masters of more ground than they actually trod upon.

'The garrisons which they had left on the military roads to keep the country in check, were continually attacked; they were obliged to construct little citadels for their safety, by repairing old ruined castles which they found on the heights, and these castles were frequently Roman or Moorish remains, which, many centuries before, had served the same purpose. In the plains, the posts of communication fortified one or two of the houses at the entrance of each village, for safety during the night, or as a place of retreat when attacked. The sentinels dared not remain without the fortified enclosures, for fear of being carried off; they therefore stationed themselves on a tower, or on wooden scaffolding built on the roof near the chimney, to observe what happened in the surrounding country. The French soldiers thus shut up in their little fortresses, frequently heard the gay sounds of the guitars of their enemies, who came to pass their nights in the neighbouring villages, where they were always well received and feasted by the inhabitants. The French armies could only obtain provisions and ammunition under convoy of very strong detachments, which were for ever harassed and frequently intercepted. These detachments met with but slight resistance in the plains, but the moment they approached the mountains, they were obliged to cut their way forward by force of arms; *and the daily loss of the French, in many parts of Spain, in their attempts to procure victuals, and to keep up their communications, were at least equal to any they could have sustained if they had had to struggle with an enemy who could have met them in open battle.*

'The people of Spain did not allow themselves to be cast down by the length of the war. In some provinces the peasants were always armed; the husbandman guided his plough with one hand, while he held in the other a sword always unsheathed, and which was only buried on the approach of the French, if they were too numerous to be fought. . . . In order to satiate their inveterate resentment, they employed, by turns, the greatest energy or the deepest dissimulation and cunning where they were weakest. Like avenging vultures eager for prey, they followed the French columns at a distance, to murder such of the soldiers as, fatigued or wounded, remained behind on a march. . . .

'The French could only maintain themselves in Spain by terror; they were constantly under the necessity of punishing the innocent with the guilty, and of taking revenge on the weak for the offences of the powerful. Plunder had become necessary for existence, and such atrocities as were occasioned by the enmity of the people, and the injustice of the cause for which the French were fighting, injured the moral feeling of the army, and sapped the very foundations of military discipline, without which regular troops have neither strength nor power.'

Among the first guerrilla leaders to take the field were Juan Martín Díaz, *El Empecinado* ('the stubborn'), who so menaced King Joseph around Madrid and actually for one day occupied the town of Guadalajara, and the priest Merino, who, charged with transporting the instruments for a French military band, took to the open country with a troop of three hundred horsemen. Rather later, Mina el Mozo or *El Estudiante* ('the student'), so-called to distinguish him from his more famous uncle, Espoz y Mina, was a constant thorn in the flesh of the French on the borders of Navarre and Aragon. For a time towards the end of

1809 and the beginning of 1810 he tied down no less than 12,000 of Suchet's men until he was finally captured in March 1810.

Francisco Espoz, who added the name of Mina to his own because it was one to conjure with, was the only guerrilla chief to publish his *Memorias* (or Memoirs). He begins by describing how he rallied the survivors of his nephew's band, incorporating in it the followers of various other leaders: 'The most notable were Sarasa (alias *Cholín*), Fidalgo, Juan de Villanueva, known as *Juanito el de la Rochapea*, his companion Juan Ignacio Noaín, Lizárraga, nicknamed *Tachuelas*, Buruchuri, Marcalain and many others, all known for their boldness and bravery. With the help of these stalwarts, and without abandoning attacks on the French, I tried to cleanse, and in effect did cleanse, the countryside of another class of enemies worse than them. These were the bands of robbers and highwaymen who in the guise of patriots wrought violence and rapine on all whom they encountered. Among others I executed the so-called *Carretero de Leire* and all the band who had terrorized the province by their atrocities. By these measures and as a result of continuous attacks on the French, always successful, I won the sympathy and support of the whole Province of Navarre and great prestige outside it.'

In recognition of these services, on 23 April 1810, the Regency awarded Mina the title of Commander General of all the partisans and guerrillas of Navarre. There remained one or two dissident chiefs who were more of a menace to the local inhabitants than the French. The most powerful and unscrupulous, Echeverría, had his headquarters in the mountain town of Estella, and Mina's account of their confrontation reads more like the script for a Western film than sober history.

'On 13 July 1810 we entered Estella in formation. We found many of Echeverría's men unarmed in the streets, and they stopped in astonishment to look at our marching order. Between cavalry and infantry, there were 900 of these men. The doors and windows of the houses were shut; and there was hardly a single peasant to be seen in the streets, because the populace foresaw a terrible clash and feared that their city would be turned into a blood bath. They well knew how sharply Echeverría and I differed; they were aware of the bad blood between our men; and they suspected—not without justification—that I was armed. Echeverría and his principal officers were quite calmly waiting in the square. Without breaking formation, I bade my men stand easy. I dismounted, and Echeverría, his adjutant and I made our way to his lodgings. We were hardly out of the square when my plans were put into execution. The positions held by Echeverría's men were taken over by my volunteers, who relieved them of their weapons; and no sooner had I sat down in his house than one of my people arrived to take Echeverría and Ayala captive. The two bitterly lamented their lack of precautions and overconfidence, and I condemned Echeverría for the atrocities he had committed and the lack of control over his men. I then led him out prisoner into the square and ordered all his followers to assemble there. In his presence, I harangued them, making them see that we had to unite to save the country and that they must behave in orderly and disciplined fashion. As I was speaking, the few townspeople whose curiosity had drawn them into the square began applauding me; Echeverría's men joined in; and on hearing the plaudits, the people inside the houses suddenly threw open doors, shutters and windows. The whole city gave itself over to celebrating the happy outcome of an event which they had imagined could only end in destruction and horror; my volunteers embraced the very men they had been prepared a minute or two before to kill; the bells began tolling and that night the whole city was lit up. As for Echeverría, Ayala, Miranda, Bona, Pomes and Comas, the chiefs of the band, they were taken to Irache in the evening and shot.'

As a result of this coup, Mina's band was swelled by 600 foot and 200 horse, and he now devoted himself to continuous attacks on the French. Operating at times with a small army of 3,000 and at others hiding in some mountain cave with half a dozen companions, he would surprise large convoys, overrun outlying strongpoints or intercept despatches and forward them to the Juntas or the English. He would never accept combat except where he had the advantage of the terrain and under conditions of local superiority, otherwise ordering his men to disperse and regroup. During the autumn of 1810 he was fruitlessly hunted by the flying columns of an entire French division under General Drouet.

In December 1811 General Abbé, Governor of Navarre, issued a proclamation ordering the execution both of guerrillas and of 'hostages' from their families and the villages that sheltered them. Mina retaliated by promising to shoot four French prisoners for every executed Spaniard—a threat which was implemented to the letter. After the French had shot four members of the 'insurrectional junta' of the Province of Burgos, one of Mina's colleagues, the priest Merino, responded by killing eighty captured French soldiers. Abbé thereupon withdrew his decree, and Mina followed suit.

It was Mina's boast that at one period early in 1812 no less than six French commanders, Dorsenne, Reille, Caffarelli, Roguet, D'Agoult and Suchet, deploying a total of 18,000 troops in his chosen territory, were separately on his trail.

Caffarelli had discovered that Mina maintained an ammunition factory, stores and a hospital in the inaccessible Pyrenean valley of Roncal. These were overrun; but Mina and his men escaped, only to be trapped on 24 March by three converging French columns. Mina made off by night over hills which to anyone else would have been impassable. The French were confident that his teeth had been drawn; but on 9 April, having made a large detour back into Navarre, he fell upon a huge convoy in the pass of Salinas near Vitoria. It comprised wounded, civilians, prisoners, stores and food, and was escorted by 2,000 soldiers, including a whole Polish regiment destined for Russia. Five hundred of the Poles were killed; and besides releasing the 450 captive Spaniards, Mina possessed himself of letters from King Joseph to his wife and Napoleon, together with several hundred thousand francs in specie and other booty.

The hunt was resumed with a vengeance and Mina repaired to the village of Robles to agree further plans with a minor guerrilla chief, Tris *el Malcarado* ('the false-faced'). Living up to his name, Tris despatched an agent to Huesca, ostensibly to spy on the French garrison, but in reality to advise General Pannetier of Mina's presence in the village. What subsequently happened forms one of the most arresting passages of the *Memorias*.

Pannetier moved up 800 infantry and 150 cavalry during the night, and Mina was awakened by the noise of the French hussars in the street. One of the cavalrymen was already forcing the gate of his lodging, when Mina emerged and struck him down with the crossbar. This gained him time to jump on to his horse; the owner of the house then threw open the gate without warning; and taking advantage of the momentary diversion, Mina burst out with a handful of his followers and cut his way through the assailants. The whole village was now aroused, and Mina and his small troop galloped up and down the streets, shouting and slashing at the French cavalrymen, so as to allow as many as possible of his men to make their escape. On the approach of the main body of infantry, he withdrew into the mountains, to return to the village a day or two later after its evacuation by the French and to exact his revenge. Tris was duly shot for his treachery, in company with the priest, the *alcalde* and various others who had been party to the plot. Mina lived on to fight another day and was soon offering assistance to Admiral Popham during his descent on the Basque coast. His exile in France and England after the end of the war and his exploits in the service of the liberals belong to a later chapter.

Further west in Biscay and the Asturian mountains, the most considerable guerrilla forces were those of Porlier, nicknamed *El Marquesito* after his uncle the Marquis of La Romana, who had fought at the Battle of Gamonal and often co-operated with another celebrated guerrilla, Longa. Some of the most spectacular of Porlier's raids were carried out with the help of a British naval squadron operating from Corunna and Ferrol, which landed muskets and ammunition for the guerrillas at the small ports along the north coast. During July 1810, in an ambitious combined operation, a convoy escorted by two British frigates put ashore 1,000 of Porlier's men at Santoña just east of Santander. The port was captured, and Porlier's irregulars, gathering strength from the local peasantry, carried out a series of raids further along the coast. In August of the same year he was again landed and took to the hills, making his headquarters at Potes in the Picos de Europa. The efforts of a whole French division under General Serras only succeeded in driving him further back into the Asturian mountains. The following summer Porlier massed his men around Santander and, in a surprise attack on 14-15 August 1811, overran the city and drove out General Rouget's garrison, retiring into the hills with some 300 prisoners as soon as reinforcements appeared.

The heaviest and most effective attacks on the north coast took place in the summer of 1812 as part of Wellington's plan for dividing and harrying the French. Admiral Sir Home Popham sailed from Corunna with two ships of the line mounting heavy guns, five frigates, and smaller vessels carrying two battalions of marines and several thousand muskets for the guerrillas. The operations were planned in concert with General Mendizábal, whose 'Seventh Army' embraced the large and fairly well-organized forces of Porlier and Longa as well as the smaller guerrilla bands of Jauregui (*El Pastor* or 'shepherd'), Renovales, Marquinez, Saornil and Merino. By landing marines and heavy guns, Popham overwhelmed a number of the coastal fortresses and on 24 January 1812 ran his squadron into the harbour of Santander. A heavy assault by the British marines and the men of one of Porlier's brigades, under his lieutenant, Campino, was repulsed with heavy losses; but soon afterwards the French decided to evacuate the fortress and broke out with 1,600 men, leaving the place in the hands of the allies. This was a most important success, since Santander was a deep-water port and was thereafter to serve as a permanent base for supplying both the Spanish in the north and also Wellington during his attack on Burgos in the autumn of 1812 and the campaign of the following year, in which the French were beaten at Vitoria and driven back across the Pyrenees.

The actual quality of guerrilla fighting in Spain, the smell of gunpowder and sense of imminent death, come out better in de Rocca's *History* than in Mina's trustworthy, but somewhat magniloquent *Memorias*. After taking part in Loison's unsuccessful operations against Porlier in the Rioja, de Rocca and his detachment of hussars were transferred to Andalusia, where Marshal Soult employed them in hunting down the guerrillas in the mountains around Ronda. This is how he describes their opponents:

'Their most popular pastime was to sit in the rocks amongst the olive groves at the end of the suburb, and tranquilly smoke their segars while they fired at our videttes. In the morning they would go out of the town with their tools, as if they were going to work in the fields, but there or at the farm-houses they found their guns, and returning at night, they would come back to the town, and sleep in the midst of us. It not unfrequently happened that our hussars recognized their hosts among their enemies, but it was impossible to make very vigorous searches, for if Marshal Soult's decree against insurgents had been carried into execution, we must have punished nearly the whole population with death. The mountaineers hung their French prisoners or burned them alive; and in return, our soldiers rarely gave quarter to a Spaniard found under arms. The women, the old men, and even children, were against us, and served as spies for the enemy. I saw a young boy of eight years old playing among our horses' feet; he offered himself as a guide, and led a small party of hussars straight to an ambuscade. When he reached it he suddenly ran off towards the rocks, throwing up his bonnet in the air, and crying with all his might, "Long live our King, Ferdinand VII!" and the firing instantly began. . . .

'The little town of Grazalema was the arsenal of the mountaineers. Marshal Soult sent a column of 3,000 men against that small place. The inhabitants defended themselves from house to house, and only abandoned the place for want of ammunition; they then escaped into the mountains, after having destroyed a considerable number of our soldiers, and the moment the army left the town they took possession again. Three regiments of the line were sent a month afterwards on the same service. They repulsed the mountaineers with ease from every point in the open country, but they could not succeed in gaining possession of Grazalema. The inhabitants had entrenched themselves in the market place, which is in the centre of the town; and had placed mattresses before the windows of the houses in which they had shut themselves up. Twelve hussars of the tenth regiment, and forty riflemen who formed the advance guard of the French division, arrived in the square without meeting any resistance; but they never returned, every one of them was struck by fire which poured from the windows on all sides; and all who were sent to the same spot perished immediately in like manner, without having done the smallest damage to the enemy. The expeditions which the French frequently sent against the highest part of the mountains almost always dispersed the enemy's troops without subduing them, and our parties returned to Ronda with great loss. Even when our troops were superior in number, the mountaineers baffled all their efforts by their manner of fighting in the mountains. On the approach of our compact bodies, they retreated from rock to rock, and from position to position, without intermitting their fire. They destroyed whole columns as they fled, without giving us an opportunity of taking revenge. This manner of fighting had procured them, even from the Spaniards themselves, the name of *mountain flies*.'

De Rocca had hitherto borne a charmed life, but while foraging for straw outside Ronda, he and a party of forty-five hussars were ambushed. Both he and his horse were severely wounded and struggled back into the town weak from loss of blood.

Amidst all the horrors of the war, it is pleasant to record this instance of humanity: 'I now had strong proof of the generosity of the Spanish character in the conduct of my hosts. They had hitherto regarded and treated me as an enemy; but no sooner did they see me wounded, than they told me, that since I could do no harm to their country, they considered me as one of their family, and without a single moment's intermission, they nursed and watched over me for fifty days.

'At day-break on 4 May the insurgents came with a stronger force than they had ever yet assembled, to attack Ronda. Balls passed so very near my windows that they were obliged to move my bed into the next room. My host and hostess came to tell me that the mountaineers were at the end of the street, and that the old town was on the point of being carried by storm; but that they were going to take precautions to shelter me from the fury of the Serranos, till the arrival of General Lerrana Valdenebro, who was their relation. They accordingly carefully hid my arms and military dress, and carried me to the top of the house behind a little chapel dedicated to the Virgin. Towards noon the firing retreated and at length ceased entirely; the enemy was repulsed from every point, and my comrades came to relate the particulars of the battle the moment they got off their horses. A few days afterwards the second hussars received orders to go to Santa Maria; it was afterwards replaced by the 43rd regiment of the line, and I was the only one of my corps left at Ronda; I did not know any of the officers of the new garrison, and I received no visits from the French, excepting indeed that a subaltern, the adjutant of a foot regiment, who was impatient of my quarters, came now and then to inquire of my host whether I was dead, or well enough to set off yet. . . .

'On 18 June, I rose for the first time since my wound. I was obliged to begin my melancholy apprenticeship of walking with crutches; I had totally lost the use of one of my legs. I went to visit the horse who was wounded with me, he had got quite well, but he did not know me at first, which showed how much I was changed. On the 22nd I left Ronda on an ammunition cart, which was going to Osuna to fetch cartridges, under a strong escort. I parted from my hosts with the same kind of regret that one feels on leaving the home of one's fathers for the first time. . . .'

After the reverses of the regular Spanish armies, guerrilla

warfare reflected a return to the mood of popular outrage which had brought into being the local juntas. Without the support of the countryfolk and villagers the guerrillas would have been helpless; and the peasants paid with their own blood and the looting and burning of their dwellings for their participation. It was not only the French who perpetrated this violence. Mina, as has been described, made it his business to punish the robbers and cut-throats who had taken advantage of the state of near-anarchy so much feared by the *afrancesados*. As far as possible, a dedicated leader like Mina levied money and requisitioned supplies only from 'bad Spaniards' who had co-operated with the invaders; and a curious example of this was his secret arrangement with the French customs officials at Irún on the border, who actually agreed to pay him 100 gold ounces a month on the understanding that goods passing into Spain would be free from the depredations of his bands. Ironically enough, he improved on Napoleon's dictum of living off the country; and an important source of arms and supplies was their seizure from the French themselves. Thus he explains in his *Memorias*: 'He who seized a horse mounted it, and from that moment he was a cavalryman; he who laid hands on a lance was, if he wished, a lancer, and in this fashion was supplied with a better gun, a better bayonet or a better sabre by the enemy.'

Apart from actual losses in the field, the French were perhaps most damaged by the constant interruption to their lines of communication, as quotations from eyewitnesses will illustrate. A French officer, Grivel, recalls that, 'To cross Spain was a military operation, and when our convoy was complete it numbered no less than 1,200 bayonets', while Saint Chaman writes: 'At that time he could not travel in Spain without an escort of less than 300 or 400 men and, frequently, more.' At the beginning of 1813 the main road between Burgos and Madrid was cut for five consecutive weeks, and orders from Paris arrived in Madrid forty-one days after being issued.

Bearing in mind Napoleon's insistence on controlling the operations of his Marshals from France, it becomes obvious that his orders often bore little relation to the rapidly changing situation on the spot. To send out a messenger without a strong escort was suicidal and only resulted in the despatches falling into the hands of the enemy, as happened in the winter of 1808, when Sir John Moore learned of Soult's isolation in the north.

The French armies were often completely blind as to the movements of their opponents: only a disastrous lack of intelligence can explain the fact that during the same campaign General Hope's artillery train was able to pass unnoticed and unscathed through the Escorial, while a huge French army lay only twenty-five miles away at Madrid. The absolute isolation of the French armies is vividly conveyed by the Duchess of Abrantes's description of Masséna's departure from Ciudad Rodrigo for Portugal: 'It was the first time that one had seen an army of 60,000 men cross a stream, reach the further bank, only to disappear the following day into a complete and absolute silence.'

It is difficult to give a global figure for the strength of the guerrillas: Canga Arguelles puts it at 36,500 and Gómez de Arteche at around 50,000; but because of the strategy of dispersal and refusal to accept pitched combat with a superior force, the number of effectives varies very greatly at any given time. Nevertheless, though relatively weak in actual numbers, the guerrillas succeeded in tying down the bulk of immensely larger French armies. Thus Liddell Hart comments: 'Napoleon ... by the end of February, 1810 had concentrated nearly 300,000 men in Spain—with more to come. Of this total, 65,000 were assigned to Masséna for the task of driving the British out of Portugal. If the number was large, its small proportion to the whole is illuminating evidence of the growing strain of the guerrilla war in Spain.'

It was in the mountains of the north that the guerrillas operated to the greatest effect; but even in Andalusia Marshal Soult had the greatest difficulty in raising 20,000 men for his expedition to the Extremadura in January 1811 and only did so by gravely weakening the garrisons in his viceroyalty. To have raised an army large enough for effective intervention in Portugal, as Napoleon demanded, would have meant abandoning two-thirds of the territory under his control. As regards the actual losses inflicted by the guerrillas, General Bigarré, aide-de-camp to King Joseph, was of opinion that they 'caused more casualties to the French armies than all the regular troops during the whole course of the war in Spain; it has been proved that they murdered a hundred of our men daily. Thus, over the period of five years they killed 180,000 French soldiers, without on their side losing more than 25,000.'

What started on a local basis as a spontaneous gesture of

popular revolt against a seemingly invincible occupying army was therefore to affect the whole future of Europe. Not only did the Spanish peasant, taking his relentless daily toll of foragers and stragglers, or a Mina or Porlier, with their bold attacks on garrisons and convoys, pin down men required for operations against Wellington, but, at a time when Napoleon was scouring the Continent for troops to fight in Russia, prolonged a war on two fronts, which in the last event it was beyond his capacity to continue.

Chapter 17

THE LEOPARD FIGHTS BACK

> The Emperor chose to cut down the numbers of his troops in Spain and to order a grand movement which dislocated them for a time, precisely at the instant when he had increased the dispersion of the Army of Portugal, by sending a detachment of 12,000 men against Valencia. He was undoubtedly aware that the English army was cantoned in a fairly concentrated position on the Agueda, the Coa, and the Mondego. But he had made up his mind—I cannot make out why—that the English were not in a condition to take the field: in every despatch he repeated this statement.
>
> MARSHAL MARMONT, Mémoires

Of all the French commanders in Spain, perhaps none was more bedevilled by out-of-date and impractical orders from Napoleon than the Duke of Ragusa during the spring of 1812. '*On ne dirige pas la guerre à trois ou quatres cents lieues de distance,*' his colleague General Thiébault remarked; but the Emperor was now so preoccupied with his preparations for invading Russia that the war in the Peninsula was a secondary issue.

When Wellington got wind of the troop movements in early January, he realized that he could at last take the initiative and at once closed in on Ciudad Rodrigo in spite of the bitter weather. The fortress was well provided with artillery, but only lightly garrisoned by some 2,000 men because of the difficulty of supplying it in the face of the British blockade. Wellington decided that he must capture it before Marmont could assemble reinforcements; and, in fact, it was taken in twelve days less than the twenty-four he had allowed. The outlying Redout Renaud was overrun by troops of the Light Division on the night of 8 January 1812; and without waiting for his heavy artillery from Almeida, Wellington at once opened fire on the main defences while his troops began digging zigzags in the half-frozen ground and moving up to the walls. By 19 January two breaches had been made and were successfully stormed—not without severe fighting in which the fiery Robert Craufurd was mortally wounded while urging forward his men, a loss which the army could ill afford. The siege was one of the few which went according to plan; but the success was marred by the disgraceful behaviour of the troops on entering the town. The uncontrolled shootings, plunder and rape were a foretaste of the even worse atrocities to be committed shortly at Badajoz.

Rightly calculating that Marmont was in no position to stage a serious attack on Portugal, Wellington moved rapidly south. Badajoz, with its garrison of 5,000 under the determined General Philippon, was a much tougher proposition than Ciudad Rodrigo, as the two earlier and unsuccessful sieges had demonstrated. The capture of the outlying Fort Picurina on 24 March allowed Wellington to bring his artillery into play. He was still without a regular siege train, but this time he did not repeat the mistake of attacking the near impregnable Fort San Cristobal and succeeded in opening three breaches along the weaker south-eastern part of the walls. Threatened by the approach of Soult from the Sierra Morena, he now decided that he must rely on the courage of his infantry to do the work of the sappers and heavy equipment which he had been denied by the government at home. The scene at the breaches on the night of Easter Sunday 1812 has been vividly described by Sergeant Cooper of the 7th Royal Fusiliers.

'When our men had approached within three hundred yards of the ditch, up went a fire ball. This showed the crowded state of the ramparts, and the bright arms of our approaching columns. Those men who carried grass bags to fill up the ditch, and ladders for escalading the walls, were now hurried forward. Instantly the whole rampart was in a blaze; mortars, cannon, and muskets roared and rattled unceasingly. Mines ever and anon blew up with horrid noise. To add to this horrible din, there was the sounding of bugles, the rattling of drums, and the shouting of combatants. Through a tremendous fire our men rushed to the top of the glacis, down the ladders, and up the breach. But entrance was impossible, for across the horrid gap the enemy had placed, in spite of our fire, a strong beam full of sword blades, etc., forming a *chevaux de frise*, behind which, intrenched, stood many ranks of soldiers, whose fire swept the breach from end to end. Besides, the top of the parapet was covered with shells, stones, sand bags, and logs of wood, etc., ready to be thrown into the ditch. As the breaches could not be forced, and as our men kept pouring down the ladders, the whole ditch was soon filled with a dense mass which could neither advance nor retreat. . . .'

The attack on the breaches ended in catastrophe. Next morning Wellington, inspecting the dead beneath the walls, broke down and sobbed. But success was to come from an unexpected quarter: Picton's 3rd Division, with nothing more than scaling ladders and at dreadful cost, swarmed over the ramparts of the castle, the arsenal and key to the French defence. When Major-General James Leith's 5th Division shortly afterwards scaled the walls on the other side of the town and broke into the streets, the defenders threw down their arms and surrendered.

The shocking aftermath, during which the British and Portuguese troops ran wild and for two days terrorized the town in a drunken orgy of murder, loot and rape, has been the subject of bitter recrimination by Spanish historians ever since. An eye-witness description forms part of the following chapter. Oman's detailed analysis of the brutal military tradition which sanctioned the sacking of a city after it had held out beyond the point of practicable defence, similar atrocities committed by the French, and the frenzy of the troops in the wake of their appalling losses may help to explain what happened, but do not condone it. Badajoz was, after all, a Spanish city.

Not all the soldiers behaved so discreditably; some risked their lives to help the victims; and the horror of Badajoz resulted in one romance. Captain Harry Smith of the 95th Rifles rescued a young Spanish girl, bleeding about the face after her earrings had been ripped out. Two days later he married Juanita de León, who was given away by Wellington in person. Her husband later became Governor of the Cape and was knighted; and Juanita gave her name to Ladysmith, the scene of another bitter siege during the Boer War.

On 16 March 1812, as Wellington was beginning the siege of Badajoz, and some weeks before his own departure for Russia, Napoleon wrote to his brother in Madrid, appointing him commander of the armies in Spain, with Marshal Jourdan as his chief of staff. The military position, as summed up in a memoir written by Jourdan in May after the fall of Badajoz, was that, following the withdrawal of troops for the Russian campaign, the total French strength in the Peninsula was 230,000 men, divided between the 48,000 men of Dorsenne's Army of the North, 60,000 of Suchet's Army of Aragon, 54,000 of Soult's Army of the South, 52,000 of Marmont's Army of Portugal, and some 16,000 of Joseph's own Army of the Centre tied down in garrison duties around Madrid. Jourdan reached the sober conclusion that this number was insufficient both to garrison the whole country and to meet the threat from Wellington and proposed that Suchet, Soult and Marmont should contribute to a strategical reserve of 20,000 at Madrid. His further recommendation—that Andalusia should be evacuated—was so obviously contentious that, without prior sanction from the Emperor, Joseph felt unable to issue the order to Soult, who, in common with his two colleagues found reasons for avoiding even the partial levy.

Wellington, too, had been doing his arithmetic, with very similar results. His conclusion was that, with the two strongest frontier forts in his possession, and having gained the initiative, he had two alternatives: to liberate Andalusia or to strike north at the French communications between the north and Madrid. He decided to attack Marmont, reckoning, rightly as it turned out, that a French defeat in the north would inevitably compel Soult to evacuate his viceroyalty. During the siege of Badajoz Marmont had advanced some fifty miles into Portugal; and on 12 April 1812 Wellington marched north in pursuit, but before he could make contact, the Duke of Ragusa, unable to obtain rations for his army in the devastated countryside, was already retreating to Salamanca.

Wellington planned his next moves with great care, so as to ensure that the French troops elsewhere in the Peninsula would be fully occupied and unable to come to Marmont's aid. Selfish as Soult was and preoccupied with Andalusia, one essential was to disrupt communications between the French armies of Portugal and the South. Among a batch of despatches, captured by the Spanish guerrillas and deciphered for Wellington by his aide Captain George Scovell, was one from Marmont to Jourdan which stressed that any effective liaison between his own army and Soult's was entirely dependent on holding the bridge across the Tagus at Almaraz in the Extremadura. Acting on this information, Wellington ordered General Rowland Hill to destroy the bridge. Moving with speed and secrecy so as to avoid interruption from Soult's commander in the Extremadura, General Drouet, Hill and his 7,000 men fell on Fort Napoleon to the south of Almaraz and, having overrun it, directed its guns on to Fort Ragusa commanding the northern approach of the bridge. The twenty large pontoons were burnt, huge quantities of stores and ammunition were captured and both forts blown up; while to safeguard his own communications Wellington had the shattered arches of Trajan's greater bridge further west at Alcántara replaced by a temporary structure carried on cables, which could be dismantled on the approach of the enemy.

So as to engage Soult fully in Andalusia, Hill was then instructed to make feints against Drouet in the west, co-ordinating his movements with those of the rumbustious General Ballesteros in the east. Ballesteros proved adept at the game, striking at the Cadiz lines or Seville, overruning Málaga in a surprise attack, and smartly retreating within shelter of Gibraltar and its guns when seriously threatened. As a result of these manoeuvres, Soult persuaded himself to the last that Wellington's real objective was Andalusia and flatly refused orders to send troops north.

In the north, another series of diversions was planned. Admiral Popham's amphibious operations, undertaken with Mendizábal's 'Seventh Army' and the guerrillas, have already been described. General Caffarelli, who had succeeded Dorsenne, was further harassed by the Army of Galicia's siege of Astorga, while the Portuguese General Silveira was called in to blockade Zamora.

The last of these diversions was mounted from an unexpected quarter. As early as January 1812 Lord William Bentinck, the commander of a British expeditionary force in Sicily, had written to the prime minister, Lord Liverpool, suggesting a landing on the east coast of Spain: 'I cannot but imagine that the occasional disembarkation at different points of a large regular force must considerably annoy the enemy, and create an important diversion for other Spanish operations.' Wellington fell in enthusiastically with the idea, offering further troops from Cadiz. In the event, the whole operation was to prove a prolonged disappointment, culminating in the court martial of Sir John Murray, who took over command during the abortive siege of Tarragona at a later stage. Bentinck was torn between the Spanish expedition and a scheme closer to his heart for invading Murat's Italy, which had been denuded of troops even more severely than Spain. He compromised by sending only 7,000 men under General Maitland, who did not arrive off the coast of Catalonia until 31 July, after Marmont had been fought and defeated. Nevertheless, earlier rumours of large transport squadrons and an impending landing kept Suchet in a constant state of suspense, so that he refused to make available reinforcements for use elsewhere in

Spain; and even the belated attacks, miserably as they were conducted, kept him fully preoccupied until he joined in the general retreat across the Ebro in 1813.

Of more immediate concern to Wellington than the timing or effectiveness of these diversions was his chronic and crippling lack of cash, so that he could write to Lord Liverpool on 22 April 1812: 'We owe not less than 5,000,000 dollars. The Portuguese troops and establishments are likewise in the greatest distress, and it is my opinion, as well as that of Marshal Beresford, that we must disband part of the army, unless I can increase the monthly payments of the subsidy. The Commissary-General has this day informed me that he is very apprehensive that he will not be able to make good his engagements for the payment of meat for the troops. If we are obliged to stop that payment, your Lordship may as well prepare to recall the army. . . . It is not improbable that we may not be able to take advantage of the enemy's comparative weakness in this campaign *for sheer want of money*.' This lack of funds was not, as Wellington was inclined to think, a deep-laid plot on Lord Liverpool's part to bring the war to a summary end, but arose from a state of near bankruptcy in England, the twin result of the protracted and exhausting struggle with Napoleon and the outbreak of war with the United States. But although, as Wellington could write, 'We are absolutely bankrupt, the troops are now five months in arrears instead of one month in advance', he was determined to seize his chance and in mid June, with an army of 28,000 British, 17,000 Portuguese and 3,000 Spaniards, began a march on Salamanca to seek out and destroy the Army of Portugal.

The British entered the old university city of Salamanca on 17 June and were rapturously welcomed by its inhabitants. Marmont, with 8,000 fewer troops, had slipped out just before, but left garrisons in three small forts in the city. Instead of pursuing him, Wellington, characteristically and, as it seems, with undue caution, spent ten long days reducing the forts, so allowing Marmont to gather up reinforcements, including 6,500 men from the Army of the North under General Bonnet, which gave him a slight numerical superiority. The next three weeks were spent amidst the blistering summer heat of the Duero valley in gruelling marching and manoeuvring, the two armies sometimes moving parallel and within sight of each other, as Marmont edged the allies south-west in an attempt to cut them off from their base at Ciudad Rodrigo. Each general was waiting for the other to make a mistake; and on 22 July 1812 it seemed that the French, who marched rather faster than their opponents, had succeeded in turning the British right flank and cutting the retreat route to Salamanca and Ciudad Rodrigo beyond. But Marmont had made the fatal mistake of confusing a dust cloud on the road for the retreating baggage train, whereas it was in fact caused by Wellington's 3rd Division marching out of Salamanca in the opposite direction.

The command posts of the two armies were established only a thousand yards apart on the low hills of the Greater and Lesser Arapiles—from which the battle took its name (in Britain it is more usually known as the Battle of Salamanca). Wellington, surveying the position through his telescope from the Lesser Arapiles to the south, now saw that, in the haste to outflank the Salamanca road, the French left wing under Generals Thomières and Maucune was dangerously over-extended and that a gap had opened between it and the centre. 'By God! that'll do,' he exclaimed, and to his Spanish liaison officer, *'Mon cher Alava, Marmont est perdu!'*

Ordering an immediate attack by Sir Edward Pakenham's 3rd Division on Thomières's advancing troops, he launched the main body of his men against the exposed right flank of the remaining French units spread out in front of him. Marmont, taken utterly by surprise, was early on hit by a cannon ball and relinquished his command to Bonnet. The leading French divisions under Thomières and Maucune were smashed within forty minutes. The fighting in the centre was murderous and much more evenly contested; Bonnet was killed; his successor, General Clausel, launched a formidable counter-attack, but was finally driven in headlong flight towards the bridge of Alba de Tormes. If General Carlos de España had guarded it, as he had been ordered, the destruction of the French army would have been complete; as it was, it suffered the enormous loss of 14,000 dead, including many senior officers, as against 5,000 allied troops.

Wellington's victory had repercussions on the whole French strategy in the Peninsula as far-reaching as the Battle of Bailén in 1808. King Joseph, in the face of a blank refusal from Soult to supply men for reinforcing the Army of Portugal, had himself with difficulty mustered 14,000 men and marched from Madrid to Marmont's aid. He was too late to avert the disaster of

Arapiles and after an agonized reappraisal of the new situation fell back to defend the capital.

Wellington, having occupied the French base at Valladolid and driven Clausel's defeated army back towards Burgos, now turned south. He has been criticized for failing to pursue Clausel with sufficient energy, and the reasons for his volte-face are not entirely clear. It would seem that, apart from the political prestige of retaking the capital, he wished to prevent a junction of King Joseph's army with the French forces in the north and by occupying the main French base in central Spain to speed Soult's long-delayed evacuation of Andalusia.

The victorious British army entered Madrid on 12 August 1812. 'I have never witnessed such a scene before,' wrote Private Wheeler of the 51st. 'For a distance of five miles from the gates the road was crowded with the people who had come out to meet us, each bringing something—laurel boughs, flowers, bread, wine, grapes, lemonade, sweetmeats, etc. The road was like a moving forest from the multitude who carried palms, which they strewed in the way for us to march over. Young ladies presented us with laurel, and even fixed it in our caps: others handed us sweetmeats and fruit. Gentlemen had hired porters to bring out wine, which they handed to us as we passed by: every individual strove to outvie us in good nature. . . .'

There remained only one French stronghold in the city to take, the fortress and arsenal in the Retiro Park, where Joseph had left a garrison in the forlorn and unfulfilled hope that Soult might after all send troops to the capital's assistance. It fell after the briefest assault; and enormous quantities of munitions and supplies were captured, including much-needed shoes for Wellington's footsore men. Still uncertain of Soult's movements to the south, Wellington remained in Madrid for some three weeks, where he received the Order of the Golden Fleece from the Cadiz Cortes and was painted by Goya on horseback in his blue Spanish cavalry cape.

King Joseph had meanwhile taken the road south to Aranjuez, accompanied by some 10,000 *afrancesados* and French civilians. Colonel D'Urban describes how the refugees, panic-stricken by the thought of their probable fate at the hands of the Spanish patriots, commandeered coaches, carts and horses, or joined the great throng on foot. Joseph had sent a last peremptory message to Soult from Segovia on 29 July, bidding him, 'Hasten, therefore, to carry out the orders which I gave you—viz. to evacuate Andalusia and march with your whole army on Toledo', but despairing of the marshal's compliance, he now turned east towards Valencia.

Even at this eleventh hour and in full knowledge of the defeat at Arapiles, Soult saw fit to reply by suggesting that, instead, the King should join forces with him to defend Andalusia and that the yawning gap between his own army and those of the north was of no account, since the Emperor would soon send reinforcements to retrieve the situation. Even he soon realized the impracticality of the scheme and began making arrangements for the evacuation, but not before he had written a furious letter to the Minister of War in Paris, insinuating that King Joseph was plotting against his brother with the Cadiz Cortes and stating his opinion that 'all the bad arrangements and all the intrigues that have been going on, have the object of forcing the Imperial armies to retreat to the Ebro, or farther, and then of representing this event as the "last possible resource", in the hope of profiting by it to come to some compromise.' He despatched this scurrilous letter by a French privateer, whose captain, forced to take shelter at Valencia, delivered it to King Joseph; and, on top of Soult's earlier intransigence, it was to result in bad blood between the two men for the remainder of the war.

With Wellington in Madrid it was now too late to retreat on Toledo, and Soult decided to withdraw to Valencia. He therefore began by calling back his troops and garrisons from the south and west of the province. The destruction of the Cadiz lines occupied several days and ended in an enormous pyrotechnic display on 24 August 1812, when the magazines were blown up and heavy guns overloaded or discharged at each other to render them unserviceable. As the French moved back, the Spanish and the British moved in behind them. Seville was taken by a mixed force on 27 August after a sharp brush with Soult's rearguard; and the last of his columns, Drouet's from the Extremadura, made junction with the main force in Córdoba on 30 August. In the east, the garrisons retiring from Málaga and Ronda were harried by the ever-active General Ballesteros; but the combined army of 45,000 which Soult concentrated at Granada was too strong to be seriously threatened. He was able to destroy the fortifications of the Alhambra at leisure, and it was not until mid September that he began the laborious march across the hills to

Valencia. Like King Joseph's, the column was accompanied by wagons piled with loot and a huge train of unfortunate *afrancesados*, who braved the mountains and the September heat on foot. By 1 October 1812 the army had linked with Suchet's and King Joseph's to make up a formidable striking force of 80,000 men; and the initiative, so long denied him by Soult's refusal to obey orders, was at last in Joseph's hands.

Wellington remained in Madrid until 31 August when, still in the dark as to Soult's movements, he decided to march north again, at the same time ordering General Hill from the Extremadura and General Skerrett, whose column from Cadiz had taken part in the capture of Seville, to move on Madrid. His reason was that the force under General Clinton, which he had left to contain the beaten Army of Portugal, was small; Clausel had now resumed the offensive and after throwing the Galicians out of Valladolid threatened to break out into the plains of León and disrupt communications with Portugal.

With the benefit of hindsight, it is evident that, in taking with him only 21,000 men, Wellington made perhaps his worst strategic mistake of the whole campaign. The 40,000 men under Hill and Skerrett were plainly insufficient to defend Madrid against an attack from the combined French forces to the east, while, with Clinton's 9,000 men, his own army was to prove too small to deal with the French in the north under Clausel and Caffarelli. It seems that Wellington planned to return to Madrid in time to face an attack by Soult; but his whole schedule was disrupted by the ill-conducted siege of Burgos and its defence by a French governor even more adroit than Philippon at Badajoz.

Clausel's army had been too severely mauled at Arapiles to offer serious opposition to Wellington's advance. Nevertheless he succeeded in so slowing its pace that it was not until 19 September that the British reached Burgos and settled down to the siege of its castle. It was not a particularly strong fortress, and orders for strengthening it issued by Napoleon during his occupation of the city in 1809 had not been fully carried out. On the other hand, its garrison of 2,000 men were picked troops, and their commander, General Dubreton, was one of the most resourceful French officers in the Peninsula. Wellington undoubtedly underestimated the difficulties of taking it or he would have brought with him more than the three eighteen-pounders which were the sum total of his heavier artillery. Although in his despatches he scrupulously shoulders the blame for the failure of the operation, he was hampered by the chronic shortage of trained engineers. It seems that after the successes at Ciudad Rodrigo and Badajoz, his officers were confident that the walls could be overrun by infantry using ladders; but the dreadful losses incurred during the earlier sieges inhibited them from using troops in sufficient numbers. As the cold, wet days wore on, Wellington seems to have become depressed—he was particularly affected by the death of one of the most brilliant of his younger officers, Major Edward Somers-Cocks—and his mood spread to the troops. After five unsuccessful assaults and the loss of 2,000 men, he received news that the combined French armies of Portugal and the North were marching on him, and gave the order to retreat westwards to Valladolid on 21 October 1812. Ironically enough, it was Trafalgar Day.

He was not yet fully aware of the threat to Madrid and Hill's army further south. Soult's arrival in Valencia had been the occasion of bitter wrangling between the self-willed marshal and the King. Joseph's first reaction on reading Soult's intercepted letter had been to complain to Clarke in Paris: '*Je demande justice. Que le Maréchal Soult soit rappelé, entendu, et puni.*' His anger had cooled somewhat since then and he contented himself with being aloof and peremptory; Soult's co-operation was, after all, essential in the march on Madrid, over which all three of his marshals, Soult, Jourdan and Suchet were in broad agreement. It was decided that the advance should be undertaken by two separate columns, both because this would ease the problem of finding food for the troops and it was envisaged that the northerly column under King Joseph might ultimately make contact with the Army of Portugal.

The quarrels began over the allocation of troops. Suchet, who was to remain in Valencia, bitterly objected to contributing any units of his Army of Aragon and indeed pleaded for its reinforcement to contain General Mackenzie's expeditionary force from Sicily, now united with the Spanish Army of Murcia. Soult protested even more strongly about transferring troops from his Army of the South to Joseph's command, but was overriden by a categorical order, which he could ignore only at the risk of being dismissed for insubordination. Finally, on 15 October, Soult set out from Albecete with 40,000 men, heading for La

Mancha and Aranjuez to the south of Madrid, while King Joseph left Valencia two days later by the northern route via Cuenca with another 25,000 troops.

In the face of this massive threat General Hill first decided to defend the line of the Tagus, passing through Toledo, Aranjuez and then east of the capital. Soult's army was already opposite Arnajuez when Hill came to the conclusion that, because of the low state of the river, it was easily fordable. He was falling back on the new river line of the Tajuna, when on 28 October he received an alarming despatch from Wellington, informing him of his own withdrawal, instructing him to abandon Madrid and, if possible, to retreat through the Escorial and across the Guadarrama mountains. Having blown up the arsenal of the Retiro, and accompanied by the now familiar crowds of refugees—this time fleeing King Joseph's wrath—the rear-guard of Hill's army evacuated Madrid on 31 October. Closely followed by Soult, Hill then carried out the dangerous retreat across the Guadarramas, while the heavily outnumbered Wellington, in his own words, 'fairly *bullied* the French into remaining quiet upon the Douro for seven days in order to give him time to make his march. . . . I have got clear, in a handsome manner, of the worst scrape I was ever in.' The two armies, comprising 30,000 British and Germans, 20,000 Portuguese and 25,000 Spaniards, were safely united behind the River Tormes and in front of Salamanca on 9 November.

King Joseph, who had reached Madrid with his Army of the Centre rather after Soult, meanwhile decided that, great as was the loss of prestige, the capital must yet again be evacuated so as to achieve decisive numerical superiority over the allies. The combined armies of the South, Centre and Portugal which faced Wellington on his chosen battleground of Arapiles, still littered with skeletons from the earlier combat, totalled some 90,000 men. The French generals were understandably nervous about a frontal attack, and Joseph finally came down in favour of a wide encircling move proposed by Marshal Soult. Wellington was not prepared to give battle except on his own terms and ordered a general retreat on his base at Ciudad Rodrigo.

Although there was no serious pursuit beyond Salamanca, the four days of this retreat were among the most depressing of the whole campaign. After the earlier triumphs of 1812 the men were out of spirits and resentful at, once again, having to retire across the Portuguese border; it rained in torrents; and, worst of all, the blundering Quartermaster-General, James Willoughby Gordon, had sent the army's supply column twenty miles astray, so that, as Donaldson of the 94th wrote on 17 November, 'The effects of hunger and fatigue were even more visible than on the preceding day. A savage sort of desperation had taken possession of our minds.... It was piteous to see some of the men, who had dragged their limbs after them with determined spirit, fall down at last among the mud, unable to proceed further, and sure of being taken prisoners if they escaped death....'

When the casualty lists were made up on 29 November 1812 it was found that, over and above some 1,200 killed and wounded, the deplorable figure of 5,000 men had gone missing during this last sad retreat. Soult was not tempted to pursue the British into the wilds of the frontier region, and both armies now settled into winter quarters. Although the news of the reverse spread gloom in England and the image of Wellington as the all-victorious conqueror suffered temporary eclipse, his own misfortunes were overshadowed by the news of Napoleon's vastly more disastrous retreat from Moscow; and after the solid achievements of 1812 final victory was now only a matter of time.

Chapter 18

VOICES FROM THE RANKS

> For thirteen pence a day did I
>   Take off the things I wore,
> And I have marched to where I lie,
>   And I shall march no more.
>
> My mouth is dry, my shirt is wet,
>   My blood runs all away,
> So now I shall not die in debt
>   For thirteen pence a day.
>
> From *Grenadier* by A. E. HOUSMAN,
> *Last Poems*

The broad canvas of the Peninsular War necessarily tends to emphasize grand strategy, political decisions, the tactics of the generals in the field and the manoeuvring of the opposing armies. It is perhaps easy to forget that armies are only as good as the individual soldiers in the ranks and that these soldiers were not so many figures on the regimental strength or ciphers on a casualty list, but human beings who were staking their lives.

As regards the actual business of fighting, of the continual battle for personal survival and the plight of the Spanish and Portuguese engulfed in a war which reached into almost every village and hamlet in the Peninsula, the accounts of the humble rankers are more illuminating than the military histories of their commanders. Half-forgotten on the shelves of many an old library are slim calf-bound volumes by the dozen, sometimes anonymous, with titles such as *Adventures of a Young Rifleman*, *Journal of a Soldier* or *Rough Notes of Seven Campaigns*. Powdering leather and yellowed paper belie the poignancy with which they are written and the stark emotion that leaps from the page.

Their authors are a mixed lot. Rifleman Harris was a Dorsetshire sheep-boy, who probably owed his life to the fact that he became a skilled cobbler in the 95th Rifles—and boots and their repairers being at a premium, he was as often as not discouraged from going into the firing line. The author of *Journal of a Soldier of the 71st, or Glasgow Regiment* begins his book by saying that,

'From motives of delicacy, which the narrative will explain, I chose to conceal my name. . . .' He was in fact Thomas Pococke, who at the age of sixteen abandoned his studies to try his luck as an actor in Edinburgh. Overcome by stage fright, he tells how, 'I shrunk unseen from the Theatre, bewildered, and in a state of despair. I wandered the whole night. In the morning early, meeting a party of recruits about to embark, I rashly offered to go with them; my offer was accepted, and I embarked at Leith, with seventeen others, for the Isle of Wight, in July, 1806.' His sense of the dramatic emerges more vividly than in any stage production, when, for example, he describes the snow-covered road as 'one line of bloody foot-marks' in a moving account of the retreat to Corunna. *The Adventures of a Young Rifleman in the French and English Armies* is particularly interesting as being written by a young German, who was first impressed into the French army after Napoleon's victories in Prussia and, having been taken prisoner by the British, changed sides.

A recurrent theme in all these narratives is the struggle for bare subsistence—against cold or heat or hunger. Thus Sergeant Cooper in his *Rough Notes of Seven Campaigns*: 'Next day [4 August, 1809] we crossed the Tagus at Arzobispo, broke down the bridge, and took up a strong position in a wood of cork and oak. No sooner was the position taken up by each regiment and the arms piled than a general attack was made upon 200 or 300 fat pigs feeding among the oaks. These were soon settled. I chased one, but Porky was too nimble for me, it ran headlong down a steep rocky bank, swam across the river we had just passed, and gave me the slip.

'In this pig-chasing, an accident happened to a sergeant of the Guards, while he with hundreds more was pursuing the grunters near the bridge of Arzobispo. Running at full speed after one, the point of his pike ran into the earth and stuck fast, causing the butt end to pass through his body. 'Twas reported that he recovered, was discharged, and afterwards kept a public house in London.

'The commissary having no bread for us, we were marched into a newly reaped field of wheat, of which each man received a sheaf instead. Laughable it was to see hundreds of soldiers bearing away their burdens, but we could make little use of the corn for want of grinding it.'

Even in midwinter on the bleak, windswept sierras the common soldiers bivouacked in the open; 'and this was the mode', explains Cooper: 'The great coat was inverted, and our legs were thrust into the sleeves; one half was put under us, and the other half above. The knapsack formed our pillow. Thus arranged, with forage cap pulled over our ears, we bid good night to the stars, and rested as we could.' During the summer the discomforts and risks were different: 'On our march to this place [Oropesa], one of the 3rd, or Old Buffs, was stung by a scorpion in the head, and died in consequence. Also, a man of our company, named John Barber, marched a league with a snake in his dress cap. It had crept in during the night, and hid itself under his forage cap.'

Even when they found a roof and shelter, the troops were scarcely less afflicted. 'I had scarcely slept an hour,' writes the unsuspecting young German rifleman of his first lodging in Spain, 'when I was awakened by an indescribable tickling all over my body. I was frightened, but soon became convinced that my suspicions were well grounded, and that this unpleasant sensation was caused by lice, of which there are quantities all over Spain, and from which my landlord was not free. These little insects had spread themselves all over their new guest, and were feasting upon my blood.' The only effective remedy was 'what was called the Hungarian washing, which was performed in the following manner: A fire was made of straw or dry wood, and the shirt, being tied up at one end, was held over it; the smoke caused it to open like a balloon, and the insects, disturbed by the heat, loosened their hold upon the linen, and fell into the flames....'

The young German devotes more space to the joys of receiving a new uniform and ridding himself of the lice than to his feelings on exchanging the French service for the English: 'At the conclusion of the surgical examination, we were all taken down to the sea-side; here we were ordered to undress; every one received a piece of soap, and leaped joyfully into the waves, to which our whole French wardrobe, with its contents, was consigned. How readily we assisted each other in getting rid of our dirt and filth, and how pleased we were when, on coming out of the water as if newly born, we found ready for each of us a shirt, a pair of linen trousers, and a flannel jacket.'

Sergeant Cooper, on his return to England in 1814 at the end of the campaign, voices the same relief: 'June 27th, we anchored in Plymouth Sound. Soon after, an order being given, over-board went all our blankets, jackets, and trowsers, with their numerous population.'

Amidst all their hardships, it is hardly surprising that, as Thomas Pococke recounts, 'The great fault of our soldiers, at this time, was an inordinate desire for spirits of any kind. They sacrificed their life and safety for drink, in many ways; for they lay down intoxicated upon the snow, and slept the sleep of death; or staggering behind, were overtaken and cut down by the merciless French soldiers: the most favourable event, was to be taken prisoners. So great was their propensity to drown their misery in liquor, that we were often exposed to cold and rain, for a whole night, in order that we might be kept from the wine stores of a neighbouring town.'

Thomas Costello, in his *Adventures of a Soldier*, tells of a chilling experience in the search for liquor at Rueda, where the wine cellars extend deep underground with ventilation shafts communicating with the open air. 'Three or four comrades and myself one evening assembled over the chimney of one of these wine-vaults, and it was proposed that one of us should descend to bring up some wine. This was no comfortable task, as the proprietors frequently watched below, and would scarcely hesitate to greet an intruder with his cuchillo or long knife.' Costello was accordingly lowered by a rope, with the empty canteens clattering at his waist. 'The place was so dark that I could scarcely see a couple of yards before me . . . and putting my hand forward, I placed it upon the cold clammy face of a corpse. My whole blood tingled, the canteens responded, and at a glance I perceived from the red wings, (for whether or not, I could see now) that it was a French soldier, exhibiting most frightful gashes, evidently inflicted by the same kind of weapon, which I at every turn, was expecting.' Costello tugged urgently at the rope and was hauled to safety empty-handed.

In the British army the punishment for looting of any kind was severe, as Costello relates of another attempt to steal wine: 'Just before we arrived at the town of Viseu, then occupied by the Foot Guards, and the headquarters of the Commander-in-Chief, I came up to some of our party who were doing their best to empty a pig-skin of wine they had stolen. . . . I was in the act of taking the jug of wine from my lips, when a party of the 16th Light Dragoons rode up and made us prisoners; the peasant, from whom the wine had been taken having made his complaint at headquarters... the Hon. Captain Pakenham, of the Adjutant-General's department, paid us a visit, and told us he had had great difficulty in saving us from being hanged.' As it was, the culprits were condemned to two dozen strokes of the lash each morning, but escaped 'this comfortable kind of breakfast' since to rejoin their regiment they were put in charge of a German officer, who delivered himself of the opinion that, 'I have been told to have you mens flogged, for a crime dat is very bad and disgraceful to de soldier—robbing de people you come paid to fight for. But we do not flog in my country, so I shall not flog you, it not being de manner of my people; I shall give you all to your Colonels, and if they like to flog you, they may.'

Eyewitness accounts of the campaign abound with descriptions of the savage floggings meted out to delinquent British soldiers. They were carried out in public, the victim being stripped and tied up in the middle of a hollow square of his companions, and the lashes being administered with the cat o' nine tails by the buglers or drummers, sometimes to a regular drumbeat. Even thieving wives were not immune; Cooper describes how one such received 'twenty-five lashes on the breach'. The justification was that looting and the theft of livestock and food by the often famished soldiers caused such bad blood between them and the Spanish and Portuguese peasants that they were hardly more popular than their French counterparts—who could at least call themselves Catholics. This serves to explain an incident such as the following, related by Sergeant Cooper.

'April 13th. [1812] We left Badajoz, and reached Aronches, where, becoming ill, I was left behind charged with the care of six sick men, and ordered to bring them on to Portalegre. How was that to be done? They were sitting on the road unable to walk. Much baggage was passing; but not one of the Spanish muleteers would take up my poor feverish men. I grew desperate. An empty car came up: I ordered my men to get into it, but the driver would not stop. I threw their knapsacks into the car; he threw them out again. Enraged, I drew my bayonet, took it by the small end, and swinging round, gave him such a blow on the mouth with the heavy end as stunned him. Then I got them on the car, and he drove on, holding his mouth as if he had got the tic....'

The worst scenes of pillage by a British army, rivalling those enacted by the French at Córdoba, occurred after the siege of Badajoz in 1812. Costello's account is worth quoting from at some length, since it goes a long way to justify the surly and unco-operative attitude described above.

'It was a dark night, and the confusion and uproar that prevailed in the town may be better imagined than described. The shouts and oaths of drunken soldiers in quest of more liquor, the reports of fire-arms and crashing in of doors, together with the appalling shrieks of hapless women might have induced any one to have believed himself in the regions of the damned.' Costello then relates how he and some of his companions broke into one of the houses.

'I had not long been seated at the fire which was blazing up the chimney, fed by mahogany chairs, broken up for the purpose, when I heard screams for mercy from an adjoining room. On hobbling in, I found an old man, the proprietor of the house, on his knees, imploring mercy of a soldier who had levelled his musket at him. I with difficulty prevented the man from shooting him, as he complained that the Spaniard would not give up his money. I immediately informed the wretched landlord in Spanish, as well as I was able, that he could only save his life by surrendering his cash. . . .

'As soon as I had resumed my seat at the fire, a number of Portuguese soldiers entered, one of whom, taking me for a Frenchman, for I had the French soldier's jacket on, my own being wet, snapped his piece at me, which luckily hung fire. Forgetful of my wounds, I instantly rushed at him, and a regular scuffle ensued between our men and the Portuguese, until one of the latter being stabbed by a bayonet, they retired, dragging the wounded man with them. After thus ejecting the Portuguese, the victors, who had by this time got tolerably drunk, proceeded to ransack the house. Unhappily they discovered the two daughters of the old patrone, who had concealed themselves up-stairs. They were both young and very pretty. The mother, too, was shortly afterwards dragged from her hiding-place.

'Without dwelling on the frightful scene that followed, it may be sufficient to add, that our men, more infuriated by drink than before, again seized the old man, and insisted on a fresh supply of liquor. And his protestations that he possessed no more were as vain as were all attempts to restrain them from ill-using him. . . .'

Costello concludes that 'men who besiege a town in the face of such dangers generally become desperate from their own privations and sufferings; and when once they get a foothold within its walls—flushed by victory, hurried on by the desire of liquor, and maddened by drink, they stop at nothing; they are literally mad, and hardly conscious of what they do in such a state of excitement. I do not state this in justification; I only remark what I have observed human nature to be on these occasions.'

The full fury of the inhabitants was reserved for the French, whose atrocities were only too often coldblooded and deliberate. Another passage from Costello, descriptive of Masséna's retreat from Portugal, is typical.

'The sun had set, its light had been supplanted by burning villages, and fires that on vale and mountain, correctly pointed out where the hostile divisions were extended.

'The following morning, the French continued their march of havoc and we closed after them, village after village, giving flaming proofs of their continued atrocities. Passing through one which had not been fired, by reason, as we were informed, of its having been the quarters of Marshal Ney and staff.

'An appalling instance of vengeance here occurred. The parents of one of our Caçadores had lived in this village, and immediately we entered, he rushed to the house where they resided. On reaching the doorway, the soldier hesitated a few seconds, but the door was open, and stretched across the threshold he beheld the mangled bodies of his father and mother, the blood still warm and reeking through the bayonet stabs, while an only sister lay breathing her last, and exhibiting dreadful proofs of the brutality with which she had been violated. The unhappy man staggered, frenzied with grief, and stared wildly around him; till suddenly burying all other feelings in the maddening passion of revenge, he rushed forth from what had probably once been a happy home. His first act was to dash at some French prisoners that unfortunately were near the spot, guarded by some of our dragoons. These he attacked with the fury of a madman. One he shot and another he wounded, and he would have sacrificed a third, had not the guard made him prisoner. . . .'

Violence begets violence; and the pages of these soldiers' reminiscences are full of detailed and stomach-turning descriptions of the brutal murders and revolting tortures perpetrated by the French, Portuguese and Spanish alike. It seems unnecessary to dwell on this distressing subject when Goya's paintings and etchings form so much more vivid a commentary on the Horrors of the War than any printed page. A passage from the narrative of the young German mercenary is indication enough.

After he had been taken prisoner by the British, 'we proceeded farther, under an escort of heavy cavalry of the German legion; and a circumstance occurred here which may serve to characterize the brutality and bloodthirstiness of the Portuguese. There was a prisoner among us, named Stern, who, on account of sickness, not being able to walk, was carried in a cart. A peasant, happening to perceive this sick man, asked a dragoon to sell him, and actually offered for him forty crusades. Upon the dragoon asking what he wanted with him, the peasant coolly replied, "To torture him". The dragoon, enraged at such inhumanity, drew his sabre, and gave the Portuguese a good drubbing. . . . With God's help we at last reached our prison [at Coimbra], which protected us from the rage of the Portuguese, who assembled round the building, and with violent outcries demanded our death. The officer in command here procured immediately a reinforcement from the garrison, and ordered his men to load. . . . One day it was my turn to go to the wine-store: our cans had been filled, and the commissary was in the act of presenting each of us with an extra glass, when a Portuguese, who was at work in the magazine, came up, seized me by the collar, and drew a long knife from under his jacket—"You French son of a w——," said he, "shall I rip you up?" I did not understand this alarming threat, but an Englishman explained it to me. "If you were not here, under English protection, your blood would soon flow." He then turned round to the English, and added—"You English are likewise rascals, and not better Christians than the French; you may all go to the devil together."'

The British, whose villages were not being burned or their families murdered, could afford to stand somewhat apart. They, too, were often appalled by what they saw and filled with fury by the wanton bloodshed and destruction, but also pay tribute to the bravery of the French on the field of battle. The ordinary French *mustachios*, when not engaged in the grim game of reprisals, were tough and likable enough; and, as between professional soldiers, a camaraderie sometimes sprang up between the troops of the two sides. Thus Costello writes of one of his companions: 'At this period [during the confrontation at

Torres Vedras] the French soldiers and ourselves began to establish a very amicable feeling, apart from duty in the field. It was a common thing for us to meet each other daily at the houses between our lines, when perhaps both parties would be in search of wine and food. In one of the houses so situated, I remember once finding Crawley in a drunken state with two French soldiers. I was mortified exceedingly by the merriment his appearance had excited, and could with difficulty get him away, as he stripped, and offered to fight the three of us for laughing at him.'

In the British army of the time it was often the custom for women, and even children, to accompany the soldiers into the field. During the Peninsular campaign their plight was perhaps worst throughout the interminable retreat to Corunna, when hundreds died of cold and exposure. Many more of the women, too exhausted to keep up, fell into the hands of the pursuing French and were brutally maltreated and raped. Like the soldiers themselves, their dependents had to live rough. So Sergeant Cooper remarks laconically that 'after passing through an immense forest of pine trees, nearly all of which were remarkably crooked, a soldier's wife was delivered of a child, after we had halted for the night. Next morning, she was placed on a horse, and marched with the column.' Costello tells a grim story of the quarrels over camp-followers, which broke out from time to time. 'I had finished my evening's meal, and was sitting drinking a tot of wine, with a sergeant of ours named Battersby.... He brought with him a very pretty looking English woman, that passed for his wife, and who was present with us, and assisted much to keep up the spirit of our conversation.' However, they were soon joined by 'a tall, fine-looking grenadier of the 61st Regiment of Foot'—and it soon transpired that he was the woman's husband.

' "So you are determined, Nelly," said he at length, "to continue this way of living?"

' "Yes," said she.

' "Well, then," he exclaimed, holding her firmly by the left hand, which she extended for him to shake, while he drew his bayonet with his right, "take that," and he drove it right through her body. The blow was given with such force that it actually tripped him over her, and both fell, the bayonet still sticking in her side....'

But the British soldier was also capable of great kindness and compassion. Rifleman Harris had a friend, Joseph Cochan, who 'was by my side loading and firing very industriously about this period of the day. Thirsting with heat and action, he lifted his canteen to his mouth: "Here's to you, old boy," he said, as he took a pull at its contents. As he did so a bullet went through the canteen, and perforating his brain, killed him in a moment.... When the roll was called after the battle, the females who missed their husbands came along the front of the line to inquire of the survivors whether they knew anything about them. Amongst other names I heard that of Cochan called in a female voice, without being replied to.' Harris had not at first the heart to speak up, but subsequently led the woman to her husband's body, when 'with hands clasped and tears streaming down her cheeks she took a prayer book from her pocket, and kneeling down, repeated the service for the dead over the body.... Mrs. Cochan then returned with me to the company to which her husband had been attached, and laid herself down upon the heath near us. She lay amongst some other females, who were in the same distressing circumstances with herself, with the sky for her canopy, and a turf for her pillow, for we had no tents with us. Poor woman! I pitied her much; but there was no remedy. If she had been a duchess she must have fared the same....' An intimacy developed between them, and Harris 'offered on the first opportunity to marry her. "She had, however, received too great a shock on the occasion of her husband's death ever to think of another soldier," she said; she therefore thanked me for my good feeling towards her, but declined my offer, and left us soon afterwards for England.'

Sudden death in the field was often preferable to treatment in hospital. Among the most graphic accounts of this are those of Sergeant Cooper, who suffered recurrent attacks of dysentery and fever: 'Next day [during the British retreat into Portugal after Talavera], which was also wet, we arrived at Villa Viciosa. Not being able to walk without support, I remained on the car till nearly night, and was then helped up the steps of a convent. The sick not being then disposed of, I was laid down on the cold flags at the stair head, and left there till removed by order of a surgeon. A relapse of fever and insensibility was the consequence. I was afterwards carried into a corridor among perhaps two hundred sick and dying men. My case was really pitiable....

One day a woman belonging to our regiment passed my bed. I called her, and asked her to bring me a little tea. I had several small loaves that I could not eat, under my pillow. These I gave her, but she forgot to bring the tea, though she often went by my couch of dried fern. . . .

'Into the bomb-proof barracks again. No ventilation, twenty sick men in the room, of whom about eighteen died. In this place there was one door and one chimney, but no windows. Relapse again; deaf as a post; shirt unchanged and sticking to my sore back; ears running stinking matter; a man lying close on my right hand, with both his legs mortified nearly to the knees and dying. A little sympathy would have soothed, but sympathy there was none. The orderlies (men who acted as nurses to the sick) were brutes. In a little time my strength and appetite began to return, consequently I asked the doctor for more bread, etc. He kindly allowed me an increase of it, and a pint of wine per day. I now got rapidly better. . . .'

Happily Sergeant Cooper, who landed in Lisbon in April 1809 and served under Wellington until the end of the campaign and the fall of Toulouse in 1814, survived the ordeals both of hospital and shot and blast. He must have possessed an iron constitution, since he died peacefully in Carlisle at the advanced age of eighty-seven.

Except on the retreat to Corunna, when the men were angry, frustrated and eager to fight, and criticism of Sir John Moore and his staff ran high, it is remarkable with what genuine respect these soldier chroniclers write of their officers. Even of that arch-martinet, Sir Robert Craufurd, Costello can say: 'While things were in this state, at an early hour General Craufurd made his re-appearance amongst us from England, and was welcomed with much enthusiasm by the division; although a strict disciplinarian, the men knew his value in the field too well not to testify their satisfaction at his return. The Caçadores, particularly, caused much laughter among us, by shouting out in Portuguese the moment they caught sight of him, "Long live General Craufurd, who takes care of our bellies!" meaning by this exclamation that they got their rations regularly, while under his command; the General seemed highly pleased, and bowed repeatedly with his hat off as he rode down their ranks.'

As a tailpiece to a chapter which has dwelt on the horrors of the war, and in contrasting mood, I reproduce a passage from

Costello, which throws an unusual sidelight on the character of the formidable Duke of Wellington: 'Head-quarters [during the winter of 1812/13] were at Grenalda [Frenada], some miles distant from where we lay, and a company of our regiment occasionally did duty over the Duke, whose quarters were in the house of the Alcalde. We had strict orders to admit no one inside the gates, leading to the house, unless some particular despatch from the front, or from Don Julian Sanchez, the Guerrilla chieftain. Indeed a report had arisen amongst us, at the time, that his Grace was not altogether right in his head—but this was mere fiction. I used to observe him walking through the Market-place, leading by the hand a little Spanish girl some five or six years' old, and humming a short tune, or dry whistle and occasionally purchasing little sweets, at the child's request, from the paysannes of the stalls.

'Here, for the first time, I saw Don Julian Sanchez, the noted Guerrilla leader, linked arm in arm with the Duke—an instance peculiar to the time of obscure merit rising of its own impulse, to an equality with the greatest man of the age.'

Chapter 19

FROM PORTUGAL TO THE PYRENEES

It being indispensable for the most rapid and certain destruction of the enemy that there should be unity in the plans and operations of the allied armies in the Peninsula, and it not being possible to attain this vital object without there being a single Commander-in-Chief of all the Spanish troops, the common and extraordinary Parliament, taking note of the urgent need to follow up the glorious triumphs of the allied forces and the favourable circumstances which are bringing nearer the moment of liberation, and greatly appreciating the distinguished talents and effective services of the Duke of Ciudad Rodrigo, Captain General of the national armies, now decree: that during the period of allied cooperation in the defence of the Peninsula, the overall command of all these forces shall be confided to him . . .

Decree of the Cadiz Cortes,
22 September 1812

Wellington did not spend the whole winter at his headquarters at the bleak little village of Frenada, which, apart from its proximity to his forces on the border, he seems to have chosen because it was situated in the best fox-hunting country in Portugal. Once his appointment as commander-in-chief had been approved by the Prince Regent in London, on 12 December 1812 he started out on the 300-mile ride to Cadiz to confer with the Cortes about his new duties and the reorganization of the Spanish army.

Alone amongst the Spanish generals, Ballesteros had opposed the appointment, on the score that it was an insult to the Spanish nation, and more particularly its army. By disobeying an order to march to Hill's aid in October he was partially responsible for the fall of Madrid to the French and he had furthermore made an outright bid for dictatorship—which resulted in his prompt arrest and exile to Ceuta in North Africa. It was with this fresh in mind and earlier memories of Cuesta, Venegas and Mendizábal and their reckless waste of troops and equipment that Wellington laid down stiff terms to Carvajal, the Spanish Minister of War. He was to be authorized to approve senior appointments; to control military expenditure; to dismiss officers whom he considered incapable; and to approve the selection of a Spanish chief of staff to be attached to his headquarters. Bearing in mind that many Spaniards were still suspicious about English designs on the Peninsula and that some of the generals whom Wellington rated most highly, like Castaños, were regarded as anglophile, the Cortes proved open-minded and accommodating—although the replacement in March 1813 of the Regency with which he had reached agreement and the appointment of a new Minister of War, in the person of General O'Donoju, with whom he had come into conflict at the time of Talavera, were to lead to later difficulties. In fact, it was with only 25,000 Spanish troops out of the 100,000 available to the Cortes that he took the field at Vitoria.

If Wellington had his problems during the winter of 1812/13, not only with the Cortes, but with the Portuguese Regency, which was grumbling about the prolonged expense of the war; with the War Office over senior appointments and the replacement of seasoned Peninsular troops by fresh units; and with the government, which kept mooting ill-conceived schemes for intervention in northern Europe, they were as nothing to those facing King Joseph and Marshal Jourdan.

Like Wellington's, the French army went into winter quarters after the confrontation at Salamanca. After the evacuation of Andalusia there were two alternatives open to the King: to reoccupy Madrid, which during his absence in the north had been taken over by *El Empecinado* and his guerrillas, or to base himself on Valladolid. Joseph, for reasons of prestige and to maintain communications with Suchet in Valencia, chose the first. Soult and his Army of the South made their headquarters at Toledo; the King returned to Madrid; and the Army of Portugal was distributed around Valladolid and Salamanca. Even with the available 95,000 French troops, the area was far too large to be held effectively.

It was on 6 January 1813 that Napoleon's celebrated '29th Bulletin', with its first veiled account of the Russian disaster, reached Madrid. Thanks to the activities of the Spanish guerrillas there was then a five weeks' gap in communications; and it was only on 14 February that Joseph was acquainted with the full extent of the calamity in a letter from an aide-de-camp, Colonel Desprez, which spoke of prisoners left in tens of thousands, bivouacs littered with frozen corpses, the appalling losses of the Young Guard and the virtual extinction of the *Grande Armée*.

This shattering news was backed up by a series of orders from Napoleon, who now resumed long-distance control of the Spanish campaign. Large numbers of troops were to be sent to France; Joseph was to retire to Valladolid, keeping Madrid only as his southern outpost; and Soult was to return to Paris—not, it is to be noted, because of Joseph's earlier complaint, but because the Emperor regarded him as 'the only military brain in the Peninsula'. The marshal, together with his stolen Murillos, left in triumph to succour France in her hour of need.

On 23 March, having pulled back the Army of the South and established his own headquarters in Valladolid, Joseph received further orders from his brother, which, besides berating him for his demands for money and inability to control the guerrillas in Navarre and Aragon, made a final French defeat inevitable. While Joseph was bidden to take the offensive against the English in Portugal, he was in the same breath instructed to send the Army of Portugal north to help Clausel subdue Biscay. That the Emperor had lost complete touch with reality is illustrated by a later despatch quoted by Oman:

> In the position in which the enemy found himself there was no reason to fear that he would take the offensive: his remoteness, his lack of transport, his constant and timid caution in all operations out of the ordinary line, all announced that we had complete liberty to act as suited us best, without worry or inconvenience. I may add that the ill-feeling between English and Spaniards, the voyage of Lord Wellington to Cadiz, the changes in his army, of which many regiments have been sent to England, were all favourable circumstances allowing us to carry out fearlessly every movement that the Emperor's orders might dictate.

In sober fact, the 50,000 men of Joseph's depleted armies of the Centre and the South were faced by a grand total of 106,000 under Wellington's command, made up of 52,000 British, 29,000 Portuguese and 25,000 Spanish. James McGrigor, the chief of the Medical Staff, had done stirling work in the hospitals during the winter and spring, and the veteran regiments had been continuously reinforced by fresh troops from England. Learning from his mistakes at Burgos, Wellington had brought up siege artillery and transported a heavy pontoon train across the length and breadth of Portugal so as to assure the army's passage across the rivers which lay in his way.

The campaign was planned with all the care of the previous year's operations. The guerrillas in the north could be relied upon to tie down large numbers of Clausel's men. In the east, Suchet was fully occupied with the Army of Murcia and the British division from Sicily, incompetently as its new commander, Sir John Murray, carried out Wellington's instructions.

After an encounter in April at Castalla, south of Valencia, in which Murray threw away his chance of inflicting a decisive defeat on Suchet, he embarked his 14,000 men at Alicante for an attack on Tarragona, on the coast of Catalonia some 200 miles to the north-east. Wellington's idea was that by so doing Murray would divert French troops both from Valencia, which would then be in danger from the Spanish armies of Murcia and the South, and from General Decaen's Army of Catalonia. Unfortunately Sir John Murray was too much influenced by Wellington's instruction that 'he would be forgiven everything excepting that the corps should be beaten or dispersed'. His great flotilla passed Valencia, thus arousing Suchet's liveliest apprehensions, and anchored south of Tarragona on 3 June. Meanwhile General Copóns, Captain General of Catalonia, had concentrated some 6,000 Spanish troops at Reus inland.

The fortifications of Tarragona were in poor repair and garrisoned by only 1,600 men, but Murray made his first mistake by establishing batteries and settling down for a conventional siege instead of using his overwhelming superiority in infantry to overrun the place. Thereafter, he was obsessed by the fear of being caught in a pincer movement between the forces of Suchet to the south and of Decaen to the north. This was unjustified by the actual movements of French troops, which, together with the Spanish, he heavily outnumbered; but on 13 June 1813, with the fortress on the point of surrender and to the dismay and anger of his officers and of Admiral Hallowell, the British naval commander, he ordered the precipitate embarkation of his men. General Copóns, who had moved up north of the city to block a French advance from Barcelona and had been promised substantial British reinforcements, was left to his fate without prior warning. It was no thanks to Murray that he succeeded in extricating his troops. On 18 June, after the evacuation had been completed, Sir Edward Pellew's blockading squadron from Toulon hove in sight, bringing with it Lord William Bentinck to take over the command. Its signal was answered by Admiral

Hallowell with: 'We are all delighted.' Bentinck arrived too late to take effective action, and Murray was subsequently to face court martial. If the siege of Tarragona was perhaps the most discreditable British action of the whole war, it had at least served its primary purpose of preventing reinforcements reaching King Joseph from the east.

Wellington had meanwhile launched his main offensive from Portugal. Spring was late in 1813. 'If the rains will but come soon and bring grass,' wrote Francis Larpent, the Judge-Advocate General for the army, 'we may, perhaps, move in the first week of May, but not before. . . .' It was in fact in the second week of the month that the army began its advance. Wellington himself, with 30,000 men under General Hill, moved on Salamanca; but this was only a large-scale diversion. He had already given orders to General Graham to march the main body of 60,000 through the wild country of the Trás-os-Montes, to use the pontoons for crossing the swift-flowing River Esla, a tributary of the Duero, and so to outflank the whole of the main French positions on the Duero river itself.

On crossing the frontier with the main army, which by now he had joined, Wellington raised his hat, and called: 'Farewell Portugal! I shall never see you again.' Such was his confidence that he had already decided to make use of Santander, ahead of him and to the north, as his supply base; and transports were waiting at Corunna to ship guns, ammunition and supplies the two hundred and fifty miles along the coast. By doing so he was able to avoid the long haul across the mountain tracks of Portugal and enormously to shorten his supply lines from England. By 2 June Wellington had established his headquarters at Toro, where he paused for Hill's army to join him; and by 4 June all 81,000 men of the allied army were concentrated north of the Duero.

King Joseph and Marshal Jourdan had spent the last days of May in Valladolid, uneasily aware that large-scale troop movements were afoot, but uncertain as to Wellington's whereabouts or the direction of the main British thrust. They even considered that he might swing south from Salamanca on Madrid. In the circumstances they decided to call back their widely dispersed troops; and General Gazan was ordered to evacuate the capital, an operation delayed by the need to escort huge numbers of *afrancesado* refugees and a massive baggage train carrying the

King's accumulated spoils. It was only on 1 June that they realized that Wellington had crossed the Esla to their rear—news which made nonsense of all their plans for defending the line of the Duero. A further retreat was ordered, and the great convoy directed back to Burgos. Instead of pressing down the main road, Wellington now began another wide encircling move with the bulk of his troops. Until now the army had been crossing the rolling plain of the Tierra de Campos. As one observer noted: 'We have been marching through one continuous cornfield. . . . The horses fed on green barley nearly the whole march, and got fat. The army has trampled down twenty yards of corn on each side of the roads by which the several columns have passed—in many places much more, from the baggage going on the side of the columns, and so spreading further into the wheat. But they must not mind the corn if we get the enemy out of their country!' The going now became rougher and more mountainous as, always keeping to the north, the army shadowed the retreating French. On the night of 13 June it was awakened by a distant and shattering explosion. Harried by Hill's men to his rear and nervous about the threat to his right flank, Joseph had decided to abandon Burgos and to blow up its castle, in the hope that by retreating still further towards Vitoria he might gain time for a junction with Clausel's Army of the North, which his scouts were urgently trying to locate.

By Wellington's own account, 'When I heard and saw the explosion (I was within a few miles, and the effect was tremendous) I made a sudden resolution forthwith—to cross the Ebro *instanter*, and to endeavour to push the French to the Pyrenees. . . .' It appears that his staff was against the plan, which involved a three-day march across mountains and through steep defiles. It could only have been possible in midsummer—and not then, if the French had opposed it—but, as Wellington roundly declared, he was in no mind to stop short at the last great river defence line. On 17 June, with the passage successfully accomplished, the two armies were in contact again near Vitoria, where Joseph at last determined to make a stand.

None of the King's urgent pleas had succeeded in bringing up the reinforcements he so urgently required. General Foy, misapprehending the seriousness of the situation, considered that, in accordance with Napoleon's personal instructions, his division was better occupied in hunting down the guerrillas and keeping open communications further north. Clausel, with his Army of the North, was still more than a day's march away in the direction of Logroño. It was therefore with some 57,000 effectives that Joseph faced Wellington's 70,000 Anglo-Portuguese and 7,000 Spaniards.

On 21 July 1813 the main French force was drawn up behind the River Zadorra, which winds across the 'plain' of Vitoria, an expanse of lower-lying ground extending south-west from the city and cupped by hills. Some miles to the north-east General Reille had been told off, with two divisions, to contain a threat to the main Bayonne road from a mixed British and Spanish force of 20,000 under General Graham and Colonel Longa, the enterprising guerrilla leader, now turned regular soldier. Wellington's aim was the complete encirclement and destruction of the French army and depended for its success on the synchronization of attacks by separate columns marching different distances across precipitous terrain. In particular, a great deal was left to the discretion of Graham, since his column was out of sight of the others and he was enjoined to cut the road, but not to be drawn into an action north of Vitoria until the main attack to the south-west was developing favourably.

Hostilities began with the seizure of the Puebla heights, overlooking the extreme left of the main French positions, by General Morillo and his Spanish division. The ground was 'so steep that while moving up it they looked as if they were lying on their faces or crawling'. Hill now sent in British and Portuguese troops to occupy the village of Subijana de Alava lower down; and such was the danger to the whole left of the French line that substantial reinforcements were diverted from the centre, where the major British attack was now developing. A brigade of the Light Division under General Kempt was able to cross the Zadorra by a bridge left negligently undestroyed by the defenders. Kempt's men were in urgent need of support, and Wellington ordered up Lord Dalhousie's 7th Division; but Dalhousie had lost his way. At this point the impetuous General Picton—an odd-looking figure, since he was suffering from an inflamed eye and had put on a broad-brimmed top hat—lost all patience and took matters into his own hands. With a shout of, 'Come on, ye rascals! Come on, ye fighting villains!', he 'swept like a comet' across the line of Dalhousie's tardy advance and with his 3rd Division punched a great hole in the French centre.

Although the French stubbornly attempted to pull back and reform, much of the spirit had gone out of them after their long retreat, and eventually the whole line began to crumple as the British and Portuguese continued to pour across the river.

On the other side of the town, Graham had overestimated the strength of Reille's force and displayed excessive caution in his advance on the Vitoria–Bayonne road. However, at five o'clock in the afternoon, Longa's Spaniards, operating on Graham's left, succeeded in occupying the village of Durana astride the road, so cutting off the main route to the north.

It was a decisive moment in the battle. There was only one other means of escape: a narrow country road leading to Salvatierra and Pamplona to the east. As the news of the defeat reached the thronged French baggage park, some 20,000 camp followers, courtiers, clerks, *afrancesados* and women folk began flooding out with their carriages and wagons. The road was soon choked with distracted humanity and broken-down vehicles; the fruitless attempts of artillery batteries and army transport to force their way through only worsened the confusion. Of the 152 French guns, just one was saved. Only Reille succeeded in extricating his two divisions and fighting a resolute rear-guard action; had it not been for this and Graham's earlier failure to engage him decisively, the whole French army might well have been destroyed. Joseph himself escaped capture by a hairsbreadth, when his coach was stopped by a detachment of the 14th Light Dragoons and he sprang out by the far door, took to his heels and made off on a horse.

The loot, in Oman's phrase, 'was such as no European army had ever laid hands on before, since Alexander's Macedonians plundered the camp of the Persian king after the battle of Issus. . . . It represented the exploitation of Spain for six long years by its conquerors.' Marauding soldiers and camp followers broke open chests containing church plate, bags of dollars, jewellery, silks and embroidery. Whole wagonloads were painted with the names of French generals or marked '*Domaine extérieur de S.M. l'Empereur*'. Among King Joseph's personal booty were found the rolled-up canvases of the choicest Italian paintings from the royal collections. The military chest contained millions in specie for the payment of the troops, only recently received from France and not yet distributed. Unfortunately, Wellington was able to recover little of it for paying his own men—they took matters into their own hands. As darkness fell, the soldiers, knowing his severity where loot was concerned, staged an impromptu torchlit auction, dressing themselves in captured military finery and selling off anything from a horse to a porcelain chamberpot for hard cash. Amidst the general feasting and festivities it seems that the prisoners, captured *afrancesados*, and what a French officer described as their army's '*bordel ambulant*' were on this occasion well treated; and it is pleasant to record that, at Wellington's express orders, the Countess Gazan was despatched in a coach to rejoin her husband, the fugitive general of the Army of the South.

It was Wellington's intention to begin the pursuit of the defeated French army at dawn next day, but as he wrote to the Secretary of State on 29 June, 'We started with the army in the highest order and on the day of battle nothing could get on better. But that event has, as usual, totally annihilated all order and discipline. The soldiers of the army have got among them about a million stirling in money. . . . The night of the battle, instead of being passed in getting rest and food to prepare for the pursuit of the following day, was spent by the soldiers in looking for plunder. The consequence was that they were incapable of marching in pursuit of the enemy and were totally knocked up.' In a further explosion of anger he added that, 'It is quite impossible for me or any other man to command a British army under the existing system. We have in the service the scum of the earth as common soldiers. . . .' In fairness, it must be recorded that these same exhausted soldiers had marched 400 miles in 40 days and that the cavalry were let down by the irresolution of their commanders.

Although casualties—8,000 French to some 5,000 allied—were fairly evenly matched and, as a result of the slow pursuit, Joseph was able to extricate 55,000 men and to withdraw them into France by the passes of the Pyrenees, the Battle of Vitoria effectively secured the French evacuation of Spain. And beyond the Peninsula its effects resounded throughout Europe. On 4 June 1813 Napoleon had signed the Armistice of Plässwitz with the Russians and Prussians; and the Allies were negotiating for a peace on terms unacceptable to Britain. The news of the Spanish reverse induced Napoleon to extend the truce for six weeks, so giving Austria time to mobilize and paving the way for his decisive defeat at Leipzig later that year.

A more immediate result of the battle was to induce General Clausel to evacuate Spain with his 15,000 men. He was at long last approaching Vitoria on 26 June when the news of the battle reached him. Turning back rapidly, his first idea was to join King Joseph and the main army. When this proved impossible, he retreated down the Ebro to Saragossa and then marched north for Jaca and the pass of Canfranc in the Pyrenees. Wellington at first considered intercepting him, but gave up the scheme, since it might well have resulted in forcing him back to join Suchet, whose Army of Aragon was the largest French force still in Spain.

Instead, Wellington now devoted himself to clearing the remaining French troops from the north. The delayed pursuit after Vitoria had enabled Joseph to leave a strong garrison in Pamplona; it was well supplied, and the fortress was plentifully provided with artillery. He therefore decided to blockade, rather than lay siege to it; and this operation was undertaken by the 11,000 Spaniards under General O'Donnell. Meanwhile, General Graham, in support of Longa and General Giron's 14,000 strong Army of Galicia, marched north into Biscay in pursuit of the 16,000 men of General Foy's Army of the North and a column under General Maucune, which had escaped from Vitoria before the cutting of the Bayonne road. Both forces were driven back across the River Bidassoa on the French frontier, but not before Foy had left a strong garrison in San Sebastián. Further to the south, General Gazan, with the last remnants of Joseph's army from Vitoria, was forced back across the Pyrenees through the pass of Maya by General Hill on 8 July. This left only two French strongholds in the north of Spain: the fortresses of Pamplona and San Sebastián.

It was with rage and incredulity that Napoleon, who was at Dresden at the time and preoccupied enough with his own problems in Germany, received a secondhand account of the defeat at Vitoria from General Foy. '*Les malheurs de l'Espagne sont d'autant plus grands qu'ils sont ridicules,*' he wrote to Savary on 20 July. The disaster was nevertheless largely the result of his own misassessment of the situation in Spain and of orders from his Minister of War, Clarke, which arrived weeks out of date. Thus, Joseph had been told to defend the Ebro when his army was already retreating in disarray across the Pyrenees. But a scapegoat had to be found, and the Emperor declared that, 'All the fault was his [King Joseph's]. . . . if there was one man too many with the army it was the King.' Through Clarke, Joseph was ordered to remain in Bayonne with his Spanish entourage; and the newspapers were forbidden to mention the matter. As the unkindest cut of all, Soult, whose transgressions against Joseph Napoleon were dismissed as *'des petitesses'*, was instructed, not only to take over the armies of Spain and resume the offensive against Wellington, but to place the ex-King under house arrest if he should try to leave Bayonne—an order which Soult later carried out.

If it was absolutely necessary for reasons of strategy and prestige to prevent Wellington from sweeping into France from the Pyrenees, the position of Suchet in the far south-east was clearly untenable. On hearing the news of Vitoria, the Duke of Albufera began the evacuation of Valencia on 5 July 1813 and thereafter divided his army into two columns, one, under his own command, retreating along the coast road and the other, under General Musnier, striking inland to Teruel and then taking a parallel course inland until both forces reunited at Tarragona. Suchet could not reconcile himself to the idea that Spain was irrevocably lost, and as a springboard for future operations and to cover the retreat, garrisons were left in numerous fortresses along the route—including Sagunto, Peñiscola, Morella, Tortosa and Tarragona—but they served little purpose except to deplete his army, since the pursuit was sluggish. The allies reached Tarragona only towards the end of July, meanwhile leaving a force to blockade Tortosa to the south. Once he had gained Catalonia, Suchet took over command from General Decaen, and in December he had some 35,000 men at his disposal to defend the province. By the end of the year Napoleon's demands for troops to contain the Allies on the Rhine reduced this number by a third; and the despatch of some 10,000 infantry and a third of his cavalry to France in the early spring compelled Suchet to evacuate Barcelona, once again leaving a garrison, and to withdraw to Figueras. An attempt by a mixed Spanish and British force to surprise the French at Molinos del Rey on 10 January 1814 was the last serious encounter between the two sides in Catalonia.

As for the far-flung garrisons, those of Lérida, Mequinenza and Monzón were tricked into surrender. A *juramentado*, Vanhalen, of Belgian or Dutch origin, having deserted from the

French Army of Catalonia, presented himself with forged orders and, to Suchet's disgust, induced their commanders to evacuate the fortresses under promise of safe conducts to France. The French troops were subsequently surrounded and imprisoned by a Spanish division under General Eroles. They were later repatriated, when the remaining garrisons surrendered to General Copóns under the terms of an armistice agreed after the fall of Toulouse and the return of Ferdinand VII to Spain. Suchet's further movements had no bearing on the outcome of hostilities, since he was unable to join forces with Soult in time to check Wellington's final advance on Toulouse.

The Duke of Dalmatia arrived in Bayonne on 11 July 1813 and, unpromising as the situation was, celebrated his long-cherished ambition to take full command of the armies in Spain with a typically rumbustious proclamation:

> Soldiers! with well-equipped fortresses in front and in the rear, a capable general possessing the confidence of his troops could by the choice of good positions have faced and defeated the motley levies opposed to you. Unhappily at the critical moment timid and downhearted counsels prevailed. The fortresses were abandoned and blown up; a hasty and disorderly retreat gave confidence to the enemy; and a veteran army, weak in numbers (it is true) but great in everything that constitutes military character, that army which had fought, bled, and conquered in every province in Spain, saw with indignation its laurels blighted, and was forced to abandon its conquests, the trophies of many sanguinary days of battle.... Soldiers! I sympathize with your disappointments, your grievances, your indignation. I know that the blame for the present situation must be imputed to others. It is your task to repair the disaster.

Acquisitive, calculating and ambitious as Nicholas Soult undoubtedly was, he was a tough and resourceful soldier and energetically set to work to weld Joseph's beaten and dispirited men into an effective fighting force. Napoleon's orders were to reorganize all the available 120,000 troops as a single Army of Spain—by now the old names of the 'Army of Portugal', 'Army of the South' and the rest were in any case somewhat embarrassing. 'General Damnation', as the British called him, achieved the near impossible within thirteen days and, although short of

FROM PORTUGAL TO THE PYRENEES

transport and artillery, mounted a full-scale attack on 23 July. His plan was a bold one: to launch 34,000 men under Reille and Clausel through the pass of Roncesvalles on the steeply climbing road from St. Jean Pied-de-Port to Pamplona and another 20,000 under General D'Erlon through the Maya pass further north. The allied army was widely dispersed, with separate forces holding the Pyrenean passes and opposite Pamplona and San Sebastián; and Wellington made his dispositions in the belief that Soult would first attempt to relieve San Sebastián. The marshal's true objective was far more ambitious: to raise the blockade of Pamplona, cut communications with San Sebastián and the coast, and then to drive into Spain towards Vitoria, so disrupting Wellington's rear.

Wellington had established his headquarters in the little village of Lesaca, midway between San Sebastián and the pass of Maya. He had barely received news on 25 July that Graham's first attempt to storm the city had failed and galloped over to order a resumption of the blockade, when the sound of distant gunfire, echoing across the hills like some evocation of Roland's horn, warned him that the passes were under attack. Sir Lowry Cole's 4th Division was under orders to hold the Roncesvalles pass at all costs and repulsed the first attack, but subsequently fell back along the road to Pamplona. Maya, too, had been held; but on hearing of Cole's retreat, Hill pulled back his men. By the morning of the 27th Soult was within half a dozen miles of Pamplona; and the situation was desperate. Wellington at once rode over to the village of Sorauen, where, with Soult's outposts approaching, he barely had time to dash off an order to Picton and Cole to deploy their troops on the ridge beyond. It was, as he said, 'a close run thing'.

It was now midday, and Soult, of whom Wellington once remarked that, 'He did not quite understand a field of battle: he knew very well how to bring his troops on to the field, but not so well how to use them when he had brought them up', decided to take a nap before launching his attack. It allowed Wellington vital time to make his dispositions and to bring up reinforcements. The attack developed as it had at Buçaco, with the dense French columns thrown against an allied line deployed behind the crest of the hill; and, as at Buçaco, the French were decisively thrown back. Soult, having failed to relieve Pamplona, regrouped and on 30 July marched across Wellington's left flank in an attempt to raise the siege of San Sebastián. If the first battle of Sorauen was Soult's Buçaco, the second proved to be his Salamanca. There was no halting the flight of his disorganized forces across the Pyrenees; during the nine days of the 'Campaign of the Pyrenees' they had suffered some 15,000 casualties. The allies now reoccupied their positions along the line of the Pyrenees and resumed the siege of San Sebastián. The city fell after appalling slaughter at the breaches; and even the sack of Badajoz pales in comparison with what followed. Thus the anglophile historian Toreno could write: 'Neither helpless old age nor tender infancy were proof against the brutality and licence of the soldiers, who in their abandon raped daughters in the laps of their mothers, mothers in the arms of their husbands, and other women indiscriminately. What shame, what an atrocity! At nightfall there followed the fire, whether accidental or deliberate we do not know. The whole city went up in flames: only sixty houses had been destroyed during the siege; now all were reduced to ashes save forty of the whole six hundred in San Sebastián. . . . It was ruin and destruction that one could not believe to be the work of soldiers of an allied nation, European and civilized, but rather of enemies and savage tribes come from Africa. The Spanish authorities raised their voices to the skies, while the city fathers and inhabitants united in agonized, but useless protests to Lord Wellington. . . .'

Wellington was bitterly attacked for these disgraceful scenes, in England as well as Spain; no doubt there was little enough that he could do to control his maddened troops, but it is strange that one of his modern biographers should pass off the affair by quoting a tribute to 'the ardour and confidence of our army'! A final attempt by Soult to relieve the city was beaten off by Spanish troops under General Freire on the day of its capture; and with the surrender of Pamplona to Carlos de España on 31 October, the French lost their last outpost in northern Spain.

Wellington might well have begun his invasion of France after Soult's defeats at Sorauen, but, uncertain as to the intentions of the Allies on the other side of Europe, he wrote to the Secretary for War: 'As for the immediate invasion of France, from what I have seen of the state of negotiations in the North of Europe, I have determined to consider it only in reference to the convenience of my own operations. . . . If peace should be made by the Powers of the North, I must necessarily withdraw into Spain.' He did not withdraw, but on 7 October 1813 marched his army across the River Bidassoa into France. His victorious progress, as he rolled back Soult across one river line after another and entered Toulouse on 12 April 1814 to be greeted with the news of Napoleon's abdication, is not the subject of a book concerned first and foremost with the Peninsula. We leave him in Toulouse as he rose to General Alava's toast *El Liberador de España* and, as his Judge-Advocate General remarked, 'bowed, confused, and immediately called for the coffee'.

PART THREE
The Aftermath

Chapter 20

A WAR FOR INDEPENDENCE

The Peninsular War has always been known in Spain as *La Guerra de la Independencia*; It was a War of Independence in more senses than the obvious one. After paying tribute to its value in diverting troops from the crucial battlefields of northern Europe, military historians habitually close the ledger with the fall of Toulouse and the expulsion of the last French troops from Spanish soil; but this is to reduce the campaign to the dimensions of a war game and to overlook what were its most significant repercussions: the last death throes of the Golden Era in Spain and the liberation of an entire continent in South America. It was the common people who with British help threw the French out of Spain and Portugal. Although their first reaction in Spain was to clamour for the return of Ferdinand VII, 'The Desired One', the consciousness that it was they, and not their absentee monarch, who were the masters of their destiny, made it impossible for a Bourbon king to rule with absolute authority in Spain, any more than his viceroys in the provinces across the ocean or the Bragdanças in Brazil.

After Napoleon had been defeated at the Battle of Leipzig in October 1813 by some 300,000 Russians, Austrians, Prussians and Swedes, it became a matter of urgency for him to seek a suspension of hostilities on his second front. On 20 November he therefore sent La Forest, the former French Ambassador in Madrid, to parley with Ferdinand VII, who had been languishing in the castle of Valençay since the notorious dealings in Bayonne of 1808. With the prerequisite that the British should evacuate the Peninsula, Napoleon offered to recognize Ferdinand as King of Spain and the Indies, stipulating among other conditions that he should grant a full pardon to the 12,000 *afrancesados* who had accompanied Joseph across the Pyrenees and also sign a trade agreement with France. Ferdinand was at first reluctant, but after Napoleon had himself spoken to the royalist Duke of San

Carlos, he finally signed the Treaty of Valençay, whether in good faith or not, on 11 December 1813.

The reality of the situation was that Ferdinand had played no part in the liberation of the country and that, as a result of his abdication, Spain now possessed a government with sovereign powers, so that he was without authority to agree terms. First the Duke of San Carlos, and later Joseph Palafox, were therefore despatched to Madrid to obtain the Regency's approval for the treaty and the King's return. Obstinately as the Duke pressed the matter, his mission was condemned to failure, since as long ago as January 1811 the Cadiz Cortes had enacted a decree invalidating all decisions taken by the King during his exile. In the face of a flurry of royalist activity, on 2 February 1814 the Cortes hurriedly passed a further decree empowering its executive, the Regency, to lay down conditions under which the King might return to Spain. Chief among these was the requirement that he should swear allegiance to the Constitution of 1812.

This Constitution, for long a model in Europe, was the keystone of the reformist activities of the Cadiz Cortes and was for decades to be the subject not only of acrimonious argument, but of armed conflict between liberals and the 'absolutists', the supporters of the traditional rights of the Crown and the Church.

The argument began over the composition and prerogatives of the Cortes, when it was first summoned in the besieged Isla de León on 24 September 1810 by the Regency, which had supplanted the Central Junta after the disaster of Ocaña. Elected by a complicated system of indirect suffrage, it was, for the first time, a national and—as far as the difficult circumstances allowed—representative parliament. From the outset it was attacked by the 'absolutists', who numbered most of the aristocracy, the clergy and the generals (but not guerrilla leaders like Porlier and Mina), as a revolutionary body unsanctioned by law or tradition. At best they were prepared to regard it and the Regency as bodies exercising temporary authority pending the restoration of the monarchy. Its composition could indeed be criticized, since with the country in a state of occupation, it was impossible for delegates from the more remote regions to attend; and its opponents always maintained that it was over-weighted by *suplentes* (or substitute deputies for the occupied areas and South America) from traditionally radical Cadiz. Its most eloquent members—and oratory counted for a great deal—were dedicated liberals like Agustín Argüelles; the historian, Toreno; and Torrero, the radical priest. Like the intellectual *afrancesados*, they had been brought up in the school of Montesquieu, Voltaire and Rousseau.

In deference to the middle-of-the-road majority, debates in the Cortes were accompanied by frequent references to traditional liberties and the *fueros*; but Argüelles summed up the basic attitude of the liberals when he declared that, 'Liberty, Equality and property are natural rights, God-given natural rights which men protect when they enter society.' In practical terms the liberal programme resulted in an attack on the entrenched privileges of the Crown, the Church and aristocrats, and embodied sweeping land reforms and centralization of government. When the liberals announced plans for dismembering Catalonia by dividing it into Lérida, Barcelona, Gerona and Tarragona, they raised up opponents outside the ranks of the élite; and the problem of Basque and Catalan separatism has been with Spain ever since.

Although the Cadiz liberals were a gifted minority, they did, however imperfectly, reflect a widespread feeling that the Peninsular War had been won by the efforts of the people themselves and their revolutionary juntas and that, as a result, sovereign power lay ultimately with the people. This attitude emerges strongly from Articles II and III of the Constitution:

Art. II   The Spanish nation is free and independent and is not nor can it ever be the property of any family or person.

Art. III   Power resides essentially in the nation, and, as such, the right to establish fundamental laws is exclusively of the nation.

Basic attitudes towards the Church and Crown are defined in Articles XII and XIV:

Art. XII   The religion of the Spanish people is, and ever shall be, the only true faith of the Roman Catholic Church. The Nation offers it protection with wise and just laws and outlaws the practice of any other.

Art. XIV   The Government of the Spanish people is a conservative hereditary monarchy.

It was in their system of controls and checks over the authority of the King that the Cortes was to find itself in outright opposition to Ferdinand VII and his 'absolutist' supporters, who argued that these could not possibly be justified by historical precedent. The King and his council of ministers were to be bound by the decisions of the Cortes; when it was not sitting his conduct was to be supervised by a Deputation; and any personal decisions made by the King were to be subject to the approval of a Council of State chosen by him from nominees of the Cortes. Implicit in all this was a deep-rooted suspicion of the arbitrary exercise of royal authority, no doubt justified by the conduct of Ferdinand's predecessor, Charles IV, but unacceptable to a self-respecting monarch at the turn of the eighteenth century.

In the face of the Regency's rotund refusal to recognize the Treaty of Valençay, Napoleon decided that he must cut his losses and set Ferdinand free, in the hope that he would abide by the agreements once he was restored to the throne. The King was met at the frontier on 24 March 1814 by General Copóns, who at once submitted to him the documents from the Regency, together with their request that he should proceed direct to Madrid, so as to take his oath to abide by the Constitution. Ferdinand's reply was evasive; instead of going to Madrid, he first paid a visit to Saragossa and then made his way to Valencia, meanwhile sounding popular opinion on the subject of his restoration. In the main it was opposed to the terms demanded by the Regency; and in Valencia he received a triumphant welcome from sixty-nine '*serviles*' or dissident right-wing deputies—the so-called 'Persians'—who petitioned him to reject the Constitution and return to traditional forms of government. At this point General Elio, a confirmed conservative, who like most of the generals from Cuesta downwards considered that they alone had won the war and were entitled to impose their authority, offered the King the support of his 2nd Army. Emboldened by this, Ferdinand snubbed and arrested the emissary of the Cortes, his uncle Cardinal de Borbón, and issued his Proclamation of 4 May.

It was a vague and windy document, offering little except a return to the traditions of the Golden Era; but on one point at least the King made himself crystal clear:

I declare that my royal intention is not only not to swear or agree to the said Constitution or any decree of the general and extraordinary Cortes and of the ordinary Cortes now in session ... but to declare that Constitution and those decrees nul and of no validity or effect, now or at any time, as if those acts had never been passed and are obliterated.

A week later General Eguía, with a division of Elio's army, entered Madrid, dissolved the Cortes and proceeded to the arrest and imprisonment of the Regents Agar and Císcar and as many of the ministers and liberal deputies as he could hunt down. Others, like Toreno, who managed to escape, were banished and joined the swelling throng of Spanish exiles in Paris and London. These included the thousands of *afrancesados*—since Ferdinand had promptly repudiated his agreement with Napoleon; and in fact the new regime made little or no distinction between patriot liberals and the ex-followers of King Joseph. Madrid was torn by riots, often instigated by the clergy; the hall of the Cortes was sacked and a stone inscribed with the Constitution broken up; while a popular ditty of the period ran:

> *Murieron los Liberales*
> *Murió la Constitución,*
> *Porque viva el Rey Fernando,*
> *Con la Patria y Religión!*

If the liberal intellectuals were out of touch with the common people and Ferdinand was swept back into power by the generals and the clergy riding a wave of patriotic fervour, the fact remains, as Miguel Artola has pointed out in Vol. XXVI of the *Historia de España*, that the overturned government 'owed its legitimacy, in the last place, to the fact of the 1808 uprising and that, whatever the juridical reservations, it was the regime which had won the war and enjoyed universal recognition of its authority'. Ferdinand proved to be bankrupt, both in his policies and literally, since his refusal to make concessions to the Spanish colonists led to final rupture with Latin America and dealt a crushing blow to the economy. In vain, he deposed minister after minister; opposition to his repressive methods grew; and soon both Mina and Porlier took to the field again with their guerrillas. Although they could not rouse the same patriotic enthusiasm as in the fight against the French—Mina fled abroad and Porlier was degraded and hanged—liberal ideas were on the upsurge. In 1820 an army destined for South America rebelled, and its revolutionary leader, Rafael de Riego, marched in triumph to Madrid. Ferdinand was thereupon compelled to swear allegiance to the Constitution, which he had so long withheld.

This was only a foretaste of the continuing struggle between liberals and 'absolutists'. The War of Independence cast forward long shadows across the Spanish history of the nineteenth century. Meeting at Verona in October 1822, the plenipotentiaries of Russia, Prussia, Austria and France decided that liberalism had gone too far in Spain; in spite of British disapproval, a French army once again crossed the Pyrenees, this time to restore the *status quo*. Before his death in 1833, Ferdinand remarked that, 'Spain is a bottle of beer and I am the cork. Without me it would all go off in froth.' His prediction was only too near the mark. Although the ensuing Carlist Wars were ostensibly a dynastic conflict between the adherents of his daughter Isabella and his brother, Don Carlos, once again the country split down the middle along the lines drawn up after the Peninsular War. Cristina, the Queen Mother, drew her support from the liberals, themselves divided between '*exaltados*' (radicals) and 'moderates', as at the time of Ferdinand, while Don Carlos recruited his followers from the equally determined members of the 'apostolic' or Church party and the dissident Basques and Catalans. And so the old feuds have rumbled on. The Civil War was fought along broadly comparable lines; Spain is still in search of an effective Cortes; and Catalan separatism is as explosive an issue as when the provinces were first divided.

When Napoleon invaded the Peninsula the Spanish possessions across the Atlantic embraced the whole of South America with the exception of Portuguese Brazil, together with Mexico, the Floridas and various outlying islands, of which the most important was Cuba. Unrest, both in Spanish America and Brazil, had been mounting for years, because the mother countries had been draining off gold, silver and colonial produce without supplying manufactured goods in sufficient bulk or at competitive prices and were unable to police the sea routes. There was therefore strong feeling among the settlers that they should be free to trade directly with other countries, especially England.

Particularly in the Spanish colonies, explosive social conflicts were also coming to the surface. The Indian slaves, who made up the bulk of the population, were politically inactive; but the *mestizos*, the half-caste children of Indian mothers and their Spanish conquerors, were becoming increasingly vocal. It was not, however, they, but the creoles, Spaniards or Portuguese of pure blood born in America, who were the mainspring of the revolt. Most of the high officials—viceroys, the judiciary, bishops and the rest—were *peninsulares* (or *gachupines*—'spurred ones') sent out from Europe. Not unnaturally, the creoles, who far outnumbered them, resented their predominance. That rebellion did not spread sooner, and that when it did the creoles first acknowledged nominal allegiance to Ferdinand VII, was probably because they themselves were a minority group and feared that it would spread to the Indians and *mestizos*.

What brought matters to a head was, in the first place, the revolutions in North America and France. 'When in the course of human events it becomes necessary for one people to dissolve the bonds which have connected them with another' were words which applied with as much force to South America as North. But it was the Peninsular War, by demonstrating the military and political impotence of Spain and Portugal which set the colonists on a course that stopped short of nothing but complete liberation.

The first article of the 1812 Constitution read:

> Art. I The Spanish nation shall be defined as the sum total of all Spaniards on both sides of the Atlantic.

By granting the colonists the same freedoms as Spaniards at home the Cadiz Cortes felt that it had removed legitimate grounds for revolt. Unfortunately the Constitution did nothing to meet the demands for free trade with Europe and North America, for which Henry Wellesley had also been pressing in Cadiz, so that he could report to Castlereagh in July 1812 that, 'No disposition exists here to make any commercial concessions, even for the important object of tranquillizing America.' The somewhat niggardly restriction of the number of American delegates to the Cortes—most of whom were in any case stand-in's from Cadiz—still further alienated the colonists. In Venezuela it was felt that the Regency which assumed power after the débâcle of Ocaña was no effective government, and taking a leaf from the Spanish book, in April 1810 the colonists set up a Junta of their own pledged to ruling the viceroyalty on behalf of

Ferdinand VII, but at the same time opening its ports to trade with other nations.

Relations between the creoles and the *peninsulares* were exacerbated by the fact that many of the high Spanish officials were nominees of the discredited Godoy; and in the earlier stages of rebellion the general pattern was self rule in the name of the King. The first of the viceroyalties effectively to free itself was that of Río de la Plata. In July 1806 a British naval squadron under Sir Home Popham had appeared off Buenos Aires and seized the city in the name of George III. Without help from Spain the *porteños* (or inhabitants of Buenos Aires) rallied, drove out the intruders and repulsed a further British expedition in 1807. They had nevertheless come to appreciate the advantages of trade with Britain; and in 1809 the Spanish viceroy submitted to demands for free trade with friendly nations. Aware by now of their own strength, the creoles created a 'Provisional Junta of the Provinces of the Río de la Plata, governing for Ferdinand VII'. A constitution was adopted and complete independence declared on 9 July 1816.

Elsewhere progress towards independence was slower and more chequered. In Mexico the revolutionary priest Miguel Hidalgo came near to liberating the whole country in 1810, but the royalists fought back successfully, as they did against that most famous of South American patriots, Simón Bolívar, in Venezuela and New Granada (Colombia) a few years later.

Had not Ferdinand VII taken a line with America even more authoritarian than that of the Regency, something might perhaps have been saved from the wreck of empire. Refusing British mediation, which envisaged concessions to the rebels and an opening up of trade, the only gesture which he ever made was a temporary offer to the creoles of participation in government. His views emerge most clearly in his Declaration to the Americas, made in 1820 shortly after swearing the Constitution. That the Constitution was long ago a dead letter in America can hardly have commended them:

> Americans, who find yourselves wandering far from the path that leads to prosperity, you now have what for so long you have been seeking at the cost of enormous efforts of ceaseless suffering, of bloody war, of awful desolation and of widespread destruction. . . . So what are you waiting for? Harken to the gentle voice of your King and father. . . .

... But if you turn down the sacred advice which comes from the depth of our heart and if you do not shake the hand which your loving country offers you and embrace the country which gave life to many of your fathers who, were they still living, would use their authority to order you to accept, then have no fear for all the fury unleashed by civil war ... and you will feel besides the terrible effects of a nation's indignation at seeing its Government insulted: a Government now strong and powerful as it has the support of the people and runs the country according to their lights. Oh, may the fatal day of such thoughtless obstinacy never dawn! Never; that we may never experience the terrible grief of having even for the shortest space of time to refrain from calling ourself your loving father, Fernando.

Ferdinand had himself already unleashed 'bloody war' by the despatch to America in 1815 of 10,000 troops under the ruthless General Morillo; but after his earlier victories in Venezuela and New Granada, Morillo was by 1819 in full retreat from the victorious Bolívar. A new expedition planned for 1820 never sailed, both because the ships provided by the Czar proved to be rotten and incapable of the voyage and, even before he issued his resounding proclamation, the army had turned against the King. Don Javier de Burgos, writing from Paris in January 1826, supplies the epitaph:

From your crown, my lord, two great and triumphal laurels with which Cortés and Pizarro wreathed the crown of Carlos I have been untimely plucked. The Spanish Monarchy has today fifteen million fewer subjects than it had in 1808. The flag of the Mexican Revolution now flutters over the battlefield of San Juan de Ulúa and it is to be feared that that of the rebels in Perú shall soon be flown over the battlements of Callao. ...

Events in Brazil followed a different course, if only because the royal family had taken up residence in Rio de Janeiro after their flight from Portugal in November 1807, and the Prince Regent showed himself a great deal more sympathetic to the needs and wishes of the people than the wooden Ferdinand VII. In January 1808 John opened all the country's ports for trade with nations friendly to Portugal; and there followed, in February 1810, a far-reaching Treaty of Commerce and Navigation with

Great Britain. In 1815 Brazil was granted dominion status within the Empire; and after the death of the mad Queen Maria, he was crowned 'John VI of the United Kingdom of Portugal, Brazil and the Algarves'. This is not to say that all was sweetness and light, since John was surrounded by a clique of luxury-loving hangers-on; and his Queen, the wanton and ill-favoured Carlota, was forever dabbling in politics. On the strength of being Ferdinand VII's sister, she at one time attempted to have herself named Queen of the Spanish province of La Plata and at another Regent of Spain itself; both projects were vetoed by the British.

In 1820 the Regency in Portugal itself was overturned by rebels, who adopted a constitution modelled on the Spanish example of 1812. This Junta, like the Cadiz Cortes, was liberal in its policies at home, but in its desire to hold Brazil, disowned many of John's reforms, including the opening of Brazilian ports to foreign commerce. At the insistence of Castlereagh, who bade him return home and 'save out of the wreck of His own Power' what he could, John sailed for Lisbon in April 1821, together with an entourage of 3,000 and all the gold which he could collect from the treasury. His last words to his son, the twenty-three-year-old Pedro, were: 'If Brazil demands independence, grant it, but put the crown upon your own head.'

John's prescience was justified. The Lisbon Côrtes continued to press its demands and summarily ordered Dom Pedro to return to Portugal. The story goes that he ripped Portuguese insignia from his uniform and shouted, 'Independence or death!'; he was crowned Emperor of a free Brazil on 1 December 1822. There remained pockets of resistance; but in the wake of the Peninsular War the Lisbon government lacked the resources to enforce its authority. The last Portuguese garrisons were evicted by the freebooting Admiral Cochrane, who, after his exploits at the siege of Rosas and elsewhere, had taken service abroad and assisted General San Martín in the liberation of Chile and Peru.

Perhaps no one has better summed up the origins and repercussions of the Peninsular War than the Spanish poet and patriot Manuel José Quintana in his long and eloquent letter to Lord Holland of 20 November 1823, written in the aftermath of the new French invasion:

... To suppose that the Spaniards faced the terrible ills and unexampled havoc of this cruel war with no other aim than to secure their independence and restore their king, and to believe that such superhuman efforts should bring no betterment of their affairs or remedy for the abuses which had brought such calamities upon them, is to nurture nothing but dreams of the human condition and the ways of the world. Ignorant and backward as we are, we are certainly not as stupid as that; and, reeling from its blows, this unhappy country learned a lesson for the future in grief and blood. Thus it is that the idea of reforming our political and civil institutions could not have resulted from the fantasies of a few hot-heads, any more than it was the criminal conspiracy of a group of agitators. . . .

. . . No, milord, these were not the authors of the great innovation which has so belatedly engaged the attention of Europe's rulers. Without doubt the true instigators are Carlos IV, with his indolence and profligacy, María Luisa, with her whims and scandalous affairs, the Prince of Peace, with his insolence, greed and incompetence, Napoleon, with his grandiose invasion, and Fernando VII, the blind instrument of a fanatical party incapable of governing the nation in accordance with the time and circumstances. In the last resort, all of them in competition helped to break the old-established springs of authority and power; and since then it has proved impossible to find alternatives.

Quintana was writing specifically about Spain, but his sentiments echoed those of patriots in Portugal and on the other side of the Atlantic. After the long centuries of absolutist rule, the Peninsular War was the catalyst which was to activate the struggle for liberty among Iberians wherever they lived.

CHRONOLOGICAL TABLE 1788-1824

1788	Death of Charles III of Spain
1789	The storming of the Bastille
1792	Godoy appointed Secretary of State in Spain
1793	The execution of Louis XVI
1793–5	Spain at war with France
1795	Godoy signs the Treaty of Basel with France and is created Prince of Peace
1796	Spain declares war on Britain
1799	Napoleon becomes First Consul
1801	Godoy leads a Franco-Spanish army into Portugal and 'wins' the 'War of the Oranges'
1802	The Treaty of Amiens establishes a brief peace between Britain, France and Spain
1803	Resumption of hostilities between Britain and France
	Godoy is compelled to hand the British Ambassador his passports and to organize the Spanish fleet for the invasion of England
1804	Napoleon is declared Emperor
1805	The Battle of Trafalgar
1806	Napoleon defeats the Prussians at Jena and Auerstadt
1807	
July	Napoleon signs the Treaty of Tilsit after his defeat of the Russians at Eylau and Friedland
12 August	French ultimatum to Portugal
27 October	The Treaty of Fontainebleau; France and Spain agree on the partition of Portugal
28–29 November	Junot enters Lisbon; the Portuguese royal family sail for Brazil
December	Napoleon orders the military occupation of Spain

CHRONOLOGICAL TABLE 1788-1824

1808

17–19 March	Fall of Godoy; abdication of Charles IV and accession of Ferdinand VII
10 April	Ferdinand VII leaves for Bayonne
2 May	Revolt of *El Dos de Mayo* in Madrid
6 May	Napoleon obtains Ferdinand VII's abdication
21 May	First Supreme Junta formed in Oviedo
15 June–14 August	First French siege of Saragossa
20 June	First French siege of Gerona
8–9 July	Joseph Bonaparte swears the Bayonne Constitution and enters Spain
20 July	Wellesley arrives in Corunna
21 July	Dupont surrenders to Castaños at Bailén
24 July–16 August	Second unsuccessful siege of Gerona
21 August	Wellesley defeats Junot at Vimeiro
30 August	Convention of Sintra; French leave Portugal
25 September	The Central Junta meets at Aranjuez
6 November	Napoleon takes over command of the French armies in Spain
November	Spanish defeats in the north of Spain and on the Ebro
November–December	Siege and capture of Rosas by the French
4 December	Madrid surrenders to Napoleon
17 December	St. Cyr relieves Barcelona
December–January 1809	Sir John Moore's retreat to Corunna
20 December–20 February 1809	Second siege and capture of Saragossa by the French

1809

13 January	Spanish defeat at Uclés enables Joseph Bonaparte to re-enter Madrid
16 January	Defeat of the French at Corunna and death of Sir John Moore
29 March	Soult captures Oporto Defeat of Cuesta at Medellín
22 April	Wellesley returns to Lisbon
12 May	Wellesley recaptures Oporto
25 May	Creation of a Provisional Junta of the Provinces of the Río de la Plata in Buenos Aires
May–June	The Spanish force Ney to evacuate Galicia

CHRONOLOGICAL TABLE 1788–1824

24 May–11 December	Third siege and capture of Gerona by the French
July	Napoleon defeats the Austrians at Wagram
27–28 July	Battle of Talavera
11 August	Venegas defeated at Almonacid
October	Resignation of Castlereagh and Canning and fall of the Portland Ministry
Autumn 1809–Spring 1810	Wellington retreats into Portugal and constructs the Lines of Torres Vedras
18 October	Del Parque defeats the French at Tamames
19 November	Spanish defeated at Ocaña

1810

January–February	French conquest of Andalusia
23–29 January	The Central Junta flees to Cadiz and hands over authority to the Regency
5 February	Victor invests Cadiz
19 April	Deposition of the Captain-General of Venezuela and establishment of a Provisional Junta in Caracas
28 May	Masséna arrives at Salamanca to take over command of the French Army of Portugal
10 September	Summoning of the Cadiz Cortes
16 September	Francisco Hidalgo proclaims revolt in Mexico
27 September	Wellington defeats Masséna at Buçaco
11 October	French arrive opposite the Lines of Torres Vedras

1811

January	Hidalgo defeated by the royalists in Mexico
3 March	Masséna orders a general retreat from Portugal
5 March	Battle of Barrosa
5 April	Masséna's army retreats into Spain
5 May	Wellington defeats Masséna at Fuentes de Oñoro
16 May	Battle of Albuera
	Joseph Bonaparte arrives in Paris to confer with Napoleon
5 July	Venezuela declares itself independent of Spain, and by early 1812 Francisco de Miranda, with Bolívar's support, becomes dictator
23 September –25 October	Suchet besieges Sagunto and defeats Blake

1812

8 January	Blake surrenders Valencia to Suchet
	Wellington recaptures Ciudad Rodrigo

CHRONOLOGICAL TABLE 1788-1824

March	Napoleon makes Joseph Bonaparte commander-in-chief in Spain
19 March	The Cadiz Cortes issues the liberal Constitution
6 April	Wellington recaptures Badajoz
April	Napoleon sets out on his Russian campaign
22 July	Wellington defeats Marmont at Arapiles (Battle of Salamanca)
24 July	Admiral Sir Home Popham and the Spanish guerrillas retake Santander
31 July	Anglo-Sicilian expedition arrives off the coast of Catalonia
12 August	Wellington enters Madrid
24 August	Soult raises the siege of Cadiz and undertakes the evacuation of Andalusia and retreat to Valencia
19 September –21 October	Wellington's abortive siege of Burgos
12 October	Napoleon begins the retreat from Moscow
22 September	Cadiz Cortes appoints Wellington commander-in-chief of its armies
15–17 October	Soult and King Joseph march from Valencia on Madrid
31 October	Hill's rearguard evacuates Madrid
October–November	Wellington withdraws into Portugal

1813

23 March	Joseph Bonaparte receives orders from Napoleon to divert the French Army of Portugal to Biscay
3–13 June	Sir John Murray's abortive siege of Tarragona
21 June	Battle of Vitoria. Joseph Bonaparte begins his withdrawal into France
5 July	Suchet begins the evacuation of Valencia
11 July	Soult arrives in Bayonne to take over command of the French Army of Spain
27–30 July	Wellington defeats Soult at the Battles of Sorauen
August	Recapture of San Sebastián
7 October	Wellington crosses the Bidassoa into France
16 October	The European Allies defeat Napoleon at Leipzig
31 October	The French surrender Pamplona
10 November	Wellington defeats Soult on the Nivelle
10–11 December	Soult's defeat at the Battle of the Nive
11 December	Ferdinand VII signs the Treaty of Valençay

1814

10 January	Molinos del Rey: Suchet's last battle on Spanish soil before retreating into France
February	Napoleon fights back against the Austrians, Prussians and Russians near Paris
24 March	Ferdinand VII returns to Spain
11 April	Napoleon abdicates
12 April	Wellington enters Toulouse
10 May	General Eguía arrests the liberal leaders in Madrid

1815

11 May	General Morillo enters Caracas and by 1816 has re-established Spanish rule in Venezuela and New Granada
14 June	Battle of Waterloo
September	Porlier's unsuccessful revolt in Galicia

1816	The Provinces of Río de la Plata declare independence
1818	San Martín defeats the Spaniards at Maipú and achieves independence for Chile
1820	Riego's *pronunciamiento*; mutiny of the Spanish army in Cadiz; Ferdinand VII accepts the Constitution of 1812
	Overturn of the Regency in Portugal; the Junta declares a liberal Constitution
	Morillo signs an armistice with Bolívar, leaving him in control of Venezuela and New Granada and returning to Spain
1821	Dom John returns to Portugal from Brazil
	Iturbide enters Mexico City and wins independence for Mexico
1822	Dom Pedro declares the independence of Brazil and is crowned Emperor
1823	French invasion of Spain; Fernando VII regains full power and annuls all the reforms of 1820-3
1824	Bolívar and Sucre set a seal to the liberation of South America with the victory of Ayacucho in Peru

NAPOLEON'S MARSHALS IN SPAIN AND PORTUGAL AND THEIR TITLES

Napoleon conferred titles on most of his marshals and some of his generals. This brief *Who was Who* may assist the reader.

Augereau, Pierre François Charles,
  Marshal—Duke of Castiglione
Beauharnais, Eugène,
  Marshal—Viceroy of Italy; Prince of Venice
Bessières, Jean Baptiste,
  Marshal—Duke of Istria
Jourdan, Jean Baptiste,
  Marshal
Junot, Androche,
  General—Duke of Abrantes
Lannes, Jean,
  Marshal—Duke of Montebello
Lefebvre, Francis Joseph,
  Marshal—Duke of Dantzig
MacDonald, Étienne,
  Marshal—Duke of Tarentum
Marmont, Auguste Fréderic Louis de,
  Marshal—Duke of Ragusa
Masséna, André,
  Marshal—Duke of Rivoli, Prince of Essling
Moncey, Bon Adrien de,
  Marshal—Duke of Conegliano
Mortier, Édouard,
  Marshal—Duke of Treviso
Murat, Joachim,
  Marshal—Grand Duke of Berg and Cleves; King of Naples,

Ney, Michel,
  Marshal—Duke of Elchingen; Prince of Moskova
St. Cyr, Laurent Gouvion,
  Marshal
Savary, Anne Jean Marie Réné,
  General—Duke of Rovigo
Soult, Nicholas,
  Marshal—Duke of Dalmatia
Suchet, Louis Gabriel,
  Marshal—Duke of Albufera
Victor, Claude Perrin,
  Marshal—Duke of Belluno

BIBLIOGRAPHY

The bibliography of the Peninsular War is so extensive that this list is necessarily selective. Apart from military histories in English, mainly devoted to the battles between the British and the French—Sir Charles Oman's great seven-volume *History of the Peninsular War* is one of the exceptions—there exist scores of memoirs written by serving officers and other ranks. I have redressed the balance by including a number of less familiar Spanish, Portuguese and French sources, dealing with, not only military operations, but also the political and social background.

Adventures of a Young Rifleman in the French and English Armies during the War in Spain and Portugal, from 1806 to 1816 (written by himself), London, 1826.
Alonso, Mariano, *La Guerra de la Independencia española y los sitios de Zaragoza*, Zaragoza, 1958.
Argüelles, Agustín, *Examen histórico de la reforma que hicieron las Cortes*, London, 1835.
Artola, Miguel, *Los Afrancesados*, Madrid, 1953.
Ayerbe, Marqués de, *Memorias*, reprinted in Biblioteca de Autores Españoles, Vol. 97, Madrid, 1957.
Azanza, José de, and O'Farril, Gonzalo, *Memoria justificativa*, reprinted in Biblioteca de Autores Españoles, Vol. 97, Madrid, 1957.
Bigarré, Auguste, *Mémoires du General Auguste Bigarré. Aide-de-Camp du Roi Joseph*, Paris, n.d.
Blakeney, Robert, *A Boy in the Peninsular War*, London, 1899.
Blaquiere, Edward, *An Historical Review of the Spanish Revolution*, London, 1822.
Bonaparte, Joseph, *Mémoires et Correspondances Politiques et Militaires du Roi Joseph*, edited by A. Ducasse, 10 vols., 1854.
The Confidential Correspondence of Napoleon Bonaparte with his Brother Joseph, translated, 2 vols., London, 1855.
Bryant, Sir Arthur, *The Great Duke*, London, 1971.
The Napoleonic Wars, 3 vols., London, 1942–50.
Canga Argüelles, José, *Observaciones sobre la historia de la Guerra de España*, London, 1829.

Carr, Raymond, *Spain 1808-1939*, Oxford, 1966.
Castlereagh, Lord, *Despatches*, 12 vols., London, 1848-53.
Ceballos, Pedro de, *Exposición de los hechos y maquinaciones que han preparado la usurpación de la Corona de España*, Biblioteca de Autores Españoles, Vol. 87, Madrid.
Chastenet, Jacques, *Godoy, Master of Spain*, translated, London, 1953.
Cole, *Memoirs of Sir Galbraith Lowry Cole*, edited by M. Lowry Cole and S. Gwynn, London, 1934.
Cooper, J. S., *Rough Notes on Seven Campaigns*, 2nd ed., Carlisle, 1914.
Costello, Edward, *The Adventures of a Soldier*, London, 1841.
Desdevizes de Dézert, *Le Conseil de Castille en 1808*, in *Revue Hispanique*, 1907.
Dundonald, Thomas, Tenth Earl of, *The Autobiography of a Seaman*, 2 vols., London, 1860.
Escoiquiz, Juan de, *Idea sencilla de las razones que motivaron el viaje del Rey Don Fernando VII a Bayona*, reprinted in Biblioteca de Autores Españoles, Vol. 97, Madrid, 1957.
Memorias, reprinted in Biblioteca de Autores Españoles, Vol. 97, Madrid, 1957.
Espoz y Mina, Francisco, *Memorias del General Don Francisco Espoz y Mina, escritas por él mismo*, 5 vols., Madrid, 1851-2. Reprinted in Biblioteca de Autores Españoles, 2 vols., Madrid, 1962.
Ford, Richard, *A Handbook for Travellers in Spain*, London, 1845.
The Campaigns of Wellington in India, The Peninsula, Belgium and France, London, 1852.
Fortescue, Sir John, *A History of the British Army*, Vols. 6-10, London, 1910-20.
Foy, Maximilien, *Vie Militaire du General Foy*, edited by Maurice Girod de l'Ain, Paris, 1900.
History of the War in the Peninsula, translated, 2 vols., London, 1827.
Glover, Michael, *Wellington's Peninsular Victories*, London, 1963.
The Peninsular War 1807-14, A Concise Military History, London, 1974.
Godoy, Manuel, *Memorias de Don Manuel Godoy*, 7 vols., Paris, 1839.
Memoirs of Don Manuel Godoy, translated, 2 vols., London, 1836.
Gómez de Arteche, *Historia de la Guerra de la Independencia*, Madrid, 1868-1903.

BIBLIOGRAPHY

Graham, William, *Travels through Portugal and Spain during the Peninsular War*, London, 1820.
Grandmaison, Geoffroy de, *L'Espagne et Napoléon*, 3 vols., 1908-31.
Grattan, William, *Adventures with the Connaught Rangers* (2 series of 2 vols. each, 1847) edited by C. Oman and republished 1902.
Gronow, *The Reminiscences and Recollections of Captain Gronow*, edited by John Raymond, London, 1964.
Hargreaves-Mawdsley, W. N., *Spain Under the Bourbons 1700-1833*, London, 1973.
Harris, John, *Recollections of Rifleman Harris*, 1848, reprinted London, 1929.
Hart, Liddell, *The Strategy of Indirect Approach*, London, 1941.
Herculano, Alexandre, *História de Portugal*, 7th ed., Lisbon, 1914-16.
Herring, Hubert, *A History of Latin America*, 3rd ed., London, 1968.
Historia de España, edited by Ramón Menéndez Pidal, Vol. XXVI, Miguel Artola Gallego, *La España de Fernando VII*, Madrid, 1968.
Holland, Lady Elizabeth, *The Spanish Journal of Elizabeth Lady Holland*, edited by the Earl of Ilchester, London, 1910.
Humphries, R. A., *Liberation in South America*, London, 1952.
Jourdan, Marshal, *Mémoires Militaires du Maréchal Jourdan*, edited by the Vicomte de Grouchy, Paris, 1899.
Jovellanos, G. M., *Vida y pensamiento de don Gaspar Melchor de Jovellanos*, Biblioteca de Autores Espanoles, Vols. 46, 50, and 85-7.
Junot, Laure (Duchesse d'Abrantes), *Memoirs*, translated, 8 vols., London, 1832.
Kincaid, Captain J., *Adventures in the Rifle Brigade*, London, 1830.
Larpent, F. S., *The Private Journal of F. Seymour Larpent, Judge-Advocate General*, edited by Sir George Larpent, 2 vols., 2nd ed., London, 1853.
Livermore, H. V., *A History of Portugal*, Cambridge, 1947.
Londonderry, Marquis of, *Narrative of the Peninsular War*, 2nd ed., London, 1828.
Longford, Elizabeth, *Wellington: The Years of the Sword*, London, 1969.
McGrigor, Sir J., *The Autobiography of Sir James McGrigor, late Director-General of the Army Medical Department*, London, 1861.

Manchester, Alan K., *British Preeminence in Brazil, Its Rise and Decline*, Chapel Hill (University of North Carolina Press), 1933.
Marbot, General, *Mémoires du Géneral Baron de Marbot*, 3 vols., Paris, 1857.
Marmont, Marshal, *Mémoires du Maréchal Marmont, Duc de Raguse*, 5 vols., Paris, 1857.
Mor de Fuentes, José, *Bosquejillo de la vida y escritos*, in Biblioteca de Autores Españoles, Vol. 97, Madrid, 1957.
Napier, W. F. P., *History of the War in the Peninsula*, 6 vols., London, 1828.
Napoleon, *Correspondance de Napoléon Ier*, 32 vols., Paris, 1854–69.
Napoleon's Memoirs, edited by S. de Chair, London, 1948.
Neale, Dr. Adam, *Letters from Spain and Portugal*, London, 1809.
Oman, Sir Charles, *A History of the Peninsular War*, 7 vols., Oxford, 1902–14.
Pérez de Guzmán, Juan, *El dos de mayo*, Madrid, 1908.
Picton, T., *Memoirs of Sir Thomas Picton*, edited by H. B. Robinson, 2 vols., London, 1836.
Pococke, Thomas, *Journal of a Soldier of the 71st, or Glasgow Regiment*, Edinburgh, 1819.
Rocca, M. de, *History of the War of the French in Spain*, translated, London, 1815.
Rudorff, Raymond, *War to the Death: the Sieges of Saragossa, 1808–1809*, London, 1974.
Schaumann, A. L. F., *On the Road with Wellington, The Diary of a War Commissary in the Peninsular Campaigns*, edited and translated by A. Ludovici, London, 1924.
Southey, Robert, *History of the Peninsular War*, London, 1823.
Stanhope, Philip Henry, 5th Earl, *Notes on Conversations with the Duke of Wellington, 1831–51*, London, 1888.
Suchet, Marshal, *Memoirs*, translated, London, 1829.
Surtees, W., *Twenty-five Years in the Rifle Brigade*, London, 1833.
Toreno, Conde de, *Historia de levantamiento, guerra y revolución de España*, reprinted in Biblioteca de Autores Españoles, Vol. 64, Madrid, 1872.
Weller, Jac, *Wellington in the Peninsula*, London, 1962.
Wellesley, H., *Diary and Correspondence of Henry Wellesley, 1st Lord Cowley, 1790–1846*, edited by the Hon. F. A. Wellesley, London, 1930.
Wellington, The Duke of, *The Dispatches of Field Marshal the*

Duke of Wellington during his various Campaigns, compiled by Lt.-Col. Gurwood, 12 vols., London, 1834–9.

Supplementary Despatches, Correspondence, and Memoranda of Field Marshal Arthur Duke of Wellington, K.G., edited by his son the Duke of Wellington (Vols. I–IX), London, 1858–64.

Wheeler, *The Letters of Private Wheeler, 1809–28*, edited with a foreword by Captain B. H. Liddell Hart, London, 1951.

Ziegler, Philip, *A Life of Henry Addington, 1st Viscount Sidmouth*, London, 1965.

INDEX

Numbers in bold refer to plates

Abrantes, Duchess of, quoted, 32, 180
Absolutists, 108–9, 226, 228, 230
afrancesados, 56, 107, 108–10, 111, 112, 114, 189, 211, 225, 229
Albuera, Battle of, 167–8
Alburquerque, Duke of, 150, 153
Alexander I, Czar, 20, 36, 92, 233
Almaraz, Bridge of, destruction of, 185–6
Almeida, French capture of, 157
Álvarez de Castro, Mariano, 134
America, Spanish, 109–10; loss of, 230–3
Amiens, Treaty of, 27
Antonio, Don Infante, Archbishop of Toledo, 49; quoted, 50; 54
Aranjuez, revolt at, 43–5
Arapiles, Battle of, 188
Araújo, António, 35
Areizaga, Juan Carlos, General, 150, 151, 152
Argüelles, Agustín, quoted, 227
Armies, strength, equipment and tactics:
  British, 71, 72, 85–6, 87
  French, 69–72
  Spanish, 68–9, 72
Artola Gallego, Miguel, quoted, 57–8, 111, 136, 150, 229
Asturias, Prince of, see Ferdinand VII of Spain
Asturias, Princess of, 38, 39
atrocities, 200–2, 220
Audiencia, defined, 57
  of Asturias, 58, 59
Augereau, Pierre François Charles, Marshal, 132, 134

Austerlitz, Battle of, 20

Badajoz, captured by Soult, 162–3; recaptured by Wellington, 183–4; British atrocities, 200–1
Bailén, Battle of, 80–1
Baird, Sir David, 99, 100, 105
Ballesteros, General, 127, 186, 207
Baltic, Campaign of, 68
Barcelona, French occupation of, 42; relieved by St. Cyr, 132
Barrosa, Battle of, 163
Basel, Treaty of, 26
Bayonne, Abdication of, 52–6
Beauharnais, François de, 39, 40
Belvedere, Count of, 93, 94
Bentinck, Lord William, 186, 210–11
Beresford, General, 124, 126, 165, 167, 168
Berg, Grand-duke of, see Murat, Joachim
Bessières, Jean Baptiste, Marshal, 43, 70; quoted, 73; 74, 83
Beuronville, French ambassador in Madrid, 28
Blake, Joaqín, General, 69, 73, 83, 93, 94, 99, 132; relieves Gerona, 133; defeated at Belchite, 134; defeated at Sagunto 137; loses Valencia, 138–9; 154
Bonaparte, Joseph, 20; named King of Spain, 55–6; crosses into Spain, 56; first entry into Madrid, 73; retreat from

INDEX

Bonaparte—*cont.*
    Madrid, 81; titles of, 107; character of, 107–8; political regime of, 108–10; lack of finance, 110–11; threatens abdication, 112–13; visits Napoleon in Paris, 114; appointed commander-in-chief, 115; at Battle of Talavera, 145–8; plans invasion of Andalusia, 151–2; accompanies Soult to Andalusia, 152–3; evacuates Madrid, 189; orders Soult to evacuate Andalusia, 189–90; joins Suchet and Soult in Valencia, 191; reoccupies Madrid, 193; ordered to retire to Valladolid, 209; retreats to Vitoria, 211–12; defeated at Vitoria, 213–15; retreats into France, 215; disgraced by Napoleon, 217, 7

Bonaparte, Louis, 20, 48
Bonaparte, Lucien, 27
Bonaparte, Napoleon, see Napoleon
Brazil, 233–4
Bryant, Sir Arthur, 123
Buçaco, Battle of, 159–60
Buenos Aires, 232
Burgos, Wellington's abortive siege of, 192; evacuated by French, 212
Burrard, Sir Harry, 88, 89, 90, 91

Caffarelli, General, 174, 186
camp followers, 203–4, 5
Canning, George, 59, 155
Captain General, defined, 57
Carlist Wars, 230
Carlota, Infanta, 32, 234
Cartaojal, General, 143, 144
Castaños, Francisco, General, 60, 80; quoted, 82; 83, 93, 94, 208
Castlereagh, Lord, 84, 88, 89, 92, 106, 120, 155, 231
Ceballos, Pedro de, 46, 49, 52
Cervellón, Count of, 77
Champagny, French foreign minister, quoted, 48, 52, 113

Charles III of Spain, 22
Charles IV of Spain, 19, 20, 21; character of, 24; quarrel with his son, 40–1; abdication at Aranjuez, 45; sent to Bayonne, 50; negotiations at Bayonne, 53–4; exile, 54; 228
Chastenet, Jacques, quoted, 26, 50
Chronological table, 236–40
Ciudad Real, Battle of, 143
Ciudad Rodrigo, defence by Spanish, 157; recaptured by Wellington, 182–3
Clausel, General, 188, 189, 191, 209, 212, 213, 216, 219
Cochrane, Lord, 130–2, 234
Cole, Sir Lowry, 167, 219
Collingwood, Admiral, 81
Constitution of 1812, Spanish, 108, 226; clauses of, 227; 228, 229, 231, 232
Continental System, 20
Cooper, Sergeant John Spence, quoted, 85–7, 146, 183, 196–7, 197–8, 199, 203, 204–5
Copóns, General, 210, 218, 228
Córdoba, sack of, 79–80
Cortes, Cadiz, 108, 207–8, 226, 231, 234, **12**
Cortes, Spanish, 57, 228, 229
Corunna, Battle of, 104–6, **6**
Costello, Thomas, quoted, 198, 198–9, 200–1, 201, 202–3, 203, 205
Cotton, Admiral, 87, 90
Council of Castile, 57, 74, 82
Cradock, Sir John, 117, 120, 142
Crauford, General Robert, 103, 149, 157, 159, 166, 182, 205
Cuesta, General, 60; defeated at Valladolid, 73; defeated at Medina de Río Seca, 73; 83, 108, 110, 124, 141; defeated at Medellín, 142–3, 144; Battle of Talavera, 145–8; 207, 228

Dalrymple, Sir Hew, 88, 89, 90, 91, 98
Daoiz, Luis, 51

INDEX

Desastres de la Guerra, 80, 11
Desdevises du Dézert, quoted, 57, drink, 198
Duhesme, General, 42, 69, 70, 78, 79, 132
Dupont, General, 42, 70, 73, 79–81
Duroc, General, 54

Echeverría, bandit, 172–3
Eguía, General, 152, 229
Elio, General, 228
Empecinado, El, 137, 171, 208
Escoiquiz, Juan de, 38, 39, 41, 46, 49, 52; quoted, 53; 54, 56
Espoz y Mina, General, 137, 171, 172–5, 176, 179, 181, 226, 229
Estudiante, El, 171–2
Etruria, Queen of, 31, 47, 50, 52
Eylau, Battle of, 20

Ferdinand VII of Spain, character and early history, 38; quarrel with Godoy, 39; intrigues against his father, 40–1; supersedes Charles IV at Aranjuez, 44–5; leaves for Bayonne; 49, abdicates at Bayonne, 52–4; exile at Valençay, 54–5; signs Treaty of Valençay with Napoleon, 225–6; returns to Spain and rejects Constitution, 228–9; coup of 1820, 229–30; Declaration to the Americas, 232–3, 2
Filangieri, General, 59
flogging, 199
Floridablanca, Count of, 26
Fontainebleau, Treaty of, 21; provisions of, 30–1
Ford, Richard, quoted, 13, 65, 66
Foy, Maximilien, General, 13, 71, 80; quoted, 121; 156, 162, 212, 216
Fox, Charles James, 25
Franco, General, 108
Fraser, Major-General Alexander, 105

Freire, Bernado, General, 118, 220
Frere, Hookham, quoted, 101; 142, 144
Friedland, Battle of, 20
Fuentes de Oñoro, Battle of, 165–6
Fusiliers, 7th, 85

Gazan, General, 211, 215
Gerona, first siege of, 78–9; second siege of, 79; third siege of, 133–4
German mercenaries, 196, 197, 202
Godoy, Manuel, 'Prince of Peace', warned by Napoleon, 19–21; early career, 24–6; ultimatum to England, 27; 'War of the Oranges', 27; designs on Portugal, 30; antagonism to Prince of the Asturias, 38–41; overthrow at Aranjuez, 43–5; released and sent to Bayonne, 50; at Bayonne, 53–4; exile, 54; 69, 232
Goya y Lucientes, Francisco José de, 51, 76, 80, 189, 202
Graham, General, 163, 211, 213, 214, 216, 219
Grey, Lord, quoted, 155
guerrillas, 65, 67, 68, 118, 122, 131, 137, 169–81; strength of, 180; casualties caused by, 180; 186, 10

Hallowell, Admiral, 210–11
Hargreaves-Mawdsley, W. N., quoted, 28
Harris, Rifleman, 195; quoted, 204
Hart, Liddell, 13; quoted, 65, 180
Herresi, General, 157
Heudelet, General, 119, 159
Hill, General Rowland, 147, 185, 191, 192, 193, 211, 212, 216, 219
Holland, Lady, 25; quoted, 25, 38, 39, 43–4, 99–100, 101, 103
Holland, Lord, 25, 100, 234
Hope, General, 101, 105, 180
hospitals, 204–5
Housman, A. E., quoted, 195

Infantado, Duke of, 39, 41, 46, 49, 82, 141
Irish soldiers in Spain, 69
Izquierdo, Eugenio, 29

Jena, Battle of, 20, 30
John VI, Prince Regent of Portugal, 32, 33; quoted 34–5, 36; evacuates Lisbon, 36, 233, 234
Jones, y La Peña, General, 80, 81, 95, 163
Jourdan, Jean Baptiste, Marshal, 92, 115; quoted, 151–2; 185, 208
Jovellanos, Gaspar Melchor de, 56, 82; conversation with Lady Holland, quoted, 99–100
Junot, General, 32; invades Portugal, 35–7, 70, 82, 88, 89
Junot, Mme., see Duchess of Abrantes
Junta de Gobierno, 49, 54, 57
Juntas, see Supreme Juntas

Kellermann, General, 89

Le Forest, French ambassador, quoted, 108, 114; 225
La Llave, General, 58
La Peña, General, see Jones y La Peña, General
Laborde, General, 88
Lacy, Luis, General, 69
Lannes, Jean, Marshal, 33, 94, 133
Lapisse, General, 119, 124
Larpent, Francis, quoted, 211
Lecchi, General, 42, 70
Lefebvre, Francis Joseph, Marshal, 93
Lefebvre-Desnouettes, General, 74–5
Leith, General James, 184
Levantamiento, 60, 61
Liberals, 227, 229, 230
lice, 197, 198
Lisbon, captured by Junot, 36; evacuated by French, 90
Liverpool, Lord, 186, 187

Loison, General, 119, 126
Longa, Colonel, 175, 176, 213, 214, 216
Longford, Elizabeth, 123
looting, 198–9, 200
Louis XIV of France, 20, 26

Macdonald, Étienne, Marshal, 135, 136
Mackenzie, General, 124
Madrid, revolt of May 2, 1808, 50–1; capture by Napoleon, 96–7
Mahy, General, 137; quoted, 138; 139
María I of Portugal, 32, 234
María Luisa of Parma, character of, 24–6; 38, 39; plea for Godoy quoted, 47; at Bayonne, 53–4; exiled, 54, 1
Marmont, Auguste Frederic Louis de, Marshal, quoted, 115; 138, 168; quoted, 182; 182–3, 185; defeated at Arapiles, 188
Marryat, Captain, 130
Marshals, Napoleon's, titles of, 241–2
Masséna, André, Marshal, 67, 112; appointed commander in Portugal, 156–7; advance into Portugal, 157–8; defeated at Buçaco, 158–60; at Torres Vedras, 161–2; 180; retreats from Portugal, 164–5; defeated at Fuentes de Oñoro, 165–6
May 2, Revolt of, 50–2
Medellín, Battle of, 142–3
Mexico, 232, 233
Mina, see Espoz y Mina, General
Mina el Mozo, see *El Estudiante miqueletes*, 61
Moncey, Bon Adrien de, Marshal, 70, 73; attack on Valencia, 77–8; 94, 133
Mondego Bay, landing at, 87
Montbrun, General, 138, 140, 161, 166
Montijo, Count of, 44, 151, 152

INDEX

Moore, Sir John, 67; troop training, 85; unpopularity of, 88; march on Salamanca, 99–100; pursues Soult, 102; retreat to Corunna and death, 102–6; 179, 205
Morla, General, 81, 97
Mortier, Édouard, Marshal, 163
Moscow, Retreat from, 68, 194, 208
Munster, Earl of, quoted, 69, 147
Murat, Joachim, Grand-Duke of Berg, appointed commander in Spain, 42; plots overthrow of Spanish Bourbons, 47–50; quells revolt of May 2, 1808, 50–2; president of *Junta de Gobierno*, 54; sends delegates to Bayonne, 55; 56, 57; quoted, 68; replacement of, 77
Murray, General, 125, 210–1

Napier, Sir William, 51
Napoleon Bonaparte, warns Godoy, 19–21; plans invasion of England, 28; orders troops into Spain and Portugal, 31; ultimatum to Portugal, 33–4; involvement in plot against Charles IV, 40–1; orders large forces into Spain, 42; at Bayonne, 52–6; misconceptions of Spain, 66–8; overall strategy in 1808, 73; quoted 78; reinforces his armies and takes command in Spain, 92–3; quoted, 92, 95; forces the Pass of Somosierra, 95–6; enters Madrid, 96–7; pursues Moore, 98, 102; returns to France, 103; decentralizes command in Spain, 111; negotiations with Joseph Bonaparte, 114–15; quoted on Wellington, 119, 121; instructions to St. Cyr, 129; and Lord Cochrane, 131–2; orders capture of Valencia, 136; orders transfer of troop from Portugal, 138; sends 'Old Guard' to Spain, 156; quoted, 156, 157; orders to Masséna, 162; interruption of despatches, 179–80; withdraws troops for Russia, 184; orders new offensive in Portugal, 209; signs Armistice of Plässwitz, 215; suspends Joseph Bonaparte and appoints Soult commander-in-chief, 217; defeated at Leipzig, 225; signs Treaty of Valençay with Ferdinand VII, 225–6; 8
Neale, Dr. Adam, quoted, 104
Neufchâtel, Duke of, 112, 114, 115
Ney, Michel, Marshal, 94, 111, 112; in Galicia, 117, 119; 126–8; at Buçaco, 159, 160; 164–5

Ocaña, Battle of, 151
O'Daly, Pedro, Colonel, 69, 129, 131
O'Donahue (O'Donajú), General, 69, 144, 208
O'Donnell, General, 69, 135, 216
Oman, Sir Charles, 13, 20; quoted, 43, 56, 122, 135, 209, 214
Oporto, capture by Soult, 118–19; recapture by Wellesley, 124–6
Oporto, Bishop of, 87, 90, 118, 158
ordenanza, 118, 155, 158, 160
Orense, Bishop of, quoted, 55

Paget, Edward, General, 103, 105
Paget, Lord Henry, quoted, 100–1; 102
Palafox, Francisco, 94, 151, 152
Palafox, José, 61; at first siege of Saragossa, 74–7; 82, 83, 93, 94, 108; at second siege of Saragossa, 132–3, 226, 4
Pamplona, seized by French, 42; blockaded by Wellington, 216
Parque, del, Duke of, 150, 151
Pelayo, King of Asturias, 58
Perceval, Spencer, 155
Pérez de Guzmán, Juan, quoted, 51

254 INDEX

Philip V of Spain, 21
Picton, General Sir Thomas, 184, 213, 219
Pococke, Thomas, quoted, 103, 196, 198
Popham, Admiral Sir Home, 175, 176, 186, 232
Porlier, Colonel, 175, 176, 181, 226, 229
Portland, Lord, 84, 155
Portugal, Alliance with Britain, 20

Quintana, Manuel José, quoted, 234–5

Reconquest, The, 23
Reding, General, 80, 81, 132
Regency, Council of, Portuguese, 37, 90, 158, 234
Regency, Council of, Spanish, 152, 153, 154, 172, 208, 226, 228
Reille, General, 79, 129, 132, 139, 213, 214, 219
Reynier, General, 158, 159, 165
Rocca, M. de, quoted, 142–3, 143, 161, 169; on guerrilla warfare, 169–71; 176–7, 178
Romana, La, Marquis of, 42, 68, 101, 103, 108, 127, 151, 152, 154, 162, 175
Ronda, Serranía de, guerrillas of, 176–8
Rosas, siege of, 129–31

Saavedra, Francisco de, 80, 152
Sagunto, siege and Battle of, 136–7
St. Cyr, Gouvion, Marshal, 129, 132, 133, 134
Salamanca, Battle of, see Arapiles, Battle of
San Carlos, Duke of, 226
San Sebastián, British siege of, 219, 220
Sanchez, Julian, 206
San Juan, General, 96
Santiago, pilgrimage to, 23
Saragossa, first siege of, 74–7, 3; second siege of, 132–3

Savary, General, 49; quoted, 52, 77
Schwartz, General, 78
Sebastiani, General, 143, 145, 146, 148, 149, 151, 152, 153, 154
Separatism, Basque and Catalan, 230
Seville, capture of by French, 152
Sheridan, Richard Brinsley, quoted, 84
Shrapnel, Henry, 89
Silveira, Francisco, General, 117, 119, 124, 186
Siniavan, Admiral, 90
Sintra, Convention of, 90
Smith, Lady (Juanita de León), 184
somatenes, 61, 78, 79
Sorauen, Battles of, 219, 220
Soult, Nicholas, Marshal, 67, 94, 102, 105, 108, 112, 115; invades Portugal, 117–19; in Oporto, 119; loses Oporto, 124–6; retreats to Galicia, 126–8; 146, 148, 151; conquest of Andalusia, 152–4; captures Badajoz, 162–3; loses Battle of Albuera, 167–8; 176, 177, 179, 180, 185, 186, 189; disobeys Joseph Bonaparte, 190; retreats to Valencia, 190–1; advances on Madrid, 192–3; pursues Wellington to Salamanca, 193, 208; returns to France, 209; attacks across Pyrenees, 218–20; defeated at Sorauen, 219–20
Spain, under the Bourbons, 22–4; geography of, 65–6
Stewart, William, General, 153
Strangford, Lord, 35, 36
Suchet, Louis Gabriel, Marshal, quoted, 110; 111, 134; at siege of Lérida, 135; siege and battle of Sagunto, 136–8; captures Valencia, 138–40; 174, 185, 186–7, 208, 210; evacuates Valencia and withdraws to France, 217, 218

Supreme Juntas, 59, 227
 American, 231–2
 of Asturias, 58, 59
 Central, 60, 81, 82–3, 93, 98, 99, 100, 110, 123, 141, 143, 150, 151, 152, 155, 169, 226
 of Galicia, 60, 99–100
 of Oporto, 87, 90
 of Seville, 60, 81
Surtees, Sergeant, quoted, 69

Talavera, Battle of, 86, 145–8
Talleyrand, 20, 28; quoted, 49; 54–5
Tamames, Battle of, 150
Tarragona, British attack on, 210–11
Tascher de la Pagerie, Marie Stéphanie, 39
Tilsit, Treaty of, 20
tirailleurs, 71
Toreno, Count of, 59, 82; quoted 220; 227, 229
Torres Vedras, Lines of, 150, 155–6, 160–1, 165
Trafalgar, Battle of, 28–9
Trant, Colonel, 158, 160
Tudela, Battle of, 94–5
Tudo, Pepita, 44

Uclés, Battle of, 140
Unamuno, Miguel, quoted, 24
uniform, British, 85–6, 87
Urquijo, Marquis of, 49, 56

Valençay, Treaty of, 225–6, 228
Valencia, first siege of, 77; capture by Suchet, 138–9
Vedel, General, 80, 81
Velarde, Pedro, 51
Venegas, General, 141, 144, 145, 146, 149, 207
Venezuela, 231–2, 233
Verdier, General, 75–7, 132, 133, 134
Victor, Claude Perrin, Marshal, 124, 140; wins Battle of Medellín, 142–3; Battle of Talavera, 145–8; 151, 153, 154
Vitoria, Battle of, 208, 213–15

Wellesley, Arthur, first Duke of Wellington, 66, 68; quoted, 71; appointed commander in the Peninsula, 84; quoted, 85; sails for Corunna, 86; superseded in command, 88; quoted, 88; wins Battle of Roliça, 88; wins Battle of Vimeiro, 88–9; signs Convention of Sintra and returns to England, 90; acquitted by Court of Inquiry, 91; pledges support to Moore, 98; return to Portugal, 120; character and military tactics of, 120–3; capture of Oporto, 124–5; pursues Soult, 126; shortage of finance, 144–5; differences with Cuesta, 145–6; Battle of Talavera, 146–8; retreat to Portugal, 148–50; constructs Lines of Torres Vedras, 155–6; retreats through Portugal, 157–8; wins Battle of Buçaco, 159–60; falls back on Torres Vedras, 160–1; pursues Masséna, 164–5; wins Battle of Fuentes de Oñoro, 165–6; abortive siege of Badajoz, 168; recapture of Ciudad Rodrigo, 182–3; recapture of Badajoz, 183–4; plans for diversions, 186; near-bankruptcy of commissary, quoted, 187; occupies Salamanca, 187; defeats Marmont at Arapiles, 188; enters Madrid, 189; unsuccessfully besieges Burgos, 191–2; retreats beyond Salamanca, 193–4; in winter quarters, 194; contact with guerrillas, 206; and Cadiz Cortes, 207–8; advances towards Vitoria, 211–12; wins Battle of Vitoria, 213–15;

Wellesley, Arthur—*cont.*
    mopping up operations in north, 216; defeats Soult in the Pyrenees, 219–20; crosses into France, 221; captures Toulouse, 221, **9**

Wellesley, Henry Marquis of, 149, 231
Wilson, Sir Robert, 118, 119, 145
Wolfe, Charles, quoted, 106

Zaragoza, Agustina, 76

Date Due

MAY 31 '92